ArtScroll Mesorah Series®

Rabbi Nosson Scherman / Rabbi Meir Zlotowitz

General Editors

הגדה של פסח

HAGGADAH

THE PASSOVER HAGGADAH
with a commentary anthologized
from the writings of
RABBI MOSHE BEN NACHMAN

by Yosef Israel

RAMBAN

Published by
Mesorah Publications, ltd

FIRST EDITION
First Impression . . . March 1996
Second Impression . . . February 2007

Published and Distributed by
MESORAH PUBLICATIONS, Ltd.
4401 Second Avenue
Brooklyn, New York 11232

Distributed in Europe by
LEHMANNS
Unit E, Viking Business Park
Rolling Mill Road
Jarrow, Tyne & Wear NE32 3DP
England

Distributed in Israel by
SIFRIATI / A. GITLER — BOOKS
6 Hayarkon Street
Bnei Brak 51127
Africa

Distributed in Australia & New Zealand by
GOLDS WORLD OF JUDAICA
3-13 William Street
Balaclava, Melbourne 3183
Victoria Australia

Distributed in South Africa by
KOLLEL BOOKSHOP
Ivy Common 105 William Road
Norwood   2192,   Johannesburg,   South

THE ARTSCROLL MESORAH SERIES®
RAMBAN HAGGADAH
© Copyright 1996, by MESORAH PUBLICATIONS, Ltd.
4401 Second Avenue / Brooklyn, N.Y. 11232 / (718) 921-9000
ALL RIGHTS RESERVED

ISBN:
0-89906-390-X (hard cover)
0-89906-391-8 (paperback)

Typography by CompuScribe at ArtScroll Studios, Ltd.
4401 Second Avenue / Brooklyn, N.Y. 11232 / (718) 921-9000

Printed in the United States of America by Noble Book Press
Bound by Sefercraft, Quality Bookbinders, Ltd. Brooklyn, N.Y.

Rabbi CHAIM P. SCHEINBERG
Rosh Hayeshiva "TORAH-ORE"
and Morah Hora'ah of Kiryat Mattersdorf

הרב חיים פינחס שיינברג

ראש ישיבת "תורה-אור"
ומורה הוראה דקרית מטרסדורף

י"א אדר-ב תשנ"ה

הנה הרה"ג המחבר הרב יוסף שליט"א עשה עבודה גדולה
שליקט פנינים יקרים מתורת רבינו הרמב"ן זצ"ל ואספם
לחיבור רב-ערך על ההגדה אשר נוסף על התועלת
הגדולה מאד שבו בהיות פירוש של אחד מגדולי
הראשונים מסודר בטוב טעם ודעת על סדר ההגדה עוד
זאת מעלה יתירה בו אשר משובצים בו יסודות הדת אשר
הנחיל לנו רבינו הרמב"ן זצ"ל בעניני מעשה בראשית
אמונה והשגחה וכו' דברים העומדים ברומו של עולם ואין
יד כל אדם משגת למצוא כל זאת בתורת הרמב"ן זצ"ל
הרחבה, ובפרט שלשונו קצר ועמוק ובנוסף על הקושי
למצוא יש גם קושי להבין, ועל כן מה גדול כח הרה"ג
המחבר שליט"א שבנוסף על עבודת הליקוט גם השכיל
להציע תורת הרמב"ן בשפה בהירה ומובנת לכל ועל כן
ברכתי שלוחה שזכותו של הרמב"ן זצ"ל יעמוד לו
להרה"ג המחבר שליט"א שיזכה להפיץ תורתו של
הרמב"ן זצ"ל כרצונו הטהור ויזכה לכל טוב בזה ובבא.

ובאתי על החתום
פה עה"ק ירושלים תובב"א

חיים פינחס שיינברג

רחוב פנים מאירות 2, ירושלים, ת. ד. 6979, טל. (02)-371513, ישראל
2, Panim Meirot St., Jerusalem, P.O.B. 6979, Tel (02)-371513, Israel

RABBI B. RAKOW
RAV OF GATESHEAD
138 WHITEHALL ROAD,
GATESHEAD   NE8   1TP
Tyne & Wear
TEL. 0632-773012

בצלאל בהרה"ג ר' יום טוב ליפמאן ראקאוו

אב"ד דגייטסהעד

ב"ה ‏_____

כ' הר' שליט"א שלח לי ספרו פניני הרמב"ן ליקוט מכתבי
הרמב"ן על עניני הגדה של פסח כאשר עיינתי קצת ראיתי
שהר' הנ"ל לא היה מלקט בעלמא אלא השקיע בזה עמל
ויגיעה וזכה להבין עומק דברי הרמב"ן כדי לקשר ולאחד
הדברים מכמה מקומות של כתבי הרמב"ן וגם הראה בזה
ידיעותיו הרחבות בדברי הרמב"ן ובזה זיכה את הרבים
לאפשר ולעיין בדברי הרמב"ן שיש בהם יסודות האמונה
בעת שעוסקים בסיפור יציאת מצרים וחיזוק אמונתינו ובודאי
זכות רבינו הרמב"ן יעמוד לו לכל טוב ובזכות חיזוק האמונה
נזכה לגאולה שלימה בקרוב

הק' בצלאל ראקאוו

This approbation was written for the Hebrew edition of this work

בס"ד אדר שני שנת תשנ"ה לפ"ק פה גייטסהעד יצ"ו

לכבוד יד"נ כמו"ה יוסף ישראל שליט"א

כאשר קבלתי הגדה פניני הרמב"ן בערב חג הפסח תשנ"ד הי'
לי אז שמחת יו"ט ממש כל ימי החג ממנו. והנה נתרשמתי
מאד כי אין החיבור הזה ליקוט בעלמא של דברי הרמב"ן על
יצ"מ אלא יגיעה רבה ניכר בה אשר עשית בהשכל ודעת
עבודת הפרדה והבדלה להתאים הדברים לכל קטא וקטא על
ההגדה. ואם אין דעת להבין בהבנה גמורה דברי הרמב"ן
הבדלה מנין להתאים דבריו לפסגם הראוי ובזאת הראית
כוחך הגדול בידיעת והבנת דברי הרמב"ן וע"ז נעשה הספר
כולה שלך וזכות הרבים תלוי בך. ובטח רבינו הגדול הרמב"ן
ימליץ טוב בעדך ובעד כל משפחתך להיות מתברכות בשפע
כל טוב מן השמים עבור הטובה הגדולה הזאת שעשית להפיץ
דבריו על פני תבל ולעשות יסודותיו לנחלת עם. גם התרגום
לשפה המדוברת עבודה חשובה היא כי הצלחת להיות נאמן
לדברי הרמב"ן במקור ולהעביר הדברים בשפה ברורה
ונעימה לאלו שעוד לא הורגלו לעיין ולהבין בלשון הקודש.
יישר כחך וחילך לאורייתא ממני הכו"ח לכבוד התורה
ולכבוד הפצת דברי קדוש ה' רבינו הרמב"ן ז"ל

מתיתי' חיים סלומון

❧ Preface

Ramban's Bible Commentary has been justifiably recognized throughout the centuries as being fundamental to *hashkafah* and our understanding of Judaism. So what could be more fitting at the *seder* night, as we transmit the basis of our beliefs to the next generation, than combining the holy and profound words of *Ramban* with this golden chain of tradition.

"We relate the entire sequence of the Exodus since this graphically reveals the might and power of the Creator, who brought the universe into existence through His Will and Power" (*Ramban, Deuteronomy* 6:20). Elsewhere, *Ramban* elaborates: "When God interrupted the natural order with the miracle in Egypt, He proved that there is a Creator. Initially the plagues confirmed Divine Providence, that the world has not been abandoned to chance and coincidence. These further demonstrated the principles of Creation, how Hashem controls His world after establishing it from absolute nothingness. The latter plagues were an awesome display of His unique power to the doubting Egyptians; nothing could withstand Him" (*Exodus* 13:16).

Nor is the concept of adapting *Ramban's* commentaries to another format quite so revolutionary. Judging by Rabbi C.B. Chavel's edition of *Kisvei Ramban,* no less than *Ramban* himself regularly reworked many of his earlier writings while lecturing on various topics, and even repeated whole passages verbatim.

Rabbeinu Moshe ben Nachman is one of the most illustrious and prominent *Rishonim* from the era of the later Tosafists. At the precocious age of fifteen, he already compiled two Talmudic *Halachah* sections, which *Rif* had earlier omitted from his code. At the relatively young age of forty-four, he was called upon to mediate in the major controversy raging over *Rambam's* philosophical writings, and vigorously defended *Rambam's* reputation while upholding the respect and honor of his learned opponents. This was strikingly similar to his other Talmudic projects. In his glosses on the *Sefer HaMitzvos,* he consistently defended *BeHaG* from the strictures of the *Rambam,* just as his glosses on the *Halachos* vindicated *Rif* from the criticisms of *Raavad* and *Baal HaMaor.*

In addition to authoring profound *chiddushim* on most tractates in Talmud, *Ramban* personally disseminated the Tosafist's school of thought in his native Spain, counting such formidable *Rishonim* as *Ra'ah* and *Rashba* among his pupils. His halachic influence in Spain remained so enduring that *Rivash* over a century later testified (*Responsa* 415): "All his words are sparks of fire. Entire communities of Catalonia rely upon his rulings as if given directly to Moses from the Almighty."

At the age of sixty-nine, he was forced into a public religious debate in the presence of the king and notable church dignitaries. Although he decisively defeated his heretic opponent, the embarrassed church intrigued to have him expelled from Aragon. Shortly afterwards, *Ramban* settled in Eretz Yisrael and re-established a permanent Jewish presence in Jerusalem, which had been ravaged by the Crusaders and Mongols.

It was in Eretz Yisrael that *Ramban* finally completed his Bible Commentary, a lifetime's endeavor begun at the age of sixteen, that he continued revising almost until his passing on 11 Nissan 5030 (1270), in his seventy-sixth year. This was to become his most popular work, designed (as he wrote in his preface) "to bring peace of mind to students weary of exiles and adversity, to attract them with words pleasing to listeners and scholars." Indeed, his commentary remains a unique blend of analytical exegesis, philosophy and mysticism.

Over the centuries, several super-commentaries were devoted to the study of *Ramban* and the last few generations have witnessed a remarkable revival of interest in *Ramban's* writings. Spearheading this phenomenon was *Chasam Sofer* who pioneered the weekly study of *Ramban* with his yeshiva students. In his responsa (6:61), *Chasam Sofer* describes the Bible Commentary as "the foundation of faith and the roots of religion," yet laments that all too few of his contemporaries — even scholars — study these words. In his last will and testament, *Chasam Sofer* urges his descendants to learn *Ramban* with their children because of its pre-eminence in instilling *emunah.*

In our own generation, this revival has gained even greater momentum. Newly corrected editions, super-commentaries, translations and anthologies have appeared, and this is not entirely surprising. There is no major religious dilemma — providence, miracles, Creation, man, soul, Eretz Yisrael, good and evil, Moshiach — that is not dealt with in his commentary.

Naturally, this Haggadah — revised from my Hebrew compilations, *Peninei HaRamban*, published in 5754 — draws heavily on the commentary, yet does not confine itself to *Ramban's* novel interpretations on the Exodus but also contains many of his comments on a diverse array of subjects. Likewise many fundamental concepts are anthologized from his numerous other writings and novellae. According to *Ritva*, a towering personality in the generations following *Ramban*, "His works strengthen the foundation of the Torah; his words bear the stamp of truth."

I deem it a great privilege that Mesorah Publications, who have displayed exemplary expertise and flair in publishing the trailblazing *ArtScroll* series, have included this *Ramban Haggadah* among their highly acclaimed Torah classics. I pray this conceptual anthology finds grace and approval in the eyes of the Almighty and Man, and may the holy *zechus* of the *Ramban* favor our family and grant us all that we lack. May this volume likewise be an *ilui neshamah* for my parents (whose *yahrzeits* are imminent) as well as an encouragement to us toward further endeavors in Torah literature.

Yosef Israel

Motzai Shabbos, Parshas Zachor,
11th *Adar* 5756 / March 1996
London, England

הגדה של פסח

RAMBAN
HAGGADAH

בדיקת חמץ

On the night of 14 Nissan, the night before the Pesach *seder*, the search for *chametz* (leaven) is made. It should be done with a candle as soon as possible after nightfall. [When the first *seder* is on Saturday night, the search is conducted on Thursday night (13 Nissan).]
Before the search is begun, the following blessing is recited.
If several people assist in the search, only one recites the blessing for all.

בָּרוּךְ אַתָּה יהוה, אֱלֹהֵינוּ מֶלֶךְ הָעוֹלָם, אֲשֶׁר קִדְּשָׁנוּ
בְּמִצְוֹתָיו, וְצִוָּנוּ עַל בִּעוּר חָמֵץ.

After the search, the *chametz* is wrapped and put aside in a safe place
to be burned in the morning. Then the following declaration is made:

כָּל חֲמִירָא וַחֲמִיעָא דְּאִכָּא בִרְשׁוּתִי, דְּלָא חֲמִתֵּה
וּדְלָא בְעַרְתֵּה וּדְלָא יְדַעְנָא לֵהּ, לִבָּטֵל
וְלֶהֱוֵי הֶפְקֵר כְּעַפְרָא דְאַרְעָא.

◆§ . . . בִּרְשׁוּתִי דְּאִכָּא . . . כָּל חֲמִירָא — *Any chametz that is in my possession.* . . According to the Talmud, this declaration (known as a בִּיטּוּל) to nullify forbidden *chametz* is sufficient to rid oneself of any *chametz*, as far as the Torah rules are concerned. Even if the *chametz* is visible and known to the householder, this simple declaration is enough. (Later, the Sages obliged us to search out and destroy all *chametz* before Passover.)

Rashi in his Talmudic commentary explains that this declaration derives from the Biblical directive תַּשְׁבִּיתוּ שְּׂאֹר מִבָּתֵּיכֶם, "you shall eliminate leaven from your homes" (*Exodus* 12:15). Since the Torah uses an ambiguous phrase, rather than words that clearly describe the *physical* destruction of the *chametz* by burning, we understand from this that a *mental* destruction of the *chametz,* by nullification, is enough. Later I found the source of *Rashi's* words in the *Baal Halachos Gedolos.*

Tosafos is not satisfied with *Rashi's* explanation and poses various questions. First, the *Tanna* Rabbi Akiva clearly associates תַּשְׁבִּיתוּ, "elimination," with "burning" (*Pesachim* 5a). Moreover, this phrase is actually referring to *chametz* in one's possession after midday on *Erev Pesach,* when the nullification is no longer effective.

Therefore, *Rabbeinu Tam* and *Tosafos* put forward a different explanation. The declaration is not a form of destroying *chametz* (as

THE SEARCH FOR CHAMETZ

On the night of 14 Nissan, the night before the Pesach *seder*, the search for *chametz* (leaven) is made. It should be done with a candle as soon as possible after nightfall. [When the first *seder* is on Saturday night, the search is conducted on Thursday night (13 Nissan).]
Before the search is begun, the following blessing is recited.
If several people assist in the search, only one recites the blessing for all.

Blessed are You, HASHEM, our God, King of the Universe, Who has sanctified us with His commandments and has commanded us concerning the removal of *chametz*.

After the search, the *chametz* is wrapped and put aside in a safe place to be burned in the morning. Then the following declaration is made:

Any *chametz* or leaven that is in my possession which I have not seen, have not removed and do not know about, should be nullified and be worthless and considered like dust.

Rashi claimed) but an announcement of הֶפְקֵר, "relinquishing ownership." We avoid the Biblical injunction against possessing *chametz* by ceasing to be the owners. Thus, according to *Tosafos*, the declaration functions by regarding the *chametz* as no longer לְךָ, "yours," rather than by "destroying" the *chametz*, as Rashi had mentioned. This is the view of the Rabbis of France.

However, I found this difficult to accept. Why does the Talmud continually refer to this declaration as a "nullification" and never as "relinquishing ownership"? (Nor indeed do we ever find relinquishing ownership being described elsewhere as nullification.) I also cannot understand why the declaration is so universally accepted as a valid method of avoiding the possession of *chametz*, when the rules of relinquishing ownership (upon which this declaration depends according to *Tosafos*) are open to argument. According to one view in the Talmudic tractate of *Nedarim*, the relinquishment of ownership actually takes effect only when it actually comes into the possession of someone else. However, the nullification declaration is apparently effective immediately, even when no other party has yet taken possession of the *chametz*. Moreover, a statement of formally relinquishing ownership ought to be a verbal public announcement, ideally in front of three people, whereas even a mental commitment to nullification is sufficient for *chametz* — as is

בִּיעוּר חָמֵץ

In the morning, after the *chametz* has been burned,
the following declaration is made:

כָּל חֲמִירָא וַחֲמִיעָא דְּאִכָּא בִרְשׁוּתִי, דַּחֲזִתֵּה
וּדְלָא חֲזִתֵּה, דַּחֲמִתֵּה וּדְלָא חֲמִתֵּה,
דְּבִעַרְתֵּה וּדְלָא בִעַרְתֵּה, לִבָּטֵל וְלֶהֱוֵי הֶפְקֵר כְּעַפְרָא
דְאַרְעָא.

apparent from the *Mishnah* and Talmud. In addition, why would the
declaration be permitted on Shabbos, when relinquishing ownership
would be forbidden, as are all other business dealings?

What also makes me doubtful about *Tosafos'* approach is part of
the phraseology in the declaration (as used by the *Rishonim* and
based on the *Yerushalmi*) that it "...should be worthless and
considered like dust." I do not know of any statement relinquishing
ownership in which a man declares that his possessions should be
considered as dust. Also, why would dust in one's property be
considered ownerless?

Therefore, I believe that the declaration functions by reducing
one's leaven products into non-leaven by considering them mere
dust — totally inedible. In fact, this exemption derives from the
ruling of the *Tanna* Rabbi Yishmael. He pointed out that, in reality,
no leaven should be considered within a person's domain during
Passover, since it can give him no benefit and becomes totally
valueless. The Torah, however, considers the householder as the
legal owner in order to render him liable for possessing *chametz*.
This applies only as long as the householder has that *chametz* in
mind and is interested in retaining it. By declaring the leaven
"worthless and considered like dust," the householder reveals that
his own wishes are in accordance with the Torah and he no longer
values or desires that *chametz* among his possessions. Thus, he
cannot be charged with owning *chametz*.

If *Rashi* is correct that the basis for nullification is the Torah's use
of the ambiguous phrase "you shall eliminate . . ." this can now be
well understood. The Torah is instructing us not to possess any
leaven and we should consider all leaven already burnt as mere dust
and ashes with no one interested in retaining it. Moreover, the term

BURNING THE CHAMETZ

In the morning, after the *chametz* has been burned,
the following declaration is made:

Any *chametz* or leaven that is in my possession, whether I have recognized it or not, whether I have seen it or not, whether I have removed it or not, should be nullified and be worthless and considered like dust.

בִּיטוּל, (which we have translated as nullification but which can also meant to interrupt, suspend or abolish), is in fact the literal translation of הַשְׁבָּתָה, "the elimination of," throughout the Torah as we can see elsewhere, as well as from *Onkelos'* translation here (תְּבַטְלוּן).

Of course, destroying one's leaven by burning is also included within the Biblical imperative to eliminate. Burning leaven is the *only* option after midday *Erev Pesach,* and throughout the festival when nullification can no longer be made. (Indeed, it makes little sense to declare something valueless when it has already lost its value.) It is only before midday that one can, according to basic Torah law, "destroy" *chametz* by any method, even with merely a mental commitment to nullify it.

The *Yerushalmi,* however, clearly translates *tashbisu* as "burning." Moreover, the *Sifre* derives the concept of nullification not from the Biblical command to "eliminate leaven" but from the statement "no *chametz* may be seen *in your possession*" (*Exodus* 13:7) — in other words, that the leaven should not be considered "yours." While these sources would appear to support *Tosafos'* view, I can still incorporate them into my premise. As I explained earlier, once a person surrenders possession of the leaven, it ceases to have any value in his eyes. It is considered mere "dust and ashes," no longer "yours," nor *halachically* "leaven." (Obviously, this refers to possessing leaven and not eating it.)

To summarize, according to the Torah there is more than one method of destroying leaven so that we do not possess any over Passover. Ideally, the best solution would be to burn it or destroy it completely. Alternatively, one can make the nullification declaration, which removes it from being considered leaven — and makes it as worthless as dust and ashes. This is also sufficient as

עֵרוּב תַּבְשִׁילִין

When Pesach falls on Thursday and Friday, an *eruv tavshilin* is made on Wednesday.
The *eruv*-foods are held while the following blessing and declaration are recited:

בָּרוּךְ אַתָּה יהוה אֱלֹהֵינוּ מֶלֶךְ הָעוֹלָם, אֲשֶׁר קִדְּשָׁנוּ
בְּמִצְוֹתָיו, וְצִוָּנוּ עַל מִצְוַת עֵרוּב.

בַּהֲדֵין עֵרוּבָא יְהֵא שָׁרֵא לָנָא לַאֲפוּיֵי וּלְבַשּׁוּלֵי
וּלְאַטְמוּנֵי וּלְאַדְלוּקֵי שְׁרָגָא וּלְתַקָּנָא וּלְמֶעְבַּד
כָּל צָרְכָּנָא, מִיּוֹמָא טָבָא לְשַׁבַּתָּא [לָנָא וּלְכָל יִשְׂרָאֵל
הַדָּרִים בָּעִיר הַזֹּאת].

הַדְלָקַת הַנֵּרוֹת

On each *Yom Tov* night of Pesach two blessings are recited. When Pesach coincides with the Sabbath, light the candles, then cover the eyes and recite the blessings. Uncover the eyes and gaze briefly at the candles. When Pesach falls on a weekday, some follow the above procedure, while others recite the blessings before lighting the candles. When Pesach coincides with the Sabbath, the words in brackets are added.
[It is forbidden to create a new flame — for example, by striking a match — on *Yom Tov*. Therefore, on the second night the candles must be lit from a flame that has been burning from before *Yom Tov*.]

בָּרוּךְ אַתָּה יהוה אֱלֹהֵינוּ מֶלֶךְ הָעוֹלָם, אֲשֶׁר קִדְּשָׁנוּ
בְּמִצְוֹתָיו, וְצִוָּנוּ לְהַדְלִיק נֵר שֶׁל [שַׁבָּת וְשֶׁל]
יוֹם טוֹב.

בָּרוּךְ אַתָּה יהוה אֱלֹהֵינוּ מֶלֶךְ הָעוֹלָם, שֶׁהֶחֱיָנוּ וְקִיְּמָנוּ
וְהִגִּיעָנוּ לַזְּמַן הַזֶּה.

far as the Torah is concerned.

The Sages, however, have instructed us to remove all leaven in case we may inadvertently come to eat it. In addition, they were concerned that perhaps a person may find and be tempted by a tasty biscuit. This would reveal that the original declaration was not performed with a total commitment. Therefore he would remain

ERUV TAVSHILIN

When Pesach falls on Thursday and Friday, an *eruv tavshilin* is made on Wednesday. The *eruv*-foods are held while the following blessing and declaration are recited:

Blessed are You, HASHEM, our God, King of the Universe, Who has sanctified us with His commandments and has commanded us concerning the *mitzvah* of *eruv*.

Through this *eruv* may we be permitted to bake, cook, insulate, kindle flame, prepare, and do anything necessary on the Festival for the sake of the *Shabbos* [for ourselves and for all Jews who live in this city].

KINDLING LIGHTS

On each *Yom Tov* night of Pesach two blessings are recited. When Pesach coincides with the Sabbath, light the candles, then cover the eyes and recite the blessings. Uncover the eyes and gaze briefly at the candles. When Pesach falls on a weekday, some follow the above procedure, while others recite the blessings before lighting the candles. When Pesach coincides with the Sabbath, the words in brackets are added.
[It is forbidden to create a new flame — for example, by striking a match — on *Yom Tov*. Therefore, on the second night the candles must be lit from a flame that has been burning from before *Yom Tov*.]

Blessed are You, HASHEM, our God, King of the Universe, Who has sanctified us with His commandments, and has commanded us to kindle the light of [the Sabbath and of] the Festival.

Blessed are You, HASHEM, our God, King of the Universe, Who has kept us alive, sustained us, and brought us to this season.

---

guilty of wanting to possess leaven. Thus, they establish that even in cases of doubt, we have to search and destroy (or sell or give to a non-Jew) all possible *chametz* before midday. (In fact, according to the Talmudic School of *Beis Shammai*, the non-Jew must consume this *chametz* before midday.)

(Chiddushim, Pesachim, Perek Rishon)

It is customary to recite the following prayer after the kindling.
The words in brackets are included as they apply.

יְהִי רָצוֹן לְפָנֶיךָ, יהוה אֱלֹהַי וֵאלֹהֵי אֲבוֹתַי, שֶׁתְּחוֹנֵן אוֹתִי [וְאֶת אִישִׁי, וְאֶת בָּנַי, וְאֶת בְּנוֹתַי, וְאֶת אָבִי, וְאֶת אִמִּי] וְאֶת כָּל קְרוֹבַי; וְתִתֶּן לָנוּ וּלְכָל יִשְׂרָאֵל חַיִּים טוֹבִים וַאֲרוּכִים; וְתִזְכְּרֵנוּ בְּזִכְרוֹן טוֹבָה וּבְרָכָה; וְתִפְקְדֵנוּ בִּפְקֻדַּת יְשׁוּעָה וְרַחֲמִים; וּתְבָרְכֵנוּ בְּרָכוֹת גְּדוֹלוֹת; וְתַשְׁלִים בָּתֵּינוּ; וְתַשְׁכֵּן שְׁכִינָתְךָ בֵּינֵינוּ. וְזַכֵּנִי לְגַדֵּל בָּנִים וּבְנֵי בָנִים חֲכָמִים וּנְבוֹנִים, אוֹהֲבֵי יהוה, יִרְאֵי אֱלֹהִים, אַנְשֵׁי אֱמֶת, זֶרַע קֹדֶשׁ, בַּיהוה דְּבֵקִים, וּמְאִירִים אֶת הָעוֹלָם בַּתּוֹרָה וּבְמַעֲשִׂים טוֹבִים, וּבְכָל מְלֶאכֶת עֲבוֹדַת הַבּוֹרֵא. אָנָּא שְׁמַע אֶת תְּחִנָּתִי בָּעֵת הַזֹּאת, בִּזְכוּת שָׂרָה וְרִבְקָה וְרָחֵל וְלֵאָה אִמּוֹתֵינוּ, וְהָאֵר נֵרֵנוּ שֶׁלֹּא יִכְבֶּה לְעוֹלָם וָעֶד, וְהָאֵר פָּנֶיךָ וְנִוָּשֵׁעָה. אָמֵן.

May it be Your will, HASHEM, my God and God of my forefathers, that You show favor to me [my husband, my sons, my daughters, my father, my mother] and all my relatives; and that You grant us and all Israel a good and long life; that You remember us with a beneficent memory and blessing; that You consider us with a consideration of salvation and compassion; that You bless us with great blessings; that You make our households complete; that You cause Your Presence to dwell among us. Privilege me to raise children and grandchildren who are wise and understanding, who love HASHEM and fear God, people of truth, holy offspring, attached to HASHEM, who illuminate the world with Torah and good deeds and with every labor in the service of the Creator. Please, hear my supplication at this time, in the merit of Sarah, Rebecca, Rachel, and Leah, our mothers, and cause our light to illuminate that it be not extinguished forever, and let Your countenance shine so that we are saved. Amen.

❧ Preparing for the *Seder*

The *seder* preparations should be made in time for the *seder* to begin as soon as the synagogue services are finished. It should not begin before nightfall, however. *Matzah*, bitter herbs and several other items of symbolic significance are placed on the *seder* plate. Most people customarily follow the arrangement of *Arizal* as shown below.

ג' מצות
3 MATZOS

Matzah — Three whole *matzos* are placed one atop the other, separated by a cloth or napkin. *Matzah* must be eaten three times during the *seder,* by itself, with *maror,* and as the *afikoman.* Each time, the minimum portion of *matzah* for each person should have a volume equivalent to half an egg. Where many people are present, enough *matzos* should be available to enable each participant to receive a proper portion.

Maror and **Chazeres** — Bitter herbs are eaten twice during the *seder,* once by themselves and a second time with *matzah.* Each time a minimum portion, equal to the volume of half an egg, should be eaten. The Talmud lists several vegetables that qualify as *maror,* two of which are put on the *seder* plate in the places marked *chazeres* and *maror*. Most people use romaine lettuce (whole leaves or stalks) for *chazeres*, and horseradish (whole or grated) for *maror*, although either may be used for the *mitzvah* of eating *maror* later in the *seder*.

Charoses — The bitter herbs are dipped into *charoses* (a mixture of grated apples, nuts, other fruit, cinnamon and other spices, mixed with red wine). The *charoses* has the appearance of mortar to symbolize the lot of the Hebrew slaves, whose lives were embittered by hard labor with brick and mortar.

Z'roa [roasted bone] and **Beitzah** [roasted egg] — On the eve of Passover in the Holy Temple in Jerusalem, two sacrifices were offered and their meat roasted and eaten at the *seder* feast. To commemorate these two sacrifices, we place a roasted bone (with some meat on it) and a roasted hard-boiled egg on the *seder* plate.

The egg, a symbol of mourning, is used in place of a second piece of meat as a reminder of our mourning at the destruction of the Temple — may it be rebuilt speedily in our day.

Karpas — A vegetable (celery, parsley, boiled potato) other than bitter herbs completes the *seder* plate. It will be dipped in salt water (according to the Gaon, in vinegar) and eaten. (The salt water is not put on the *seder* plate, but it, too, should be prepared beforehand, and placed near the *seder* plate.)

קַדֵּשׁ

Kiddush should be recited and the *seder* begun as soon after synagogue services as possible — however, not before nightfall. Each participant's cup should be poured by someone else to symbolize the majesty of the evening, as though each participant had a servant.

On *Shabbos* begin here:

(וַיְהִי עֶרֶב וַיְהִי בֹקֶר)

יוֹם הַשִּׁשִּׁי: וַיְכֻלּוּ הַשָּׁמַיִם וְהָאָרֶץ וְכָל צְבָאָם. וַיְכַל אֱלֹהִים בַּיּוֹם הַשְּׁבִיעִי מְלַאכְתּוֹ אֲשֶׁר עָשָׂה, וַיִּשְׁבֹּת בַּיּוֹם הַשְּׁבִיעִי מִכָּל מְלַאכְתּוֹ אֲשֶׁר עָשָׂה. וַיְבָרֶךְ אֱלֹהִים אֶת יוֹם הַשְּׁבִיעִי וַיְקַדֵּשׁ אֹתוֹ, כִּי בוֹ שָׁבַת מִכָּל מְלַאכְתּוֹ אֲשֶׁר בָּרָא אֱלֹהִים לַעֲשׂוֹת.¹

KIDDUSH CONTINUES ON THE NEXT PAGE.

◄§ מִכָּל מְלַאכְתּוֹ אֲשֶׁר בָּרָא אֱלֹהִים לַעֲשׂוֹת — *All His work which God created to make.* In addition to their literal meaning, the days of Creation also represent the evolving history of the world, each day alluding to different millennia of existence. As the Sages teach us, *The day of the Holy One, Blessed is He, is a thousand years* (*Bereishis Rabbah* 19:14). During the first two days of Creation, water totally covered the globe and nothing was completed, yet a primeval light illuminated the first day of existence. So too, *During the first two thousand years there was desolation* (*Avodah Zarah* 9a, *Sanhedrin* 97a) when few people served Hashem. Yet, the Creator, the "light of the world," was still recognized throughout the existence of Adam — a life-span of nearly one thousand years. Perhaps the pagan worship of idolatry did not dawn until the death of Adam.

The second day witnessed the creation of the firmament and the division of the waters above and below. This mirrored the experience of the second millennium at the Generation of the Flood, when the righteous Noah and his sons were separated from the wicked, who were punished by water. On the third day, dry land appeared with the growth of vegetation and the ripening of fruits. This foreshadowed the third millennium that began when Abraham was forty-eight years old and proclaimed the Name of Hashem. Abraham persuaded many to acclaim God's existence and instructed his household and descendants to tread Hashem's path, and to behave with righteousness and justice. Eventually the nation he gave birth to received the Torah, *"the fruits of the world,"* at Sinai and brought His Commandments to fruition.

KADDESH

Kiddush should be recited and the *seder* begun as soon after synagogue services as possible — however, not before nightfall. Each participant's cup should be poured by someone else to symbolize the majesty of the evening, as though each participant had a servant.

On *Shabbos* begin here:

(And there was evening and there was morning)

The sixth day. And the heavens and the earth and all their array were completed. And God completed on the seventh day His work which He had done. And He rested on the seventh day from all His work which He had done. And God blessed the seventh day and sanctified it, for on it He rested from all His work which God created to make.[1]

KIDDUSH CONTINUES ON THE NEXT PAGE.

(1) *Genesis* 1:31-2:3.

Constellations of stars were created on the fourth day accompanied by the large and small luminaries. Similarly, the fourth millennium witnessed the two Temples where *The Glory of HASHEM filled the House of God.* In the First Temple, under the dynasty of King David, the Divine fire waxed strong, consuming the sacrifices, until, as the waning of the moon, the Jews were exiled to Babylon. In the Second Temple, under the Hasmonean dynasty, the fire was much smaller. Both luminaries set towards the evening of this millennia and the Second Temple, too, was destroyed.

On the fifth day, the seas swarmed with living creatures, the great sea serpents were created and birds flew above the earth. This foreshadowed a dark period when atheistic nationalism would rule supreme and the mass of humanity would have no more value or leadership than the fish or birds. Every individual would be susceptible to be trapped at will and none would seek Hashem.

From before daybreak of the sixth day, the earth produced animals and beasts until Man was finally created in the image of Hashem. So too, the sixth millennium will first be marked by beastly behavior, before the Divinely inspired Messiah will finally appear as predicted in *Daniel*. It seems also apparent that at the onset of the sixth millennium, a new, terrible and extremely powerful empire will come closer to attaining the ultimate truth than any preceding kingdom. The seventh and final thousand years of existence refers to the World to Come which is "entirely Sabbath, bringing everlasting peace."

(*Genesis* 2:3 and *Ramban's* lecture *Toras Temimah*)

On all nights other than Friday, begin here; on Friday night include all passages in parentheses.

סַבְרִי מָרָנָן וְרַבָּנָן וְרַבּוֹתַי:

בָּרוּךְ אַתָּה יהוה אֱלֹהֵינוּ מֶלֶךְ הָעוֹלָם, בּוֹרֵא פְּרִי הַגָּפֶן:

בָּרוּךְ אַתָּה יהוה אֱלֹהֵינוּ מֶלֶךְ הָעוֹלָם, אֲשֶׁר בָּחַר בָּנוּ מִכָּל עָם, וְרוֹמְמָנוּ מִכָּל לָשׁוֹן, וְקִדְּשָׁנוּ בְּמִצְוֹתָיו. וַתִּתֶּן לָנוּ יהוה אֱלֹהֵינוּ בְּאַהֲבָה (שַׁבָּתוֹת לִמְנוּחָה וּ)מוֹעֲדִים לְשִׂמְחָה, חַגִּים וּזְמַנִּים לְשָׂשׂוֹן, אֶת יוֹם (הַשַּׁבָּת הַזֶּה וְאֶת יוֹם) חַג הַמַּצּוֹת הַזֶּה, זְמַן חֵרוּתֵנוּ (בְּאַהֲבָה) מִקְרָא קֹדֶשׁ, זֵכֶר לִיצִיאַת מִצְרָיִם, כִּי בָנוּ בָחַרְתָּ וְאוֹתָנוּ קִדַּשְׁתָּ מִכָּל הָעַמִּים, (וְשַׁבָּת) וּמוֹעֲדֵי קָדְשֶׁךָ (בְּאַהֲבָה וּבְרָצוֹן) בְּשִׂמְחָה וּבְשָׂשׂוֹן הִנְחַלְתָּנוּ. בָּרוּךְ אַתָּה יהוה, מְקַדֵּשׁ (הַשַּׁבָּת וְ)יִשְׂרָאֵל וְהַזְּמַנִּים.

On Saturday night, add the following two paragraphs:

בָּרוּךְ אַתָּה יהוה אֱלֹהֵינוּ מֶלֶךְ הָעוֹלָם, בּוֹרֵא מְאוֹרֵי הָאֵשׁ.

בָּרוּךְ אַתָּה יהוה אֱלֹהֵינוּ מֶלֶךְ הָעוֹלָם, הַמַּבְדִּיל בֵּין קֹדֶשׁ לְחוֹל, בֵּין אוֹר לְחֹשֶׁךְ, בֵּין יִשְׂרָאֵל לָעַמִּים, בֵּין יוֹם הַשְּׁבִיעִי לְשֵׁשֶׁת יְמֵי הַמַּעֲשֶׂה. בֵּין קְדֻשַּׁת שַׁבָּת לִקְדֻשַּׁת יוֹם טוֹב הִבְדַּלְתָּ, וְאֶת יוֹם הַשְּׁבִיעִי מִשֵּׁשֶׁת יְמֵי הַמַּעֲשֶׂה קִדַּשְׁתָּ, הִבְדַּלְתָּ וְקִדַּשְׁתָּ אֶת עַמְּךָ יִשְׂרָאֵל בִּקְדֻשָּׁתֶךָ. בָּרוּךְ אַתָּה יהוה, הַמַּבְדִּיל בֵּין קֹדֶשׁ לְקֹדֶשׁ.

On all nights conclude here:

בָּרוּךְ אַתָּה יהוה אֱלֹהֵינוּ מֶלֶךְ הָעוֹלָם, שֶׁהֶחֱיָנוּ וְקִיְּמָנוּ וְהִגִּיעָנוּ לַזְּמַן הַזֶּה.

The wine should be drunk without delay, while reclining on the left side. It is preferable to drink the entire cup but at the very least, most of the cup should be drained.

◌§ מִקְרָא קֹדֶשׁ — *A holy convocation.* This phrase denotes that every-one should gather on the festivals. They shall publicly sanctify the festivals with prayer and praise to God; they should also honor the

On all nights other than Friday, begin here; on Friday night include all passages in parentheses.

By your leave, my masters and teachers:

Blessed are You, HASHEM, our God, King of the Universe, Who creates the fruit of the vine.

Blessed are You, HASHEM, our God, King of the Universe, Who has chosen us from among all peoples, raised us above all languages, and sanctified us with His commandments. And You have given us, HASHEM, our God, lovingly, (*Shabbasos* for rest, and) appointed times for gladness, festivals and holidays for rejoicing, this day of (*Shabbos* and this day of) the Festival of Matzos, the time of our freedom, (lovingly,) a holy convocation in commemoration of the Exodus from Egypt. For You have chosen us and sanctified us from among all peoples and (*Shabbos* and) Your sacred holidays (with love and goodwill) with gladness and joy You have granted us a heritage. Blessed are You, HASHEM, Who sanctifies (the *Shabbos* and) Yisrael and the Festivals.

On Saturday night, add the following two paragraphs:

Blessed are You, HASHEM, our God, King of the Universe, Who creates the lights of the fire.

Blessed are You, HASHEM, our God, King of the Universe, Who distinguishes between the sacred and the profane, between light and darkness, between Yisrael and the other peoples, between the seventh day and the six days of labor. You have made a distinction between the sanctity of *Shabbos* and the sanctity of a holiday, and sanctified the seventh day over the six days of labor. You have separated and sanctified Your people Yisrael with Your holiness. Blessed are You, HASHEM, Who distinguishes between one sanctity and another.

On all nights conclude here:

Blessed are You, HASHEM, our God, King of the Universe, Who has kept us alive, and maintained us and enabled us to reach this time.

The wine should be drunk without delay, while reclining on the left side. It is preferable to drink the entire cup but at the very least, most of the cup should be drained.

---

festivals by donning clean, fresh clothes and by eating festive meals. (*Leviticus* 23:2. See also 23:24, *Ramban's Rosh Hashanah* lecture.)

וּרְחַץ

The head of the household washes his hands as if to eat bread (pouring water from a cup, twice on the right and twice on the left), but without reciting a blessing.

כַּרְפַּס

All participants take a vegetable other than *maror* and dip it into salt water.
A piece smaller in volume than olive size should be used.
The following blessing is recited (with the intention that it also applies to the *maror* which will be eaten during the meal) before the vegetable is eaten.

בָּרוּךְ אַתָּה יהוה אֱלֹהֵינוּ מֶלֶךְ הָעוֹלָם, בּוֹרֵא פְּרִי הָאֲדָמָה.

יַחַץ

The head of the household breaks the middle *matzah* in two. He puts the smaller part back between the two whole *matzos,* and wraps up the larger part for later use as the *afikoman.* Some briefly place the *afikoman* portion on their shoulders, in accordance with the Biblical verse (*Shemos* 12:34) recounting that Israel left Egypt carrying their *matzos* on their shoulders, and say, בְּבֶהָלוּ יָצָאנוּ מִמִּצְרָיִם, "In haste we went out of Egypt."

מַגִּיד

The head of the household lifts the broken *matzah* for all to see,
and recites the following brief explanation of the proceedings.

הָא לַחְמָא עַנְיָא דִי אֲכָלוּ אַבְהָתָנָא בְּאַרְעָא דְמִצְרָיִם. כָּל דִּכְפִין יֵיתֵי וְיֵכוֹל, כָּל דִּצְרִיךְ יֵיתֵי וְיִפְסַח. הָשַׁתָּא הָכָא, לְשָׁנָה הַבָּאָה בְּאַרְעָא דְיִשְׂרָאֵל. הָשַׁתָּא עַבְדֵי, לְשָׁנָה הַבָּאָה בְּנֵי חוֹרִין.

The *seder* plate is removed and the second of the four cups of wine is poured.
The youngest present asks the reasons for the unusual proceedings of the evening.

מַה נִּשְׁתַּנָּה הַלַּיְלָה הַזֶּה מִכָּל הַלֵּילוֹת?

שֶׁבְּכָל הַלֵּילוֹת אָנוּ אוֹכְלִין חָמֵץ וּמַצָּה, הַלַּיְלָה הַזֶּה — כֻּלּוֹ מַצָּה.

הָא לַחְמָא עַנְיָא ⇐ — *This is the bread of affliction*. The *Haggadah* describes *matzah* as the bread of poverty and affliction. *Matzah* recalls our

URECHATZ

The head of the household washes his hands as if to eat bread (pouring water from a
cup, twice on the right and twice on the left), but without reciting a blessing.

KARPAS

All participants take a vegetable other than *maror* and dip it into salt water.
A piece smaller in volume than olive size should be used.
The following blessing is recited (with the intention that it also applies to the *maror*
which will be eaten during the meal) before the vegetable is eaten.

Blessed are You, HASHEM, our God, King of the Universe,
Who creates the fruit of the soil.

YACHATZ

The head of the household breaks the middle *matzah* in two. He puts the smaller part back
between the two whole *matzos,* and wraps up the larger part for later use as the *afikoman.*
Some briefly place the *afikoman* portion on their shoulders, in accordance with the Biblical
verse (*Shemos* 12:34) recounting that Israel left Egypt carrying their *matzos* on their
shoulders, and say, בְּבְהֵלוּ יָצָאנוּ מִמִּצְרַיִם, "In haste we went out of Egypt."

MAGGID

The head of the household lifts the broken *matzah* for all to see,
and recites the following brief explanation of the proceedings.

This is the bread of affliction which our fathers ate in the
land of Egypt. Let anyone who is hungry come in and eat.
Let anyone who is needy come in and make Pesach.
This year we are here; next year we will be in the Land of
Israel. Now we are slaves; next year we will be freemen.

The *seder* plate is removed and the second of the four cups of wine is poured.
The youngest present asks the reasons for the unusual proceedings of the evening.

Why is this night different from all other nights?
1. On all other nights we eat *chametz* and *matzah*.
On this night — only *matzah*.

---

ancestors' ill treatment in Egypt and their diet of "meager bread and
scant water" (*Isaiah* 30:20). However, *matzah* also symbolizes the bread
of freedom, when our ancestors were freed in such haste that their dough
had no time to rise and become leaven. (*Deuteronomy* 16:2)

⊷§ חָמֵץ וּמַצָּה — *Chametz and matzah*. Wine or strong drink that has

שֶׁבְּכָל הַלֵּילוֹת אָנוּ אוֹכְלִין שְׁאָר יְרָקוֹת,
הַלַּיְלָה הַזֶּה — מָרוֹר.
שֶׁבְּכָל הַלֵּילוֹת אֵין אָנוּ מַטְבִּילִין אֲפִילוּ פַּעַם אֶחָת,
הַלַּיְלָה הַזֶּה — שְׁתֵּי פְעָמִים.
שֶׁבְּכָל הַלֵּילוֹת אָנוּ אוֹכְלִין בֵּין יוֹשְׁבִין וּבֵין מְסֻבִּין,
הַלַּיְלָה הַזֶּה — כֻּלָּנוּ מְסֻבִּין.

The *seder* plate is returned. The *matzos* are kept uncovered as the *Haggadah* is recited in unison. The *Haggadah* should be translated if necessary, and the story of the Exodus should be amplified upon.

עֲבָדִים הָיִינוּ לְפַרְעֹה בְּמִצְרָיִם, וַיּוֹצִיאֵנוּ יהוה אֱלֹהֵינוּ
מִשָּׁם בְּיָד חֲזָקָה וּבִזְרוֹעַ נְטוּיָה. וְאִלּוּ לֹא הוֹצִיא
הַקָּדוֹשׁ בָּרוּךְ הוּא אֶת אֲבוֹתֵינוּ מִמִּצְרַיִם, הֲרֵי אָנוּ וּבָנֵינוּ
וּבְנֵי בָנֵינוּ מְשֻׁעְבָּדִים הָיִינוּ לְפַרְעֹה בְּמִצְרָיִם. וַאֲפִילוּ כֻּלָּנוּ
חֲכָמִים, כֻּלָּנוּ נְבוֹנִים, כֻּלָּנוּ זְקֵנִים, כֻּלָּנוּ יוֹדְעִים אֶת הַתּוֹרָה,

---

soured and turned to vinegar is known as *chometz*, a similar-sounding word derived from "loss" or "robbery" (see *Psalms* 71:4, 73:21) since the original taste of the wine has been removed. Leaven naturally has the power to alter other foodstuff, so it symbolizes the Divine Attribute (*Middah*) of Justice, according to those learned in the Kabbalistic secrets. However, this world was created by a combination of two separate Attributes — that of Justice and that of Mercy (*Bereishis Rabbah* 12:15). Thus, any sacrifice that contained fermenting agents (or sweetening agents such as honey) was usually not acceptable before Hashem. For this reason, the thanksgiving sacrifice, containing both leaven and *matzah*, will be sacrificed even in the World to Come — since in the future, harmony will reign there. (*Leviticus* 23:17)

≈§ לְפַרְעֹה בְּמִצְרַיִם — *To Pharaoh in Egypt.* When our forefather Abraham
descended to Egypt because of famine, the Egyptians persecuted him unfairly by abducting his wife. God punished the Egyptians and rescued Sarah, and then Abraham and Sarah left the country laden with gold, silver and cattle. Pharaoh also arranged to have Abraham escorted out of Egypt.

All this foreshadowed how his descendants would later be forced down to Egypt because of famine. Likewise, the Egyptians would persecute

2. On all other nights we eat all kinds of vegetables.
On this night — *maror.*
3. On all other nights we do not dip even once.
On this night — twice.
4. On all other nights
we eat either sitting straight or reclining.
On this night we all recline.

The *seder* plate is returned. The *matzos* are kept uncovered as the *Haggadah* is recited in unison. The *Haggadah* should be translated if necessary, and the story of the Exodus should be amplified upon.

W e were slaves to Pharaoh in Egypt, and HASHEM, our God, took us out of there with a strong hand and an outstretched arm. If the Holy One, Blessed is He, had not taken our forefathers out of Egypt, we and our children and our children's children would still be enslaved to Pharaoh in Egypt. Even if all of us were wise, all of us understanding, all of us aged, all of us knowledgeable in Torah,

them wickedly, even murdering their sons, while seeking to keep their females for themselves. God punished their wickedness with colossal plagues until Abraham's descendants emerged with gold, silver and a great wealth of cattle and sheep. The Egyptians also exerted great pressure that they should leave their country.

Nothing happened to Abraham which his progeny did not later experience. The Sages teach us (*Midrash Tanchuma, Lech Lecha* 9), "Whatever occurred to the Patriarchs was symbolic of what would later transpire with their children." Many of the Patriarchs' actions were symbolic in nature, to pave the way for their descendants.[1]

It should also be understood that our father Abraham, by fearing for his life as he descended to Egypt, unwittingly transgressed — according to his high level of faith in God — and brought his righteous wife close to sin. Instead, he should have placed his trust in God the All-Powerful to protect him, his wife and belongings. Leaving the land to which God had specifically directed him was also a sin. Surely God would have rescued him from starvation. His descendants were exiled specifically to Egypt, under the Pharaohs, since justice is generally meted out at the place of the original sin.   (*Genesis* 12:6, 10)

1. We also find other prophets who were instructed to do a symbolic act so that their prophecies would come to pass; see *Jeremiah* 51:63 ff., and *II Kings* 13:17 ff.

מִצְוָה עָלֵינוּ לְסַפֵּר בִּיצִיאַת מִצְרָיִם. וְכָל הַמַּרְבֶּה לְסַפֵּר בִּיצִיאַת מִצְרָיִם, הֲרֵי זֶה מְשֻׁבָּח.

מַעֲשֶׂה בְּרַבִּי אֱלִיעֶזֶר וְרַבִּי יְהוֹשֻׁעַ וְרַבִּי אֶלְעָזָר בֶּן עֲזַרְיָה וְרַבִּי עֲקִיבָא וְרַבִּי טַרְפוֹן שֶׁהָיוּ מְסֻבִּין בִּבְנֵי בְרַק, וְהָיוּ מְסַפְּרִים בִּיצִיאַת מִצְרָיִם כָּל אוֹתוֹ הַלַּיְלָה. עַד שֶׁבָּאוּ תַלְמִידֵיהֶם וְאָמְרוּ לָהֶם, רַבּוֹתֵינוּ הִגִּיעַ זְמַן קְרִיאַת שְׁמַע שֶׁל שַׁחֲרִית.

אָמַר רַבִּי אֶלְעָזָר בֶּן עֲזַרְיָה, הֲרֵי אֲנִי כְּבֶן שִׁבְעִים שָׁנָה, וְלֹא זָכִיתִי שֶׁתֵּאָמֵר יְצִיאַת מִצְרָיִם בַּלֵּילוֹת, עַד שֶׁדְּרָשָׁהּ בֶּן זוֹמָא, שֶׁנֶּאֱמַר, לְמַעַן תִּזְכֹּר אֶת יוֹם צֵאתְךָ מֵאֶרֶץ מִצְרָיִם כֹּל יְמֵי חַיֶּיךָ.[1] יְמֵי חַיֶּיךָ הַיָּמִים, כֹּל יְמֵי חַיֶּיךָ הַלֵּילוֹת. וַחֲכָמִים אוֹמְרִים, יְמֵי חַיֶּיךָ הָעוֹלָם הַזֶּה, כֹּל יְמֵי חַיֶּיךָ לְהָבִיא לִימוֹת הַמָּשִׁיחַ.

בָּרוּךְ הַמָּקוֹם, בָּרוּךְ הוּא. בָּרוּךְ שֶׁנָּתַן תּוֹרָה לְעַמּוֹ יִשְׂרָאֵל, בָּרוּךְ הוּא. כְּנֶגֶד אַרְבָּעָה בָנִים דִּבְּרָה תוֹרָה: אֶחָד **חָכָם**, וְאֶחָד **רָשָׁע**, וְאֶחָד **תָּם**, וְאֶחָד **שֶׁאֵינוֹ יוֹדֵעַ לִשְׁאוֹל.**

◆§ **וְכָל הַמַּרְבֶּה לְסַפֵּר בִּיצִיאַת מִצְרָיִם** — *And whoever expands upon the story of the Exodus.* The story of our Exodus from Egypt is so important, it must constantly be repeated. In the Ten Commandments, the Creator is described as ". . . taking you out of Egypt." The Exodus clearly revealed Hashem as the Creator Who is All-Powerful and directs the world and its inhabitants with His Will. The miracles and wonders which accompanied the Exodus proved for all time that Hashem our God is the God of Heaven and Earth, and no other deity or power exists besides Him. *(Deuteronomy 6:20)*

◆§ **שֶׁתֵּאָמֵר יְצִיאַת מִצְרָיִם בַּלֵּילוֹת** — *To show that the Exodus from Egypt must be said at night.* Though the actual Exodus from Egypt took place in broad daylight, they had already become free men the previous night.

we would still be commanded to tell the story of the Exodus from Egypt, and whoever expands upon the story of the Exodus merits praise.

An incident took place in which Rabbi Eliezer, Rabbi Yehoshua, Rabbi Elazar ben Azaryah, Rabbi Akiva, and Rabbi Tarfon were reclining in Bnei Brak and recounting the tale of the Exodus from Egypt all that night, until their students came and told them: "Our Rabbis! The time for the recitation of the morning *Sh'ma* has arrived."

Rabbi Elazar ben Azaryah said: "Behold, I am like a seventy-year-old man, yet I have never been privileged to show that the Exodus from Egypt must be said at night until Ben Zoma explained it. It says: 'So that you will remember the day of your departure from Egypt all the days of your life.'[1] 'The days of your life" indicates the days. 'All the days of your life' indicates the nights. The other Sages say, 'the days of your life' indicates the world in its present state. 'All the days of your life' includes the days of *Mashiach*.

Blessed is the Omnipresent. Blessed is He. Blessed is He Who gave the Torah to His people, Israel. Blessed is He. The Torah addresses itself to four sons — one is wise, one is wicked, one is perfect, and one is unable to ask.

---

(1) *Deuteronomy* 16:3.

Moses and Aaron remained within the city that night, close to the royal palace. After the firstborn sons were struck down at midnight, Pharaoh finally relented and urged them to leave immediately, but they refused to steal out quietly like thieves in the night.

Moreover, God had expressly forbidden the Jews to venture out of doors until morning. When the message reached the Land of Goshen where most of the Children of Israel lived, it was already morning. They all gathered at Rameses to begin their journey out of Egypt "*with an upraised hand, before the eyes of all Egypt*" (*Numbers* 33:3).

(*Exodus* 12:31, 51)

◆§ לִימוֹת הַמָּשִׁיחַ — *The days of Messiah*. Since Creation, man has had the freedom of choice to do either good or evil. Our decision earns us either reward or punishment. This free choice will continue until the

חָכָם מָה הוּא אוֹמֵר? מָה הָעֵדֹת וְהַחֻקִּים וְהַמִּשְׁפָּטִים אֲשֶׁר צִוָּה יהוה אֱלֹהֵינוּ אֶתְכֶם?[1] וְאַף אַתָּה אֱמָר לוֹ כְּהִלְכוֹת הַפֶּסַח, אֵין מַפְטִירִין אַחַר הַפֶּסַח אֲפִיקוֹמָן.

רָשָׁע מָה הוּא אוֹמֵר? מָה הָעֲבֹדָה הַזֹּאת לָכֶם?[2] לָכֶם וְלֹא לוֹ, וּלְפִי שֶׁהוֹצִיא אֶת עַצְמוֹ מִן הַכְּלָל, כָּפַר בְּעִקָּר – וְאַף אַתָּה הַקְהֵה אֶת שִׁנָּיו וֶאֱמָר לוֹ, בַּעֲבוּר זֶה עָשָׂה יהוה לִי בְּצֵאתִי מִמִּצְרָיִם.[3] לִי וְלֹא לוֹ,

---

coming of the Messiah. In the messianic era, however, men will return to the state of Adam before the Sin. Everyone's natural inclination will then be to behave correctly and do only good. As described by the prophets, they will no longer lust after wickedness (see *Jeremiah* 31:30 ff., *Ezekiel* 36:26 ff.). Since the evil inclination will no longer plague us, the Sages teach us (*Shabbos* 151b) that in the days of the Messiah we will not have the opportunity for merit or guilt.

(*Deuteronomy* 30:6. See also *HaGeulah* Ch. 2)

◆§ מָה הָעֵדֹת וְהַחֻקִּים וְהַמִּשְׁפָּטִים — *What are the testimonies, the statutes, and the laws?* The wise son asks several questions. First he queries the basis behind the commandments known as עֵדֹת, "testimonies" — what exactly do they testify? Commandments such as eating *matzah,* erecting a *succah,* observing Passover or the Sabbath, donning *tefillin* and affixing a *mezuzah* bear witness to Hashem's miracles. We perform these duties to commemorate God's wonders.

This son then inquires: What do the "statutes" signify? Indeed, the Torah deliberately does not offer the reasons behind these decrees known as "*chukim.*"

He further asks: What is the purpose of the מִשְׁפָּטִים, "laws" — particularly the less understandable ordinances such as stoning those who breach the Sabbath, burning alive those who behave incestuously or inflicting forty lashes for sowing forbidden seed mixtures?

In reply, we relate the whole sequence of the Exodus that graphically revealed the might and power of the Creator. Surely it is fitting that we display our gratitude to God for showing us such great kindness. He is our God and we are His people, part of His flock, and we are obliged to carry out His Will. It is our intrinsic duty to honor His Commandments and obey His "testimonies, statutes, and laws." Moreover, these are all designed for our benefit; none contain any harm — even the "statutes"

What does the wise son say? "What are the testimonies, the statutes, and the laws which HASHEM, our God, has commanded you?"[1] And you, too, should tell him the laws of Pesach: It is forbidden to eat anything after the *Pesach* sacrifice."

What does the wicked son say? "What is this service to you?"[2] "To you," but not to himself. Since he excludes himself from the group, he denies that which is fundamental. You, too, should set his teeth on edge, and say to him: "It is because of this that HASHEM did so for me when I went out of Egypt."[3] "For me," but not for him.

---

(1) *Deuteronomy* 6:20. (2) *Exodus* 12:26. (3) 13:8.

---

whose exact reasons are not revealed. Although we already owe everything to Him and deserve no payment, God in His charity will reward us.

(*Deuteronomy* 6:20 ff.)

◀§ אֵין מַפְטִירִין אַחַר הַפֶּסַח אֲפִיקוֹמָן — *It is forbidden to eat anything after the Pesach sacrifice.* We ate nothing afterwards to ensure that the paschal lamb should not be served while members of the household were hungry. This made it less likely that the Biblical injunction against breaking the bones of this sacrifice (*Exodus* 12:46) would be infringed. Our Rabbis further restricted eating after the sacrifice even foods or tidbits that are not satisfying in themselves but are served only as desserts. Furthermore, according to the *Rishonim*, these restrictions were in force all night long.

Since the destruction of the Temple, a piece of *matzah* is customarily eaten in memory of the paschal lamb, which was consumed when the Temple stood. Similar rules now apply against the eating of other foods after partaking of this *matzah*, though obviously the concern of "breaking the bones" does not apply to *matzos*. Therefore, this *matzah* (that we now describe as an *afikoman* whereas the original meaning of *afikoman* was dessert) completes the *seder* meal nowadays.

Imbibing more wine after the fourth cup is certainly forbidden. This is not because of the *matzah* (since we drink the last two cups of wine *after* the *afikoman* anyway), but since it might appear as if we are adding to the four cups of wine or even beginning a new *seder*.

(*Milchamos, Pesachim 119*)

◀§ רָשָׁע — *The wicked son.* As the bitter root that produces gall, the wicked son is the "twig that grows from his father's roots" (*Isaiah* 11:1). By contrast, no bitter plant will sprout from sweet-tasting roots. So

אִלּוּ הָיָה שָׁם לֹא הָיָה נִגְאָל.

תָּם מָה הוּא אוֹמֵר? מַה זֹּאת? וְאָמַרְתָּ אֵלָיו, בְּחֹזֶק יָד הוֹצִיאָנוּ יהוה מִמִּצְרַיִם מִבֵּית עֲבָדִים.[1]

וְשֶׁאֵינוֹ יוֹדֵעַ לִשְׁאוֹל, אַתְּ פְּתַח לוֹ. שֶׁנֶּאֱמַר, וְהִגַּדְתָּ לְבִנְךָ בַּיּוֹם הַהוּא לֵאמֹר, בַּעֲבוּר זֶה עָשָׂה יהוה לִי בְּצֵאתִי מִמִּצְרָיִם.[2]

יָכוֹל מֵרֹאשׁ חֹדֶשׁ, תַּלְמוּד לוֹמַר בַּיּוֹם הַהוּא. אִי בַּיּוֹם הַהוּא, יָכוֹל מִבְּעוֹד יוֹם, תַּלְמוּד לוֹמַר בַּעֲבוּר זֶה. בַּעֲבוּר זֶה לֹא אָמַרְתִּי אֶלָּא בְּשָׁעָה שֶׁיֵּשׁ מַצָּה וּמָרוֹר מֻנָּחִים לְפָנֶיךָ.

מִתְּחִלָּה, עוֹבְדֵי עֲבוֹדָה זָרָה הָיוּ אֲבוֹתֵינוּ, וְעַכְשָׁו קֵרְבָנוּ הַמָּקוֹם לַעֲבוֹדָתוֹ. שֶׁנֶּאֱמַר,

---

too, anyone whose heart is at peace with God and spares no thought for idolatry will not give birth to a son who agrees with pagan worship. (Deuteronomy 29:17)

◀§ מֵרֹאשׁ חֹדֶשׁ — *From the first of the month.* To commemorate the miracle of the Exodus, the lunar months start from *Nissan.* Although the new year begins in *Tishrei*, it remains the seventh month of the year. The Torah does not ascribe names to the months of the year; rather it describes them respectively as "the third month" (*Exodus* 19:1), or "the second month" (*Numbers* 29:1, see also *Genesis* 8:13 ff.). This is deliberate. By calculating each month from the month of the Exodus, we are continually reminded of the miracle of our freedom.

Also, for the same reason, the Torah has no specific names for the days of the week. Instead we describe each individual weekday as the "first day of the Sabbath," the "second day of the Sabbath," and so on. In this way we are constantly recalling the wonders of Creation.

The foreign names of the months (*Nissan, Iyar, Sivan*, etc.) were first mentioned in Scriptures by Ezra, Nehemiah, Zechariah and Esther since they originate from the Persian empire. As the Sages teach us, "The titles of the months came out with us from Babylon" (*Yerushalmi, Rosh*

Had he been there he would not have been redeemed.

What does the perfect son say? "What is this?" Say to him: "HASHEM took us out of Egypt, from the house of slaves, by strength of hand."[1]

And regarding the one who is unable to ask, you open a conversation with him, as it says: "And you will tell your son on that day, saying, 'It is because of this that HASHEM did so for me when I went out of Egypt.'"[2]

We might have held from the first of the month, but the Torah tells us: "On that day." Since it says "on that day," we might have held that we should begin while it is still day. But the Torah says: "Because of *this*." I only say "because of *this*" at a time when *matzah* and *maror* are placed before you.

At first our ancestors were idolaters, but now the Omnipresent has brought us close to His service, as it says: "And

---

(1) *Exodus* 13:14. (2) 13:8.

Hashanah 1:2 and *Bereishis Rabbah* 48:9). These names are now used to commemorate our redemption from the Babylonian Exile.
(*Exodus* 12:2 and *Rosh Hashanah* lecture)

◆§ בַּעֲבוּר זֶה — *Because of this. . .* This is an elliptical sentence and really means, "It is because of what Hashem did for me when I left Egypt that I now observe this *mitzvah*." Apparently the word "this" invites the father to describe to his son how he personally sees what God did for us then. According to Kabbalah the use of the term "this," זֶה, refers to the use of the word in the Song of the Sea, "This (זֶה) is my God and I will glorify Him." Thus, it was because of His Name and Glory that He brought us out of Egypt. The Sages, however, understand זֶה to refer to the *matzah* and *maror* placed on the Passover *seder* table.   (*Exodus* 13:8, 16)

◆§ וְעַכְשָׁו קֵרְבָנוּ הַמָּקוֹם לַעֲבוֹדָתוֹ — *But now the Omnipresent has brought us close to His service.* Often, many commandments are based on one general principle. When idol worship first began in the days of Enoch, people denied true belief in God in various ways. Some insisted that the universe was permanent, had always existed, and was never created by God. Others denied only הַשְׁגָּחָה פְּרָטִית, *Divine Providence.* They claimed

וַיֹּאמֶר יְהוֹשֻׁעַ אֶל כָּל הָעָם, כֹּה אָמַר יהוה אֱלֹהֵי
יִשְׂרָאֵל, בְּעֵבֶר הַנָּהָר יָשְׁבוּ אֲבוֹתֵיכֶם מֵעוֹלָם, תֶּרַח

that either God was unaware of the individual and his concerns or He awards no retribution (in reward or punishment) for individual actions. Thus, when God interrupts the natural world order on behalf of a nation or individual, He exposes these false theories for what they are.

Each great miracle proves that this world has a Creator, continually monitoring events and changing the rules at will. Furthermore, if a prophet predicted this miracle, the ensuing wonder simultaneously confirms that Hashem speaks unto man (*Deuteronomy* 5:28, *Amos* 3:7), thereby bolstering the foundations of the Torah, likewise a prophetic transmission.

Initially, the plagues in Egypt proved the existence of Divine Providence, that God has not abandoned this world to chance. Therefore, the Torah here declares, "so that you will know that I am HASHEM in the midst of the land" (*Exodus* 8:18). Then the plagues clearly showed the principle of Creation, *so that you shall know that the Earth is HASHEM'S* (ibid. *Exodus* 9:29), that Hashem owns this world after creating it from absolute nothingness. Finally, the plagues displayed to the doubting Egyptians the unique power of Hashem — "so that you shall know that there is none like Me in all the world" (ibid. v. 14), none can withstand Him. The absolute truth as to the existence of the Creator of the universe (and also the integrity of the Torah) was firmly and publicly established by the great signs and wonders performed in Egypt.

God does not intend to continually refute every heretic and sinner by performing miracles in each generation. Therefore He instructed us to observe various commandments that act as "signs" and "memorials" to the events that we witnessed with our own eyes. Thus, those irrefutable truths are transmitted to our descendants throughout the generations. This transmission is considered so important that one is liable to the severest Heavenly punishment for deliberately omitting the paschal sacrifice or eating *chametz*.

We also testify to these fundamental truths by wearing, close to our hearts and minds, the *tefillin* — recalling the signs and wonders we witnessed in Egypt. The *mezuzah* scrolls fixed to our doorposts contain the same inscriptions and we also recite these Biblical passages each morning and evening with supporting prayers. Many other commandments are similarly designed to commemorate the Exodus and record

Joshua said to all of the people, So says HASHEM the God of
Israel, Of old, your forefathers dwelt beyond the river — Terah,

---

those miracles for posterity. The lessons they teach should never be
forgotten; nor allow anyone the opportunity for heresy.

By purchasing a *mezuzah* and fixing it to a doorpost with the correct
intentions, a person declares his belief in Creation, the Knowledge and
Providence of a Supreme Being, the principle of prophecy and all the
fundamentals on which the Torah is based. Furthermore, he publicizes
how enormous the Creator's Mercy is upon those who observe His Will.
For it was due to the merit of our forefathers, who feared God, that we
were delivered from slavery to liberty and great honor.

This then is the underlying purpose of the commandments: to believe
in God and display our gratitude for His having created us. Why else was
Man formed? What demands does the Almighty place on the creatures
of this world, other than that the human race recognize the Creator and
display their gratitude? Thus, we set aside places of worship, assemble
for prayers and raise our voices to express our heartfelt appreciation for
Hashem's Creation and His continued support. We openly declare that
we are all His creatures.

By accepting the explicit miracles, one comes to recognize that
everything that happens to the individual or the community is truly
miraculous; nothing is merely "natural" or "ordinary." How else could
observing the commandments bring success or breaching them invite
punishment? Equally, all the blessings and curses contained in the
Torah (*Leviticus* 26:3 ff. and *Deuteronomy* 28:1 ff., and 29:28 ff.) depend
on hidden, implicit miracles. Yet, one becomes aware how unnatural
the events are when any of these hidden miracles occur to a large body
of people.   (*Exodus* 13:16 and *Ramban*' lecture *Toras Temimah*)

⇐§ בְּעֵבֶר הַנָּהָר יָשְׁבוּ אֲבוֹתֵיכֶם מֵעוֹלָם — *Of old, your forefathers dwelt*
beyond the river. Abraham was known as an עִבְרִי, a Hebrew from
across the great Euphrates River. Also, he was a Semite, a descendant
of Shem. Therefore, he could not have been native to Ur of the
Chaldees, since the Chaldeans were descendants of Ham who inhabited
the rest of Babylon.

In fact, both Abraham and his brother Nachor were born in
Mesopotamia, between the Euphrates and Tigris rivers, which was
the domain of the Semitic nations. Only Haran, their youngest
brother, was later born in Ur, when Terach journeyed there with
his family (leaving Nachor behind in Haran). As mentioned by the

אֲבִי אַבְרָהָם וַאֲבִי נָחוֹר, וַיַּעַבְדוּ אֱלֹהִים אֲחֵרִים. וָאֶקַּח
אֶת אֲבִיכֶם אֶת אַבְרָהָם מֵעֵבֶר הַנָּהָר, וָאוֹלֵךְ אוֹתוֹ בְּכָל
אֶרֶץ כְּנָעַן, וָאַרְבֶּה אֶת זַרְעוֹ, וָאֶתֶּן לוֹ אֶת יִצְחָק. וָאֶתֵּן
לְיִצְחָק אֶת יַעֲקֹב וְאֶת עֵשָׂו, וָאֶתֵּן לְעֵשָׂו אֶת הַר שֵׂעִיר
לָרֶשֶׁת אוֹתוֹ, וְיַעֲקֹב וּבָנָיו יָרְדוּ מִצְרָיְמָה.[1]

Sages (*Bava Basra* 91a), Abraham was initially imprisoned in Kuta. Many of my students have told me that Kuta is a large city about six days' journey from Haran (on the route from Haran to Assyria) which makes it nowhere near Babylon where the descendants of Ham lived.

The tome of Egyptian agriculture, quoted by the *Guide to the Perplexed* (3:29), confirms that Abraham was born in Kuta where he disputed the dominant cult of sun worship, until the king imprisoned him. Even in prison, Abraham continued to propound his logical arguments for many days. Eventually, the king became concerned Abraham might convert his people against sun worship. After confiscating all his possessions, he expelled Abraham to Canaan.

According to the Sages, however, an open miracle saved Abraham, rescuing him from a fiery furnace. The phraseology of the Torah, "taking out," also seems to imply a miraculous escape from imprisonment and perhaps the name Ur refers to these fires of the Chaldeans .
(Genesis 11:28, 12:1,
and Ramban's lectures on Koheles and Toras Temimah)

◆§ תֶּרַח אֲבִי אַבְרָהָם — *Terach, the father of Abraham*. I have found written in a *Midrash* that Abraham saved the soul of his father, Terach. Thus the Torah records, "And you shall come to your father in peace" (*Genesis* 15:15).

In a similar fashion, continues the *Midrash*, olive wood and wood of the vine were both spared from being burnt on the Altar in the Temple. This was because the fruit of these trees — oil and wine — were already designated as part of the Temple offerings.
(Genesis 11:32)

◆§ וָאֶתֵּן לְעֵשָׂו אֶת הַר שֵׂעִיר — *I gave unto Esau Mount Seir.* When his brother Jacob was still in Haran, Esau was already a leader of four hundred armed men and resided around the area of Seir. Perhaps

the father of Abraham and the father of Nahor, and they worshiped other gods. And I took your father Abraham from beyond the river, and I led him throughout all the Land of Canaan, and I multiplied his seed, and I gave Isaac unto him, and I gave Jacob and Esau unto Isaac, and I gave unto Esau Mount Seir to inherit, but Jacob and his sons went down to Egypt."[1]

---

(1) *Joshua* 24:2-4.

---

the Horite tribe, native to Seir, were afraid of him and refused him access to their territory or inside their fortifications. Eventually the Edomites would overpower and rule over the Horites, thus fulfilling Isaac's blessing to Esau, "And you shall live by the sword" (*Genesis* 27:40).

When Jacob returned from Haran, Esau finally vacated Canaan — the rightful inheritance of his brother — and settled permanently in Seir. While the chiefs of Esau had already taken possession of their inheritance, Jacob remained a foreigner — as his fathers before him — fulfilling God's covenant to Abraham. Thus, "Your descendants shall be strangers in a foreign land" applied solely to Jacob and his progeny.

In fact, Seir belonged to Canaan and therefore was really part of Abraham's inheritance. God awarded Seir to Esau just as He gave the lands of Amman and Moab to Lot's descendants. As the Torah records, "Yet HASHEM destroyed these before them so that they dwelt in their stead" (*Deuteronomy* 2:21). Indeed, these three states were captured from their powerful inhabitants by Divine miracles; similarly to how Canaan was later awarded to Israel. Therefore, the Children of Israel were warned not to take these lands from them.

(*Genesis* 36:6, 31, 37:1, *Deuteronomy* 2:10)

⊷§ וְיַעֲקֹב וּבָנָיו יָרְדוּ מִצְרָיִם — *But Jacob and his sons went down to Egypt.* Jacob's exile with his family into Egypt was also an allusion to our current exile under Rome — "the fourth beast" in Daniel's vision (*Daniel* 7:7). The parallels are remarkable. The children of Jacob brought the Egyptian exile on themselves by selling Joseph. Later, Jacob descended into Egypt because of the famine. He believed he would be safe among Joseph's fraternity since his son was treated by Pharaoh as one of his own family. Also, the children of Jacob intended to return to Canaan as soon

בָּרוּךְ שׁוֹמֵר הַבְטָחָתוֹ לְיִשְׂרָאֵל, בָּרוּךְ הוּא. שֶׁהַקָּדוֹשׁ בָּרוּךְ הוּא חִשַּׁב אֶת הַקֵּץ, לַעֲשׂוֹת כְּמָה שֶׁאָמַר לְאַבְרָהָם אָבִינוּ בִּבְרִית בֵּין הַבְּתָרִים, שֶׁנֶּאֱמַר, וַיֹּאמֶר

---

as the famine was over, but this took far longer than they had hoped. Jacob died there and his body was only released when Pharaoh's ministers and sages accompanied the funeral cortege with great honor.

This is similar to our relationship with Rome, the nation of Edom. Our own brothers first initiated our downfall by making a covenant with the Romans (*Avodah Zarah* 8b). Later, Agrippa, the last king during the Second Temple, sought Rome's military assistance prior to the *Churban,* destruction of the Temple. Jerusalem ultimately fell to the Romans because of the famine, and the resultant exile has lasted far longer than anyone dared fear, reducing us to "dry bones." Unlike previous exiles, the end of the present *Galus* was left unknown. Finally, we will be extricated from the nations, who will be mortified at the great honor we will then receive, while we shall witness the Divine vengeance. (*Genesis* 47:28, see also 43:14)

◆§ בָּרוּךְ שׁוֹמֵר הַבְטָחָתוֹ לְיִשְׂרָאֵל — *Blessed is He Who keeps His promise to Israel.* Hashem is the God of Truth; none of His promises shall ever prove groundless. He honored the Covenant with the Patriarchs just as He has punished His evil enemies. His destruction of the Egyptians followed without delay. The wicked only flourish as long as the All-Merciful allows them to enjoy the fruits of any good deeds they may have done in this world. For there are only two salient strands in Divine Justice: rewarding the good and punishing evil. Perhaps, those who are utterly evil and deny His existence are punished immediately without any respite.

Abraham's whole life story is an object lesson in Divine Providence, in reward and restitution, and reflects Abraham's trust in God. One would not require a great element of trust to believe in ultimate reward, since good deeds automatically receive their recompense in the World to Come. However, God also promised Abraham great rewards in this world, which is a less natural event.
(*Deuteronomy* 7:9 and his lecture *Toras Temimah*)

◆§ חִשַּׁב אֶת הַקֵּץ — *Calculated the end* [*of the exile*]. From the time the Egyptian exile was decreed, God waited and looked forward

Blessed is He Who keeps His promise to Israel. Blessed is He. For the Holy One, Blessed is He, calculated the end [of the exile], to do as He said to Abraham our father at the Covenant Between the Parts, as it is said, "And He said

---

to this fateful night of redemption, and hastened to redeem His people.

The length of time the Jews spent in Egypt is not entirely clear. Whereas the Covenant Between the Parts, God's Covenant with Abraham (*Genesis* 15:13), speaks of 400 years, at the time of the actual redemption, the Torah describes the time they dwelt in Egypt as 430 years (*Exodus* 12:40).

Rashi explains that the extra thirty years were calculated from the time the Covenant Between the Parts took place until Abraham was blessed with his child Isaac. The 400 years began with Isaac's birth, and the decree, "Your children shall be strangers," then came into effect. Therefore, according to the *Seder Olam,* the Covenant took place when Abraham was 70 years old, and five years before he left Haran forever. Also, it is possible that the Covenant implicitly refers to these 430 years where it mentions, "And the fourth generation shall return here, for the iniquity of the Amorite shall not yet be full until then" (*Genesis* 15:16), which could allude to those missing years. The *Ibn Ezra* explains that the thirty years represent the time between Abraham leaving Haran and the date of the Covenant.

However, according to the simple reading of the Torah, Abraham was approximately 80 years old when God spoke to him at the Covenant. Thus, the Children of Israel were exiled in Egypt for around 220 years. (Another 80 years passed until Jacob was born, and he was 130 at his appearance before Pharaoh in Egypt. That left another 220 years to reach 430.) There is a tradition of 210 years, hinted at when Jacob used the word רְדוּ, "*go down*" (which has the numerical value of 210: ר = 200, ד = 4, ו = 6; 200 + 4 + 6 = 210), to describe the Egyptian exile. Since those years began only after Jacob's passing, following seventeen years' sojourn in Egypt, the total exile amounted to 227 years.

The best explanation of these thirty missing years is, I believe, that the decree of exile was originally intended to last only until four hundred years after the date of the Covenant. Yet the conclusion of the exile was left deliberately vague — "Afterwards they will go out with great possessions" — without specifying or promising how long

לְאַבְרָם, יָדֹעַ תֵּדַע כִּי גֵר יִהְיֶה זַרְעֲךָ בְּאֶרֶץ לֹא
לָהֶם, וַעֲבָדוּם וְעִנּוּ אֹתָם, אַרְבַּע מֵאוֹת שָׁנָה. וְגַם אֶת
הַגּוֹי אֲשֶׁר יַעֲבֹדוּ דָּן אָנֹכִי, וְאַחֲרֵי כֵן יֵצְאוּ בִּרְכֻשׁ
גָּדוֹל.¹

---

that "Afterwards" would actually be. Since the Hebrews sinned in
Egypt, as the prophets elaborate (*Ezekiel* 20:8 and also *Joshua*
24:14), they were punished by their redemption being postponed
another thirty years. Their wickedness held back the Exodus
unnecessarily, similar to how the sin of the spies later delayed their
entry into Eretz Yisrael by forty years.

Perhaps that was why members of the tribe of Ephraim left Egypt
thirty years early (see *Megillah* 9b). Their reasoning was mathemati-
cally correct, but they were entrapped by their sins.

(*Exodus* 12:40, 42; see also *Emunah and Bitachon* Ch.12)

⊷ **כִּי גֵר יִהְיֶה זַרְעֲךָ** — *Your offspring will be a stranger.* God warned
Abraham that his children would not receive the Promised Land
before four hundred years had passed. Also, they would have to
undergo exile and suffering. Although He informed Abraham of the
proposed date of redemption, God did not actually specify the depth
of suffering nor the length of exile. (*Genesis* 15:13)

⊷ **וְגַם אֶת הַגּוֹי אֲשֶׁר יַעֲבֹדוּ** — *But also the nation whom they will
serve.* Even though exile and suffering had been decreed for the
Jews, nonetheless the nation that enslaves and oppresses them will
be judged and punished. They would be assessed on whether they
merely carried out the Divine decree or willingly increased the
oppression on the Hebrews as we see elsewhere (*Exodus* 18:11,
Zechariah 1:15, *Isaiah* 47:6 and *Nehemiah* 9:10). Indeed, the
Egyptians persecuted them excessively by drowning their children
in the Nile, embittering their lives and plotting to eradicate their
memory.

Rambam (*Hilchos Teshuvah* 6:5), however, explains that they
deserved punishment because each individual Egyptian could have
personally avoided tormenting the Hebrews; the Divine decree of
inflicting exile and suffering had not specified any particular
Egyptian. However I find this theory unacceptable. Once God

to Abram, Know that your offspring will be a stranger in a land not theirs, and they will serve them and they will torment them for four hundred years. But also the nation whom they will serve I will judge. Afterward, they will go out with great possessions."[1]

---

(1) *Genesis* 15:13-14.

---

ordered unnamed individuals to torment the children of Israel, everyone who undertook that unpleasant task with alacrity deserved due credit for fulfilling God's commandments. Those who evaded their duties deserved nothing. Does not the Covenant here clearly state, *"The nation whom they will serve. . ."* with the obvious implication that the whole nation was to be involved?

God punished the Egyptians for enslaving the Hebrews by force and for throwing their children into the river, actions that could have destroyed this nation completely. Plotting to "Deal cunningly with them lest they multiply" or "embittered their lives with hard work" (*Exodus* 1:10,14) was not part of the Divinely inspired enslavement (*Bereishis Rabbah* 30:15).

To cite another example, when a person had been judged in Heaven on *Rosh Hashanah* and condemned to be killed, his murderer cannot be acquitted with the defense that he was merely enforcing a Divine decree. On the contrary, the victim's blood will be demanded from the killer. However, in the event that a prophet announces a Divine decree, different rules apply. Someone who overheard the prophet and hastens to carry out God's will should not be punished, of course, but has earned merits instead. We see this with Jehu who eliminated the wicked house of Ahab (*II Kings* 10:30).

However, if someone acts out of personal animosity or hopes to acquire the victim's wealth, then he will be punished for his sinful intentions. Sennacherib was punished for his impure motives (*Isaiah* 10:5 ff. and *Jeremiah* 50:17 ff.). Nebuchadnetzer, the Assyrian king, acted out of arrogance to increase his own power. Although he knew it was God's wish that Jerusalem be destroyed, he too was punished (*Jeremiah* 25:9, 32:28 ff., 40:2 ff., and *Isaiah* 13:11, 14:13 ff., 47:8). Babylon likewise deserved punishment for having exceeded the Divine decree (*Isaiah* 13:129 ff., 14:22, 47:6, and *Jeremiah* 51:11 ff.).

(*Genesis* 15:14)

The *matzos* are covered and the cups lifted as the following paragraph is proclaimed joyously. Upon its conclusion, the cups are put down and the *matzos* are uncovered.

וְהִיא שֶׁעָמְדָה לַאֲבוֹתֵינוּ וְלָנוּ, שֶׁלֹּא אֶחָד בִּלְבַד עָמַד
עָלֵינוּ לְכַלּוֹתֵנוּ. אֶלָּא שֶׁבְּכָל דּוֹר וָדוֹר
עוֹמְדִים עָלֵינוּ לְכַלּוֹתֵנוּ, וְהַקָּדוֹשׁ בָּרוּךְ הוּא מַצִּילֵנוּ מִיָּדָם.

צֵא וּלְמַד מַה בִּקֵּשׁ לָבָן הָאֲרַמִּי לַעֲשׂוֹת לְיַעֲקֹב אָבִינוּ,
שֶׁפַּרְעֹה לֹא גָזַר אֶלָּא עַל הַזְּכָרִים, וְלָבָן בִּקֵּשׁ לַעֲקוֹר
אֶת הַכֹּל. שֶׁנֶּאֱמַר:

אֲרַמִּי אֹבֵד אָבִי, וַיֵּרֶד מִצְרַיְמָה וַיָּגָר שָׁם בִּמְתֵי מְעָט,
וַיְהִי שָׁם לְגוֹי, גָּדוֹל עָצוּם וָרָב.[1]

וַיֵּרֶד מִצְרַיְמָה — אָנוּס עַל פִּי הַדִּבּוּר.

◆§ וְהַקָּדוֹשׁ בָּרוּךְ הוּא מַצִּילֵנוּ מִיָּדָם — *But the Holy One, Blessed is He, saves us from their hand.* The tactics Jacob employed in his confrontation with Esau demonstrated to future generations that Esau's descendants will not be able to wipe us out completely, as the *Midrash* tells us (*Bereishis Rabbah* 76:3). Although we may be persecuted physically or financially in one kingdom, another government will simultaneously exercise compassion and shelter the refugees.

Generally, once we were exiled, we were treated equally to the other inhabitants as Hashem promised us, ". . .in the land of their enemies, I will not have been revolted by them nor will I have rejected them to obliterate them. . ." (*Leviticus* 26:44). Our possessions and produce were no longer cursed as they were in the decade preceding the Destruction of the Temple.

In our present exile, the merits of the Patriarchs no longer protect us, and we shall only be finally redeemed with the Eternal Grace of Hashem (as it says in *Ezekiel* 20:41 ff.; see also *Tosafos, Shabbos* 55). The reason for our survival in this long exile is fundamental. Man was created to acknowledge the Creator and show gratitude to God. When the world sinned and denied His Presence, only one nation remained loyal to God. Through them, God revealed His miracles and displayed His Almighty power to the nations of the world. Should that nation vanish and its memory be obliterated, then God's deeds and wonders will also be forgotten and the purpose of Creation will

The *matzos* are covered and the cups lifted as the following paragraph is proclaimed joyously. Upon its conclusion, the cups are put down and the *matzos* are uncovered.

It [the Covenant Between the Parts] has stood firm for our fathers and for us. For it was not one alone who stood against us to annihilate us, but in every generation there are those who stand against us to annihilate us. But the Holy One, Blessed is He, saves us from their hand.

Go and ascertain what Laban the Aramean intended to do to Jacob our father, for Pharaoh decreed destruction only for the males, but Laban intended to eradicate everything. As it is said,

An Aramean would destroy my father, and he went down to Egypt, and he sojourned there with few people, and he became there a nation, great, mighty, and many.[1]

And he went down to Egypt — forced by HASHEM's word.

---

(1) *Deuteronomy* 26:5.

---

remain unfulfilled.   (*Genesis* 32:9, and *Deuteronomy* 28:42, 32:26)

מַה בִּקֵּשׁ לָבָן הָאֲרַמִּי לַעֲשׂוֹת — *What Laban the Aramean intended to do.* According to the *Pirkei D'Rabbi Eliezer* (Ch. 26) it seems that Laban first returned to his home town to gather together all the strong warriors, men of war, to chase after Jacob.

(*Genesis* 31:22, but see there 31:46)

אָנוּס עַל פִּי הַדִּבּוּר — *Forced by Hashem's word.* The *Midrash* (*Bereishis Rabbah* 94:5) reveals that as the descent into Egypt approached, Jacob realized that this was the beginning of the exile, both for him and his household. So he went down to Beer Sheba, previously a site of prayer sanctified by his father Isaac. Here, Jacob had earlier sought Divine permission when he left the Land to travel to Haran. Now he offered up many sacrifices to appease the Attribute of strict Divine Justice symbolized by, "God of his father" (who exemplified God's Attribute of Justice). Moreover, unlike previous sacrifices brought by Noah and the other Patriarchs, Jacob did not sacrifice *burnt-offerings,* but rather *peace-offerings* that appease the Divine Judgment (*Toras Kohanim* 16:1).

By the merit of these sacrifices, the God of his father Isaac appeared in a night vision (which symbolized that the Divine Justice had indeed been moderated). God reassured him that he would be

וַיָּגָר שָׁם – מְלַמֵּד שֶׁלֹּא יָרַד יַעֲקֹב אָבִינוּ לְהִשְׁתַּקֵּעַ
בְּמִצְרַיִם, אֶלָּא לָגוּר שָׁם. שֶׁנֶּאֱמַר, וַיֹּאמְרוּ אֶל פַּרְעֹה,
לָגוּר בָּאָרֶץ בָּאנוּ, כִּי אֵין מִרְעֶה לַצֹּאן אֲשֶׁר לַעֲבָדֶיךָ, כִּי
כָבֵד הָרָעָב בְּאֶרֶץ כְּנָעַן, וְעַתָּה יֵשְׁבוּ נָא עֲבָדֶיךָ בְּאֶרֶץ
גֹּשֶׁן.¹

בִּמְתֵי מְעָט – כְּמָה שֶׁנֶּאֱמַר, בְּשִׁבְעִים נֶפֶשׁ יָרְדוּ
אֲבֹתֶיךָ מִצְרָיְמָה, וְעַתָּה שָׂמְךָ יהוה אֱלֹהֶיךָ כְּכוֹכְבֵי
הַשָּׁמַיִם לָרֹב.²

וַיְהִי שָׁם לְגוֹי גָּדוֹל – מְלַמֵּד שֶׁהָיוּ יִשְׂרָאֵל מְצֻיָּנִים
שָׁם.

---

judged virtuous in the Egyptian exile. Although Jacob will be
oppressed, eventually he would be redeemed.

Interestingly, although Heaven had previously informed him "No
longer will it be said that your name is Jacob, but Israel" (*Genesis*
32:29), in this vision God again addressed him as "Jacob." The
reason for this is that the name "Israel" symbolized "battling with
men and angels and proving victorious." This would no longer be the
case. Instead, he was about to descend into slavery and the name
"Jacob" more accurately described his contemporary status. Indeed,
for this reason the Torah then relates, "These are the names of the
children of Israel who were coming to Egypt, Jacob and his children
. . ." (ibid. 46:8). (*Genesis* 46:1 ff.)

◆§ כִּי אֵין מִרְעֶה לַצֹּאן — *For there is no pasture for the flocks.* I fail to
understand the reason they gave Pharaoh. The famine was
directed against Egypt in particular, and its situation was certainly as
severe as in Canaan, if not worse. It would seem the Egyptian grazing
lands were also not spared from the catastrophic hunger.

It is possible, however, that since no food had been left in Canaan
for human consumption, its population had been reduced to eating
grass, leaving their herds with no sustenance at all. In Egypt, on the
other hand, there were preplanned stocks of food, so the animals
were not so completely deprived. Also, some pasture possibly
remained in Egypt due to the Nile, the canals and surrounding
marshes. (*Genesis* 47:4, see also 47:11)

He sojourned there — This teaches us that our father Jacob did not descend to Egypt to settle, but only to sojourn there temporarily, as it says, "They (the sons of Jacob) said to Pharaoh, We have come to sojourn in the land, for there is no pasture for the flocks of your servants, because the famine is severe in the Land of Canaan. And now, please let your servants dwell in the Land of Goshen."[1]

With few people — as it says, "With seventy souls your fathers went down to Egypt, but now HASHEM, your God, has made you numerous as the stars of the heavens."[2]

There he became a nation — This teaches us that the Jews were distinctive there.

---

(1) *Genesis* 47:4. (2) *Deuteronomy* 10:22.

⋅§ בְּשִׁבְעִים נֶפֶשׁ — *With seventy souls.* Jacob's household's dramatic increase in Egypt, from seventy souls to a huge multitude, was a miracle.

As the Sages teach us, the number 70 is profoundly significant (*Bereishis Rabbah* 66:8). Originally, the world's human population divided itself into seventy nations with seventy separate languages (*Genesis* 10), each guided by their own constellation and angel (*Daniel* 10:13 ff. — see also *Pirkei D'Rebbi Eliezer* Ch. 24). For this reason, seventy young bulls were sacrificed on Succos (*Succah* 58b). Also, at the Giving of the Torah, the Divine Glory rested on the seventy Elders — the perfect number — with Moses at their head. Additionally, the *Sanhedrin,* who sat in Hashem's House, numbered seventy judges (with the President at their head) to include all conflicting opinions. The great Ineffable Name of Hashem contains seventy-two letters reflecting the angel of each nation (including Israel) and the One God, the Sole Master over all.

(*Genesis* 46:15 and *Numbers* 11:16)

⋅§ מְצֻיָּנִים שָׁם — *Were distinctive there.* It became customary for the Children of Israel to group themselves into large "families." Each family would trace their lineage back to the head of the family — usually those who had descended with Jacob into Egypt — naming their family in honor of this ancestor. (Similarly, the Jews in Moslem countries call their extended family by names such as "Ibn Ezra" or "Ibn Shushan.") With the Children of Israel, this practice presumably

עָצוּם – כְּמָה שֶׁנֶּאֱמַר, וּבְנֵי יִשְׂרָאֵל פָּרוּ וַיִּשְׁרְצוּ
וַיִּרְבּוּ וַיַּעַצְמוּ בִּמְאֹד מְאֹד, וַתִּמָּלֵא הָאָרֶץ אֹתָם.[1]

וָרָב – כְּמָה שֶׁנֶּאֱמַר, רְבָבָה כְּצֶמַח הַשָּׂדֶה נְתַתִּיךְ,
וַתִּרְבִּי וַתִּגְדְּלִי וַתָּבֹאִי בַּעֲדִי עֲדָיִים, שָׁדַיִם נָכֹנוּ
וּשְׂעָרֵךְ צִמֵּחַ, וְאַתְּ עֵרֹם וְעֶרְיָה; וָאֶעֱבֹר עָלַיִךְ וָאֶרְאֵךְ
מִתְבּוֹסֶסֶת בְּדָמָיִךְ, וָאֹמַר לָךְ, בְּדָמַיִךְ חֲיִי, וָאֹמַר לָךְ,
בְּדָמַיִךְ חֲיִי.[2]

וַיָּרֵעוּ אֹתָנוּ הַמִּצְרִים, וַיְעַנּוּנוּ, וַיִּתְּנוּ עָלֵינוּ עֲבֹדָה
קָשָׁה.[3]

וַיָּרֵעוּ אֹתָנוּ הַמִּצְרִים – כְּמָה שֶׁנֶּאֱמַר, הָבָה נִתְחַכְּמָה
לוֹ, פֶּן יִרְבֶּה, וְהָיָה כִּי תִקְרֶאנָה מִלְחָמָה, וְנוֹסַף גַּם הוּא

---

began in Egypt to retain their communal identity and not to become
assimilated. From the time they began to "be fruitful and multiply,"
each tribe adopted this custom. Thus, they remained easily recogniz-
able as a separate and homogeneous group. This tradition continued
among the Jews for many generations.   (*Numbers* 26:13)

◆§ וּבְנֵי יִשְׂרָאֵל פָּרוּ — *And the children of Israel were fruitful.* One can
  discern an odd phenomenon with the tribe of Levi. In the desert,
the Levites were counted from the age of one month, whereas the
other tribes were only included in the census from the age of twenty.
Yet the number of Levites aged one month and over totaled only
22,000. When those above thirty years old were counted, there were
just over eight and a half thousand Levites. The Levites must have
numbered less than half of the smallest tribe. Why were there so few
Levites?

This phenomenon cannot be attributed to the Levites carrying the
Holy Ark, which decimated those unworthy to transport it (*Bamidbar
Rabbah* 5:1), since at the time of the census, they had not yet begun
carrying the Ark. To my mind, this supports the view of the *Midrash*
(*Tanchuma, Vaeira* 6) that the tribe of Levi were exempt from the
slavery. When the other tribes were afflicted and embittered with
hard labor to reduce their number, God intervened so that they
multiplied mightily, in direct challenge to the Egyptian plots to

Mighty — as it says, "And the Children of Israel were fruitful, increased greatly, multiplied, and became very very mighty; and the land was filled with them."[1]

Numerous — as it says, "I made you as numerous as the plants of the field; you grew and developed, and became charming, beautiful of figure; your hair grown long; but you were naked and bare. I passed over you and saw you downtrodden in your blood and I said to you: 'Through your blood you shall live!' And I said to you: 'Through your blood you shall live!' "[2]

The Egyptians did evil to us and afflicted us; and imposed hard labor upon us.[3]

The Egyptians did evil to us — as it says, "Let us deal cunningly with them lest they multiply and, if we happen to be at war, they may join our enemies and

---

(1) *Exodus* 1:7. (2) *Ezekiel* 16:7,6. (3) *Deuteronomy* 26:6.

---

eliminate them. This miracle was repeated during the evil decree to kill the Hebrews' sons (*Exodus* 1:16) when Hashem responded, "Let us see whose plan succeeds, Mine or theirs!"

However, the tribe of Levi were not oppressed by the slavery. Consequently, they were not subject to the miracle of Divine intervention. Their birthrate remained normal and they did not enjoy the extraordinary increase of the other tribes.

(*Numbers* 3:14, see also *Exodus* 5:4)

◈§ הָבָה נִתְחַכְּמָה לוֹ — *Let us deal cunningly with them.* Pharaoh and his advisers hesitated to put the Hebrews to the sword without justification. That would constitute a gross betrayal of an innocent nation which had been welcomed into their land. The native Egyptians would not have accepted such treachery. There was also the danger that the Hebrews, who had become numerous and powerful, would have forcefully resisted these evil designs. Cunningly, Pharaoh schemed to make it appear that his new decrees were not directed primarily against them.

To conceal his enmity, he introduced a levy on the Children of Israel, conscripting them into laboring on royal projects. National schemes were commonly imposed on foreign citizens then. (King

עַל שֹׂנְאֵינוּ, וְנִלְחַם בָּנוּ, וְעָלָה מִן הָאָרֶץ.[1]

וַיְעַנּוּנוּ – כְּמָה שֶׁנֶּאֱמַר, וַיָּשִׂימוּ עָלָיו שָׂרֵי מִסִּים, לְמַעַן עַנֹּתוֹ בְּסִבְלֹתָם, וַיִּבֶן עָרֵי מִסְכְּנוֹת לְפַרְעֹה, אֶת פִּתֹם וְאֶת רַעַמְסֵס.[2]

וַיִּתְּנוּ עָלֵינוּ עֲבֹדָה קָשָׁה – כְּמָה שֶׁנֶּאֱמַר, וַיַּעֲבִדוּ מִצְרַיִם אֶת בְּנֵי יִשְׂרָאֵל בְּפָרֶךְ.[3]

וַנִּצְעַק אֶל יהוה אֱלֹהֵי אֲבֹתֵינוּ, וַיִּשְׁמַע יהוה אֶת קֹלֵנוּ, וַיַּרְא אֶת עָנְיֵנוּ, וְאֶת עֲמָלֵנוּ, וְאֶת לַחֲצֵנוּ.[4]

Solomon imposed a similar levy — *II Chronicles* 2:16 ff.) Later, Pharaoh secretly instructed the midwives to clandestinely kill the male infants at birth. Again, this was contrived so that even the mothers should not realize Pharoah's role.

Afterwards he asked the general populace to throw all newborn boys into the river. Yet he did not entrust this duty to his public executioners. If parents complained of their infants' murder, he could disclaim all responsibility and demand they provide witnesses and proof. With the removal of state retribution, the Egyptians voluntarily searched Hebrew homes at night and abducted the baby boys, thus forcing Jewish mothers to conceal their babies.

It seems that this particular decree did not last many years. It had not been enacted yet at the birth of Aaron. Apparently it was revoked three years later, after Moses' rescue, perhaps by Pharoah's daughter interceding with her father to rescind the decree. Alternatively, it was canceled on the advice of the astrologers, as the *Midrash* says (*Shemos Rabbah* 1:29). All Pharoah's wicked plots were contrived so that his criminal designs should not become public knowledge. (*Exodus* 1:10)

◆§ וְעָלָה מִן הָאָרֶץ — *And then leave the country. Rashi* explains this phrase to mean that Pharaoh was concerned that he and his people would be forced out of Egypt and the Children of Israel would inherit their land. It is equally plausible that Pharaoh feared that the Hebrews would take advantage of any future military conflict

fight against us and then leave the country."[1]

And afflicted us — as it says, "And they set taskmasters over them in order to oppress them with their burdens. And he built store-cities for Pharaoh — Pithom and Raamses."[2]

They imposed hard labor upon us — as it is says, "The Egyptians subjugated the Children of Israel with hard labor."[3]

W e cried out to HASHEM, the God of our fathers; and HASHEM heard our cry, and saw our affliction, our burden, and our oppression.[4]

---

(1) *Exodus* 1:10. (2) 1:11. (3) 1:13. (4) *Deuteronomy* 26:7.

---

between Egypt and its enemies. He thought that the Children of Israel would then join forces with Egypt's enemy to loot and rob Egypt before escaping to Canaan with all the spoils, and Egypt would be unable to exact revenge. (*Exodus* 1:10)

◈§ שָׂרֵי מִסִּים לְמַעַן עַנֹּתוֹ — *Taskmasters over them in order to oppress them.* Pharaoh imposed a levy, conscripting Hebrews for his projects. To oversee this tax, he appointed Egyptian officials with the authority to compel men to join the work squads. They would take turns at laboring, for a month or more at a time, on the king's building projects: constructing towns and storage cities. After the Egyptians realized that the Hebrews were unharmed by the enforced labor, they were consumed by disgust. From then on, the law forced the Hebrews to serve the Egyptian people, encouraging individual Egyptians to freely exploit the Israelites for their private use.

Furthermore, they forced them to labor with bricks and mortar. At first the Hebrews were provided with bricks and were only conscripted into construction. Later the entire Jewish nation was forcibly involved in all aspects of the projects: compelled to provide the clay, manufacture the mortar and supply the bricks. Only the straw was initially supplied by the royal household.

All heavy work in the fields, including digging and carting away the dung, was also imposed on them. Nor were they allowed to rest. The Hebrews were subject to constant pressure and physical and verbal abuse. (*Exodus* 1:11, see also *Numbers* 11:5)

וַנִּצְעַק אֶל יהוה אֱלֹהֵי אֲבֹתֵינוּ — כְּמָה שֶׁנֶּאֱמַר, וַיְהִי
בַיָּמִים הָרַבִּים הָהֵם, וַיָּמָת מֶלֶךְ מִצְרַיִם, וַיֵּאָנְחוּ בְנֵי
יִשְׂרָאֵל מִן הָעֲבֹדָה, וַיִּזְעָקוּ, וַתַּעַל שַׁוְעָתָם אֶל הָאֱלֹהִים
מִן הָעֲבֹדָה.[1]

וַיִּשְׁמַע יהוה אֶת קֹלֵנוּ — כְּמָה שֶׁנֶּאֱמַר, וַיִּשְׁמַע
אֱלֹהִים אֶת נַאֲקָתָם, וַיִּזְכֹּר אֱלֹהִים אֶת בְּרִיתוֹ אֶת
אַבְרָהָם, אֶת יִצְחָק, וְאֶת יַעֲקֹב.[2]

וַיַּרְא אֶת עָנְיֵנוּ — זוֹ פְּרִישׁוּת דֶּרֶךְ אֶרֶץ, כְּמָה שֶׁנֶּאֱמַר,
וַיַּרְא אֱלֹהִים אֶת בְּנֵי יִשְׂרָאֵל, וַיֵּדַע אֱלֹהִים.[3]

וְאֶת עֲמָלֵנוּ — אֵלּוּ הַבָּנִים, כְּמָה שֶׁנֶּאֱמַר, כָּל הַבֵּן הַיִּלּוֹד
הַיְאֹרָה תַּשְׁלִיכֻהוּ, וְכָל הַבַּת תְּחַיּוּן.[4]

וְאֶת לַחֲצֵנוּ — זוֹ הַדְּחַק, כְּמָה שֶׁנֶּאֱמַר, וְגַם רָאִיתִי אֶת
הַלַּחַץ אֲשֶׁר מִצְרַיִם לֹחֲצִים אֹתָם.[5]

⇒§ וַיְהִי בַּיָּמִים הָרַבִּים הָהֵם — *It happened in the course of those many days.* There were many days of exile and suffering, for the exile stretched interminably. The lengthy duration of their enslavement moved them to cry out in anguish — "And their cry rose up to God." *Rashi* and the *Midrash* (*Shemos Rabbah* 1:41) explain that Pharaoh had not actually died but was punished with leprosy. As a cure, he bathed himself in the blood of slaughtered Jewish babies.

The simple meaning of this passage is that all those subject to tyrannical rule eagerly await the day their ruler will die. Yet, when the Children of Israel saw that Pharaoh had died, they were extremely perturbed that his successor may even exceed him in cruelty and wickedness. In their despair, they preferred death to their dismal existence. They groaned as one fatally wounded and close to death. (*Exodus* 2:23, see also 13:16)

⇒§ וַיִּשְׁמַע אֱלֹהִים אֶת נַאֲקָתָם — *God heard their groaning.* At first, God hid His Presence and they were left totally defenseless. Later, this Heavenly veil lifted, God heard their groaning and felt their predicament. He understood their pain, saw everything inflicted on them and knew what they needed.

Although the allotted period of exile and enslavement had ended,

We cried out to HASHEM the God of our fathers — as it says, "It happened in the course of those many days that the king of Egypt died, and the Children of Israel groaned because of the servitude and cried; their cry because of the servitude rose up to God."[1]

And HASHEM heard our cry — as it says, "God heard their groaning and God recalled His covenant with Abraham, with Isaac, and with Jacob."[2]

And saw our affliction — that is the disruption of family life, as it says, "God saw the Children of Israel, and God took note."[3]

Our burden — refers to the children, as it says, "Every son that is born you shall cast into the river, but every daughter you shall let live."[4]

Our oppression — refers to the pressure, as it says, "I have also seen how the Egyptians are oppressing them."[5]

---

(1) *Exodus* 2:23. (2) 2:24. (3) 2:25. (4) 1:22. (5) 3:9.

---

they still did not deserve to be liberated, as the prophet Ezekiel elaborates (20:6 ff.). Here, the Torah details evolving stages in their liberation: *God heard their groaning; God recalled His covenant with Abraham, with Isaac, and with Jacob; God saw the Children of Israel and God took note (Exodus 2:24,25).* Many reasons and stages were involved because it was only due to their cries that God, in His mercy, accepted their prayers.

This is the meaning of the passage here: *"The Children of Israel groaned because of the servitude. And they cried. And their cry because of the servitude rose up to God. And God heard their groaning."* Later Hashem told Moses, *"Behold the Children of Israel's cries have reached Me. For I know their pains." (Exodus 3:7)* We also recite here (from *Deuteronomy* 26:7) *"And we cried out to HASHEM, the God of our fathers; and HASHEM heard our cry and saw our affliction, our burden, and our oppression."* All this clearly shows that they were unworthy of redemption, although the end of exile had arrived. Hashem accepted their groans and weeping only because of the unbearable agony they were suffering. *(Exodus 2:25 and 12:42)*

וְגַם רָאִיתִי אֶת הַלַּחַץ אֲשֶׁר מִצְרַיִם לֹחֲצִים אֹתָם ﹽ— *I have also seen how the Egyptians are oppressing them.* This phrase means that God

וַיּוֹצִאֵנוּ יהוה מִמִּצְרַיִם בְּיָד חֲזָקָה, וּבִזְרֹעַ נְטוּיָה, וּבְמֹרָא גָּדֹל, וּבְאֹתוֹת וּבְמֹפְתִים.[1]

וַיּוֹצִאֵנוּ יהוה מִמִּצְרַיִם — לֹא עַל יְדֵי מַלְאָךְ, וְלֹא עַל יְדֵי שָׂרָף, וְלֹא עַל יְדֵי שָׁלִיחַ, אֶלָּא הַקָּדוֹשׁ בָּרוּךְ הוּא בִּכְבוֹדוֹ וּבְעַצְמוֹ. שֶׁנֶּאֱמַר, וְעָבַרְתִּי בְאֶרֶץ מִצְרַיִם בַּלַּיְלָה הַזֶּה, וְהִכֵּיתִי כָל בְּכוֹר בְּאֶרֶץ מִצְרַיִם מֵאָדָם וְעַד בְּהֵמָה, וּבְכָל אֱלֹהֵי מִצְרַיִם אֶעֱשֶׂה שְׁפָטִים, אֲנִי יהוה.[2]

וְעָבַרְתִּי בְאֶרֶץ מִצְרַיִם בַּלַּיְלָה הַזֶּה — אֲנִי וְלֹא מַלְאָךְ. וְהִכֵּיתִי כָל בְּכוֹר בְּאֶרֶץ מִצְרַיִם — אֲנִי וְלֹא שָׂרָף. וּבְכָל

---

would now punish Pharaoh and his nation. By their extensive oppression, the Egyptians had exceeded the Divine Decree.

Although God had already declared that he had "heard their cry," He further reiterated that their cries had "reached unto Me." This implied that their prayers had reached Hashem's Throne of Glory. God would no longer tolerate Pharaoh's exceedingly harsh enslavement.

Earlier the Torah stated, "Their cry because of the servitude rose up to God" (*Exodus* 2:23). God took mercy upon them not for their merits but because of their enforced labor. God beheld the tears of the weak and oppressed.

Likewise, He delivers those who have no protection from the strength of their oppressors. Therefore, one should also beware of persecuting the widow or orphan. For God hears their cry — as He heard yours in Egypt. They too have no one to rely on but the Almighty.   (*Exodus* 3:9, 22:20)

◆§ וַיּוֹצִאֵנוּ — *He [HASHEM] brought us out.* God made a fourfold promise (using four different phrases): (a) וְהוֹצֵאתִי — to remove them entirely from Egypt, so that they will suffer the heavy burden no longer; (b) וְהִצַּלְתִּי — to save them from hard labor, by freeing them from Egyptian rule and absolving them from tribute; (c) וְגָאַלְתִּי — to liberate them, by punishing the Egyptians so severely until they willingly surrender the Hebrews to save their own lives; (d) וְלָקַחְתִּי — Finally, He promised to choose the Children of Israel as His people. Indeed, when they arrived at Sinai to accept the Torah, God described them as "His treasure" (*Exodus* 19:5).

Hashem brought us out of Egypt with a mighty hand and with an outstretched arm, with great awe, with signs, and with wonders."[1]

Hashem brought us out of Egypt — not through an angel, not through a *seraph,* not through a messenger, but the Holy One, Blessed is He, in His glory, Himself, as it says, "I will pass through the land of Egypt on that night; I will slay all the firstborn in the land of Egypt from man to beast; and upon all the gods of Egypt will I execute judgments. I am Hashem."[2]

"I will pass through the land of Egypt on that night" — I and no angel. "I will slay all the firstborn in the land of Egypt" — I and no seraph. "And upon all the

---

(1) *Deuteronomy* 26:8. (2) *Exodus* 12:2.

וּבִזְרוֹעַ נְטוּיָה §— *and with an outstretched arm.* The term זְרֹעַ נְטוּיָה — *an outstretched arm* — means that Hashem's hand would extend over them until they had been safely brought out.   (*Exodus* 6:6)

אֲנִי וְלֹא מַלְאָךְ §— *I and no angel.* Since these words were spoken by Moses to the Children of Israel, they should have been written in the third person (i.e. "And Hashem will pass through the land of Egypt and *He* will strike the firstborn," instead of in the first person, "And *I* will pass through. . .").

Therefore, the *Midrash* explains here, that unlike a king who punishes through his official executioners, God acted alone. He did not send an angel who inflicts plagues (as in the time of King David and Sennachirib — *II Samuel* 24:16 and *II Kings* 19:35). God alone struck down the firstborn and did not involve one of the fiery angels who consumed His enemies as in the time of Elijah (*II Kings* 1:10). God alone destroyed the Egyptian gods without recourse to the great angel *Mattatron,* whose name means "the guide," who is sent to perform whatever is necessary upon earth. The *Midrash* explains the concluding phrase "*I am Hashem*" to mean that Hashem is unique in all Creation — there is no other power or god to protest against Him.

Although the angel of death was not actively involved on the night of Passover, nonetheless the Children of Israel were warned not to venture out of doors that night. As Hashem passed from place to

אֱלֹהֵי מִצְרַיִם אֶעֱשֶׂה שְׁפָטִים – אֲנִי וְלֹא הַשָּׁלִיחַ. אֲנִי יהוה – אֲנִי הוּא, וְלֹא אַחֵר.

בְּיָד חֲזָקָה – זוֹ הַדֶּבֶר, כְּמָה שֶׁנֶּאֱמַר, הִנֵּה יַד יהוה הוֹיָה בְּמִקְנְךָ אֲשֶׁר בַּשָּׂדֶה, בַּסּוּסִים בַּחֲמֹרִים בַּגְּמַלִּים בַּבָּקָר וּבַצֹּאן, דֶּבֶר כָּבֵד מְאֹד.[1]

וּבִזְרֹעַ נְטוּיָה – זוֹ הַחֶרֶב, כְּמָה שֶׁנֶּאֱמַר, וְחַרְבּוֹ שְׁלוּפָה בְּיָדוֹ, נְטוּיָה עַל יְרוּשָׁלָיִם.[2]

---

place, He was preceded by His Heavenly guardsmen who go before Him and ensure that mortals do not meet or see the Divine Presence. (Similarly, Moses had to be concealed within the rock to protect him from the *seraphim* and Heavenly hosts — *Exodus* 33:22.)

According to the *Midrash* (*Bereishis Rabbah* 19:7 based on *Isaiah* 52:12), we will be granted even closer contact with the Divine Presence during the Final Redemption. Whereas God traveled with us by day and the Heavenly Court by night, when we left Egypt, in the Messianic Era, God will march before us; the dark night will shine as bright as day and the Attribute of Justice will be elevated and united with the Attribute of Mercy. (*Exodus* 12:12, 22, 13:21)

◆§ אֶעֱשֶׂה שְׁפָטִים — *Will I execute judgments.* God brought judgment upon the idols of Egypt. Those of wood rotted while those of metal melted. Since idolatry is nothing more than worthless vanity, the Torah does not elaborate on these punishments.

Moreover, it took place simultaneously with the striking down of all Egyptian firstborn and the firstborn of their cattle. Naturally, Egypt's prime concern was for the fate of their children. This judgment of the firstborn was already revealed during the night, as it says, "Pharaoh rose up at midnight, he and all his servants, and all Egypt" (*Exodus* 12:30). However, the fate of their idols was only discovered later in the morning when they entered their temples. The Torah later confirms this sequence of events when it relates (*Numbers* 33:4), "And the Egyptians buried those struck down by HASHEM, all the firstborn; and upon their gods did HASHEM bring justice."

I believe that this phrase, "upon their gods [of Egypt]," also refers to their Heavenly masters (similar to *Isaiah* 24:21, alluding to punishment of the Heavenly angel). God lessened the power of their

gods of Egypt will I execute judgments" — I and no messenger. "I, HASHEM" — it is I and no other.

With a mighty hand — refers to the pestilence, as it says, "Behold, the hand of HASHEM shall strike your cattle which are in the field, the horses, the donkeys, the camels, the herds, and the flocks — a very servere pestilence."[1]

With an outstretched arm — refers to the sword, as it says, "His drawn sword in his hand, outstretched over Jerusalem."[2]

---

(1) *Exodus* 9:3. (2) *I Chronicles* 21:16.

---

representatives in Heaven. However, the Torah hints only briefly at hidden Kabbalistic wisdom. *(Exodus 12:12)*

⧫§ בְּמִקְנְךָ אֲשֶׁר בַּשָּׂדֶה — *Your cattle which are in the field.* Generally, cattle are left out in the field, but in the plague of דֶּבֶר, "all the livestock of Egypt died" *(Exodus 9:6)* — even those sheltering in the houses. The Egyptians regarded "every shepherd as an abomination" *(Genesis 46:34)*. Probably, the Egyptians kept their herds far from their cities, except for the horses and asses they needed either for riding or as beasts of burden. Their cattle grazed near Goshen and would mingle with the flocks of the Hebrews. Therefore, God had to differentiate between the herds belonging to Egypt and those of Israel.

Perhaps too, God brought about this pestilence through atmospheric changes. Therefore, by the rules of nature, the plague should have afflicted the whole district indiscriminately, had Hashem not miraculously intervened. *(Exodus 9:3)*

⧫§ וּבִזְרֹעַ נְטוּיָה — *With an outstretched arm.* Hashem redeemed them with an "outstretched arm," clearly visible to all the nations. Thus, the Children of Israel recognized that it is God Who performs signs and wonders. They knew that Hashem is their God, Who wrought this all for their sake, since He considers them "part of His portion" *(Deuteronomy 32:9)*.

The term "His outstretched arm" implies that God allowed the Egyptians no escape or relief from the time His hand extended over them. He did not withdraw His hand from consuming them until they were totally destroyed.

(Exodus 6:7, Deuteronomy 11:2 — see also 34:12)

וּבְמֹרָא גָּדֹל — זוֹ גִּלּוּי שְׁכִינָה, כְּמָה שֶׁנֶּאֱמַר, אוֹ הֲנִסָּה אֱלֹהִים לָבוֹא לָקַחַת לוֹ גוֹי מִקֶּרֶב גּוֹי, בְּמַסֹּת, בְּאֹתֹת, וּבְמוֹפְתִים, וּבְמִלְחָמָה, וּבְיָד חֲזָקָה, וּבִזְרוֹעַ נְטוּיָה, וּבְמוֹרָאִים גְּדֹלִים, כְּכֹל אֲשֶׁר עָשָׂה לָכֶם יהוה אֱלֹהֵיכֶם בְּמִצְרַיִם לְעֵינֶיךָ.[1]

וּבְאֹתוֹת — זֶה הַמַּטֶּה, כְּמָה שֶׁנֶּאֱמַר, וְאֶת הַמַּטֶּה הַזֶּה תִּקַּח בְּיָדֶךָ, אֲשֶׁר תַּעֲשֶׂה בּוֹ אֶת הָאֹתֹת.[2]

וּבְמֹפְתִים — זֶה הַדָּם, כְּמָה שֶׁנֶּאֱמַר, וְנָתַתִּי מוֹפְתִים בַּשָּׁמַיִם וּבָאָרֶץ –

◈ לְעֵינֶיךָ — *Before your eyes.* As a reward for "believing in Hashem and His servant Moses," the Children of Israel witnessed great miracles. As the *Midrash* teaches us (*Mechilta* 15:2), "A single maidservant saw more at the Splitting of the Sea than Ezekiel son of Buzi and the other prophets ever saw."

Since our own eyes observed these trials, miraculous signs and wonders when God publicly took us as His people — from within another nation — we should never serve anything but God.

In theory, God could have rescued us from Egypt, punished Pharaoh and his people, led us to Canaan and overpowered the Canaanites without displaying open miracles. Earlier, God had revealed Himself to the Patriarchs only with the Holy Name of שַׁדַּי (see *Exodus* 6:3), which means "The Victorious Who defeats the forces of Heaven" (as the *Ibn Ezra* explains in the name of Rabbi Shmuel Hanagid). That Name refers to the power to overrule the natural laws and perform hidden miracles. This was the "source" of the many miracles that our Patriarchs merited: being delivered from famine, the sword, and being awarded honor and riches.

However, there were no obvious alterations to the world's natural order. (This Divine Power also lay behind the countless clandestine miracles alluded to throughout the Torah, when describing reward and punishment. These, too, do not openly challenge nature and are not obviously miraculous to the casual onlooker.)

Here, God in His Mercy performed greater miracles through Moses: The Ten Plagues, the Splitting of the Sea, manna, the miraculous well, and similar wonders openly and visibly challenged

With great awe — alludes to the revelation of the *Shechinah,* as it says, "Has God ever attempted to take unto Himself a nation from the midst of another nation by trials, miraculous signs, and wonders, by war and with a mighty hand and outstretched arm and by awesome revelations, as all that HASHEM your God did for you in Egypt, before your eyes?"[1]

With signs — refers to the miracles performed with the staff, as it says, "Take this staff in your hand, that you may perform the miraculous signs with it."[2]

With wonders — alludes to the blood, as it says, "And I will show wonders in the heavens and on the earth:

---

(1) *Deuteronomy* 4:34. (2) *Exodus* 4:17.

---

nature. Thus, He revealed Himself to Moses with the Holy Name of י-ה-ו-ה with which He created the world and everything within it. This was the Divine Power behind these clearly supernatural miracles.

(*Genesis* 17:1, 18:1; *Exodus* 3:13, 6:2 and *Deuteronomy* 4:32)

⊷§ זֶה הַמַּטֶּה — *The staff.* I have seen a *Midrash* (*Shemos Rabbah* 5:6) which queries the verse ". . . see all the miracles that I have placed in your hand and perform these before Pharaoh. . ." (*Exodus* 4:21). Which signs and wonders, asks the *Midrash*, is God referring to? It cannot be Moses' staff becoming a snake, his hand infected with leprosy or the waters turning to blood. These three signs should have been displayed to the Children of Israel rather than Pharaoh. We do not find anywhere that Moses showed all these supernatural signs to Pharaoh.

"Miracles placed in your hand" can therefore only refer to Moses' staff that had the plagues inscribed on it in an abbreviated form — דְּצַ"ךְ עַדַ"שׁ בְּאַחַ"ב — the initials of the Ten Plagues. Thus, continues the *Midrash*, Moses was instructed to examine the inscriptions on his staff "placed in his hand," describing all the miracles he would eventually inflict on Pharaoh. (*Exodus* 4:21, see also 4:17 and 17:5)

⊷§ וּבְמֹפְתִים — *With wonders.* There is a difference in meaning between "signs" and "wonders." A "sign" need not necessarily be a miracle. Yet once it had been foretold by a prophet, the sign acts as confirmation of his prophetic powers. This word for sign, אוֹת, derives from the word אָתָא, meaning something about to come.

As each of the words דָּם, "blood," אֵשׁ, "fire," and עָשָׁן, "smoke," is said,
a bit of wine is removed from the cup, with the finger or by pouring.

דָּם וָאֵשׁ וְתִמְרוֹת עָשָׁן.¹

דָּבָר אַחֵר — בְּיָד חֲזָקָה, שְׁתַּיִם. וּבִזְרֹעַ נְטוּיָה, שְׁתַּיִם. וּבְמֹרָא גָּדֹל, שְׁתַּיִם. וּבְאֹתוֹת, שְׁתַּיִם. וּבְמֹפְתִים, שְׁתַּיִם.

אֵלּוּ עֶשֶׂר מַכּוֹת שֶׁהֵבִיא הַקָּדוֹשׁ בָּרוּךְ הוּא עַל הַמִּצְרִים בְּמִצְרַיִם, וְאֵלּוּ הֵן:

As each of the plagues is mentioned, a bit of wine is removed from the cup.
The same is done at each word of Rabbi Yehudah's mnemonic.

דָּם. צְפַרְדֵּעַ. כִּנִּים. עָרוֹב.

However, a "wonder" must describe an incredible event, outside the normal rules of nature. The word מוֹפֵת, "wonder," is a shortened form of מוּפְלָאת meaning supernatural or a marvel (similar to פֶּלֶא, meaning unusual or remarkable).

Among the miracles performed at the Exodus were both "signs" and "wonders." In each case, the term used depended on whether these had been foretold or occurred without warning. When Moses warned them of an imminent plague he would say, "Tomorrow this **sign** will happen..." However, when Pharaoh received no prior warning, it was called a "wonder." Moses' staff converting to a serpent was described as a "sign" to the Children of Israel, since they had been previously told of his mission. Yet when this selfsame miracle was performed in front of Pharaoh, it was called a "wonder," because it happened without any warning.

(*Deuteronomy* 13:2, see also 31:11)

◆§ דָּם — *Blood.* Aaron lifted up the staff and stretched his hand over Egypt in all directions. Then he struck the river, in front of Pharaoh. All the water, as far as Pharaoh could see, turned to blood — as did all the water throughout Egypt. For the next seven days the Egyptians dug around the Nile, since they could not drink from the river.

This plague began in the morning, when it was usual for royalty to relax along the water. Since this was the first plague, Moses was instructed to confront Pharaoh directly without the slightest show of

Blood, fire, and columns of smoke."[1]

Another explanation of the preceding verse: [Each phrase represents two plagues,] hence: **mighty hand** — two; **outstretched arm** — two; **great awe** — two; **signs** — two; **wonders** — two.

These are the ten plagues which the Holy One, Blessed is He, brought upon the Egyptians in Egypt, namely:

As each of the plagues is mentioned, a bit of wine is removed from the cup.
The same is done at each word of Rabbi Yehudah's mnemonic.

1. Blood 2. Frogs 3. Lice 4. Wild Beasts

---

(1) *Joel* 3:3.

---

fear. This bold confrontation was repeated prior to the plague of wild beasts and again before hail. Since those two plagues might possibly prove fatal, God wanted those warnings to be as public as possible — in front of the large entourage accompanying the royal procession to the water. Perhaps, when they heard Moses' dire predictions, they would remonstrate with their ruler and persuade him to repent from his wicked ways. Should they not do so, they too would deserve the impending punishments.

For the rest of the plagues, warnings conveyed to the Egyptian king alone were sufficient. Therefore Moses was commanded to enter the Royal Palace. However, the plagues of lice and boils could not be performed inside a palace, paved with precious marble. Aaron had to strike the dust (to summon the lice) and Moses had to hurl the soot into the skies (to summon the boils). These actions had to be carried out in the royal gardens or parks, before Pharaoh.

(*Exodus* 7:20, 23, 8:15)

עָרוֹב ‎§ — *Wild beasts.* The first three plagues (blood, frogs and lice) were unlikely to spread naturally. So it was not entirely surprising that these remained within Egypt and did not afflict the land of Goshen. However, the wild beasts emerging from their dens and mountain haunts would naturally migrate throughout Egypt, invading Goshen, which contained the best grazing lands (and most herds) in the area. Yet God proclaimed that the land of Goshen would be spared and shown to be different, since the

דֶּבֶר. שְׁחִין. בָּרָד. אַרְבֶּה.

Children of Israel constituted the majority of its inhabitants.

Similar discrimination was exercised within Egypt proper. If the wild beasts came upon a Hebrew, they did not harm him. Instead, they attacked and consumed the Egyptians, as it is written (*Psalms* 78:45), "The packs of wild beasts were sent among them to devour them."

(Exodus 8:18)

◈§ שְׁחִין — *Boils.* According to the *Midrash* (*Shemos Rabbah* 10:6), the soot in Moses' hand miraculously spread out across the entire Egypt. As this burning hot dust settled on man and beast, it brought forth boils and blisters. Possibly the wind drove the dust into the houses so that even if one was indoors he was not afforded protection. (A similar curse is mentioned in the Torah: "HASHEM will turn your rain into dust and earth" — (*Deuteronomy* 28:24). Indeed, during periods of drought, some sort of dust seems to fall with the dew.

However, according to the literal interpretation, the soot in Moses' hand produced a dust that polluted the atmosphere, which, as part of the Divine Decree, caused boils to erupt all over Egypt.

(Exodus 9:9)

◈§ בָּרָד — *Hail.* The Torah describes this hail "as so heavy as had not been experienced in Egypt since the day it was first founded" (*Exodus* 9:18). Afterwards, the Torah relates that "Nothing like this had happened in the whole land of Egypt ever since they became a nation" (ibid. 9:24). This implies that equally heavy hailstones can occur in other parts of the world, outside Egypt.

Indeed, God earlier rained fire and brimstone down on Sodom; and later God showered the Canaanites with large stones (*Joshua* 10:11). Even so, for Egypt a country not normally accustomed to regular rainfall, this heavy hail was indeed a great wonder. The expression "since the day it was first founded" probably means their ancestors had also never witnessed anything like it. The hail was an unnatural punishment for the Egyptians; their ancestors had never suffered similar afflictions for their sins.

I do not understand the *Midrash* (*Shemos Rabbah* 12:3) which contradicts this when it states that similar hailstorms have never occurred — neither in Egypt nor anywhere else.

Once Moses had brought the hail down from Heaven, it should naturally have rained down on Goshen too, since it shares the same

5. Pestilence 6. Boils 7. Hail 8. Locusts

climate as the rest of Egypt. So the Torah again elaborates how Goshen was spared because of its Hebrew inhabitants.

(*Exodus* 9:12, 26)

אַרְבֶּה — *Locusts.* The locusts are described as eating everything "that grows out of the field" (*Exodus* 10:5). Therefore, some commentators believe a long time must have elapsed since the plague of hail (that had previously destroyed all growth).

However, my view is that there was only a relatively short time between these two plagues. We are taught (*Eduyos* 2:10) that the complete judgment of Egypt lasted only twelve months. Also, the Torah stresses that the locusts ate "the remains which had escaped the hail" and "even that left by the hailstones" (*Exodus* 10:5, 12), clearly implying that both plagues were inflicted during the same season.

We are forced to assume that the hailstones rained down during the month of *Adar* — and certainly not earlier. By then the barley was already sprouting while the wheat was still too young to be damaged (and it was anyhow early enough in its growth to repair any damage). Vines had not yet budded and the fruit trees were not yet in flower, though their branches and trunks were damaged by the hail.

By the next month, *Nissan,* the wheat and spelt (the "remains which had escaped") were growing and the trees were already in blossom. Then the plague of locusts descended and consumed everything — without leaving a fruit blossom or a flower to propagate. In this month, the Children of Israel were finally liberated.

The Torah describes this plague of locusts as unique, predicting its equal would never occur again. However, *Rashi* writes that the plague described by the prophet Joel (2:2) was altogether worse than that of Egypt, since it included several species (causing greater damage in total). I find *Rashi's* words hard to accept. Clearly, Egypt's locusts also included other insects as elaborated in *Psalms* (78:46, 105:34).

Presumably, the Torah means here that a similar substantial plague of locusts will never be repeated within Egypt, probably because Egypt is continually irrigated by the Nile and locusts usually arrive only in times of drought (as did those described by Joel).

The *Gaon, Rabbeinu Chananel,* writes in his Bible Commentary that, "From the time Moses prayed for the locusts' removal until this day, locusts do not harm Egypt. Even when they attack *Eretz Yisrael* and move towards the Egyptian border, they do not consume Egypt's

חֹשֶׁךְ. מַכַּת בְּכוֹרוֹת.

רַבִּי יְהוּדָה הָיָה נוֹתֵן בָּהֶם סִמָּנִים:

דְּצַ״ךְ ● עֲדַ״שׁ ● בְּאַחַ״ב.

The cups are refilled. The wine that was removed is not used.

רַבִּי יוֹסֵי הַגְּלִילִי אוֹמֵר: מִנַּיִן אַתָּה אוֹמֵר שֶׁלָּקוּ
הַמִּצְרִים בְּמִצְרַיִם עֶשֶׂר מַכּוֹת, וְעַל הַיָּם
לָקוּ חֲמִשִּׁים מַכּוֹת? בְּמִצְרַיִם מָה הוּא אוֹמֵר, וַיֹּאמְרוּ
הַחַרְטֻמִּם אֶל פַּרְעֹה, אֶצְבַּע אֱלֹהִים הוּא.[1] וְעַל הַיָּם מָה

---

produce. Apparently this fact is widely publicized.

"Compare this with the plague of frogs (which *Rabbeinu Chananel* understands to mean crocodiles). Once Moses announced, 'Let them remain in the river,' the crocodiles have remained in the Nile until this day. However, with the locusts, 'not a single locust remained within the entire border of Egypt' (*Exodus* 10:19). Of this type of phenomenon, it states in *Psalms* (105:2), "Relate all His Wonders." These are the views of *Rabbeinu Chananel*.

Personally, I understand the literal meaning of the verse differently. Locusts naturally occur in every generation. Even the Egyptian plague arrived on the east wind, thus appearing as a natural occurrence. Therefore the Torah is at pains to stress that this plague was far greater than may have occurred naturally — either before or since. By the enormity of the affliction, the Egyptians realized how it came from God. Likewise, the prophet Joel describes his plague of locusts as being of Divine origin. (*Exodus* 10:4, 14)

◆§ חֹשֶׁךְ — *Darkness*. This was not merely an absence of sunlight — as if the sun had set and it was as dark as night. This darkness that descended from Heaven had actual substance, similar to an extremely thick cloud. Therefore, Moses was instructed to "stretch your hand toward the Heavens" (*Exodus* 10:21), bringing down great darkness that enveloped the Egyptians and extinguished all candles. Similarly, no candle can remain alight in deep excavations or anywhere extremely dark. Also, those who cross the legendary Mountains of Darkness report that no fire or candle will burn. Thus, the Egyptians "could not see each other nor arise from their seats" (ibid. 10:23) because they were unable to light candles to brighten the darkness.

9. Darkness 10. Plague of the Firstborn.
Rabbi Yehudah abbreviated them thus:
D'tzach, Adash, B'achav.

The cups are refilled. The wine that was removed is not used.

Rabbi Yosi the Galilean said: "How does one derive that the Egyptians were struck with ten plagues in Egypt, but with fifty plagues at the sea? Concerning the plagues in Egypt the Torah states: The magicians said to Pharaoh: 'It is the finger of God.'[1] However, of those at the Sea, the Torah relates:

---

(1) *Exodus* 8:15.

This is the significance of the verse in *Psalms* (105:28), "He sent darkness, and it was dark" — not merely an absence of daylight, but an actual darkness. Perhaps it was a very thick fog that contained substance, as our Rabbis teach us (*Shemos Rabbah* 14:1). Sometimes this happens on the Atlantic Ocean, as Rabbi Abraham Ibn Ezra himself witnessed. (*Exodus* 10:23)

◆§ מַכַּת בְּכוֹרוֹת — *Plague of the firstborn.* According to the literal meaning of the Torah, the firstborn sons killed in Egypt were the first to be born from their mothers, although their fathers may have had other children earlier. Likewise, Pharaoh's firstborn who "sat on his throne" (*Exodus* 12:29) was the firstborn of his mother, since it was customary for the reigning queen to have been unmarried until she married the king (as we see from Ahasuerus — *Esther* 2:3). Therefore, the commandment of redeeming the Jewish firstborn is limited to the first to be born of the womb.

However, according to our Rabbis, God struck down all the first-born: the first child of either mother or father, and also the most important family member. Apparently, the verse in *Psalms* (78:51) confirms that the firstborn of the fathers were also struck down in Egypt. Even so, when our firstborn were sanctified to Hashem, only those born first to their mother were chosen because that is much easier to ascertain. Likewise, regarding the commandment to consecrate the firstborn of cattle, only the mother's firstborn are sanctified, since these alone can be usually identified. (*Exodus* 12:30)

◆§ הַחַרְטֻמִּם — *Magicians.* The strict meaning of this word is not clear.

Rabbi Abraham Ibn Ezra considers it to be of either Egyptian or Chaldean origin since it is used (here in *Exodus* and in *Daniel*) only in

הוּא אוֹמֵר, וַיַּרְא יִשְׂרָאֵל אֶת הַיָּד הַגְּדֹלָה אֲשֶׁר עָשָׂה
יהוה בְּמִצְרַיִם, וַיִּירְאוּ הָעָם אֶת יהוה, וַיַּאֲמִינוּ בַּיהוה
וּבְמֹשֶׁה עַבְדּוֹ.[1] כַּמָּה לָקוּ בְאֶצְבַּע? עֶשֶׂר מַכּוֹת. אֱמוֹר
מֵעַתָּה, בְּמִצְרַיִם לָקוּ עֶשֶׂר מַכּוֹת, וְעַל הַיָּם לָקוּ חֲמִשִּׁים
מַכּוֹת.

---

connection with those two nations. Yet it is more likely to be Aramaic, as *Rashi* explains, originating from חר טמי — "stimulated by bones." These sorcerers used the bones of dead animals or humans for their practices. The Sages describe their two types of sorcery as being executed either through "angels of destruction" or with demons summoned by incantations (*Sanhedrin* 67b). The "magicians" here comprise both their "wise men" who knew the occult art of incantations and also magicians who employed the fiery angels of destruction. These were the leaders and elders of Egypt.

The Ten Plagues were performed in front of these magicians, experts in every type of sorcery and demonology, until they admitted God's existence and power. When the magicians were unable to duplicate the plague of lice, they finally accepted that this was of Divine origin, as the *Midrash* teaches us (*Shemos Rabbah* 10:7), and not caused by demons. They no longer tried to equal Moses' power and Pharaoh never consulted them again. Later, they were unable even to protect themselves from the plague of boils and they had to stay at home out of embarrassment and shame.

The first two plagues (converting water into blood, which is similarly a liquid, or collecting frogs from the Nile) did not involve actually creating anything. These were easier to copy by means of magic. However, converting dust into living lice is something only the Creator alone can perform. Although the magicians uttered incantations ordering the demons to do their bidding, they failed miserably. They were unable even to collect lice from elsewhere and display these before Pharaoh. [The reason for this, the Sages tell us, is that the demons have no power over creatures smaller than a lentil (*Sanhedrin* 67b).]

I found this very strange until I consulted demonologists and I was informed how extremely difficult they find handling or collecting insubstantial objects. This was an established maxim among their fraternity, but I cannot reveal their secret practices. Perhaps,

'Israel saw the great "hand" which Hashem laid upon the Egyptians, the people feared Hashem and they believed in Hashem and in His servant Moses.'[1] How many plagues did they receive with the finger? Ten! Then conclude that if they suffered ten plagues in Egypt [where they were struck with a finger], they must have been made to suffer fifty plagues at the Sea [where they were struck with a whole hand]."

_____
(1) *Exodus* 14:31.

_____

Pharaoh's sorcerers thought it was worth making the extra effort to produce lice but found it impossible.

The most reasonable explanation appears to me that God intended to destroy the magicians' power and prestige by confusing their aptitude for logical thought. Similarly, the false prophets of Baal were confounded when Elijah confronted them on Mount Carmel. (Had those false prophets not mistakenly believed they were capable of producing fire, they would have never accepted Elijah's challenge.) God destroys the supernatural powers of magicians and idolaters. So they were eventually forced to accept Hashem's supreme authority.

In recognizing God's hand, the sorcerers used the more anonymous term אֱלֹהִים, rather than the title יְ־ה־ו־ה that would have implied recognition of His Existence and control. Pharaoh and his courtiers used God's Proper Name only when they spoke to Moses (as this was the designation Moses himself used). They also described this plague merely as a "finger", rather than a "hand," which would have been more usual. Again, the magicians were attempting to play down the significance of the plague.

(*Exodus* 7:11, 8:15, 9:11 and *Ramban's* lecture *Toras Temimah*)

וְעַל הַיָּם לָקוּ §— — *Made to suffer . . . at the Sea.* Egypt did not recover from this catastrophe for at least a generation. On his wild pursuit, Pharaoh had taken with him all the horses, chariots and horsemen still available in Egypt and these all perished. From then on, it was a despised kingdom, possessing neither an army, chariots, horses nor prowess.

Truly it was sheer madness for the Egyptians to follow the Children of Israel into the Sea. Already it had miraculously split before the Israelites, so that they walked on dry land, amidst the Sea. Yet, God hardened their hearts and confused their thoughts. After the striking down of the firstborn, Pharaoh greatly feared the Hebrews, even

רַבִּי אֱלִיעֶזֶר אוֹמֵר. מִנַּיִן שֶׁכָּל מַכָּה וּמַכָּה שֶׁהֵבִיא הַקָּדוֹשׁ בָּרוּךְ הוּא עַל הַמִּצְרִים בְּמִצְרַיִם הָיְתָה שֶׁל אַרְבַּע מַכּוֹת? שֶׁנֶּאֱמַר, יְשַׁלַּח בָּם חֲרוֹן אַפּוֹ – עֶבְרָה, וָזַעַם, וְצָרָה, מִשְׁלַחַת מַלְאֲכֵי רָעִים.[1] עֶבְרָה, אַחַת. וָזַעַם, שְׁתַּיִם. וְצָרָה, שָׁלֹשׁ. מִשְׁלַחַת מַלְאֲכֵי רָעִים, אַרְבַּע. אֱמוֹר מֵעַתָּה, בְּמִצְרַיִם לָקוּ אַרְבָּעִים מַכּוֹת, וְעַל הַיָּם לָקוּ מָאתַיִם מַכּוֹת.

רַבִּי עֲקִיבָא אוֹמֵר. מִנַּיִן שֶׁכָּל מַכָּה וּמַכָּה שֶׁהֵבִיא הַקָּדוֹשׁ בָּרוּךְ הוּא עַל הַמִּצְרִים בְּמִצְרַיִם הָיְתָה שֶׁל חָמֵשׁ מַכּוֹת? שֶׁנֶּאֱמַר, יְשַׁלַּח בָּם חֲרוֹן אַפּוֹ, עֶבְרָה, וָזַעַם, וְצָרָה, מִשְׁלַחַת מַלְאֲכֵי רָעִים.[1] חֲרוֹן אַפּוֹ, אַחַת. עֶבְרָה, שְׁתַּיִם. וָזַעַם, שָׁלֹשׁ. וְצָרָה, אַרְבַּע. מִשְׁלַחַת מַלְאֲכֵי רָעִים, חָמֵשׁ. אֱמוֹר מֵעַתָּה, בְּמִצְרַיִם לָקוּ חֲמִשִּׁים מַכּוֹת, וְעַל הַיָּם לָקוּ חֲמִשִּׁים וּמָאתַיִם מַכּוֹת.

---

asking for their blessing. Certainly he had lost all inclination to chase after them. Had God not strengthened his heart, Pharaoh probably favored Moses doing anything he desired.

By appearing to use the east wind, God allowed the Egyptians leeway to believe that the Sea had perhaps naturally congealed into dry land. Although no wind could possibly split the Sea into separate portions, the Egyptians ignored this out of their malevolent desire to harm the hated Hebrews. Their hearts were so hardened, they believed the Children of Israel were trapped within their grasp. They forgot that God Himself was fighting for Israel against the Egyptians.

Only God is capable of performing great — and apparently incompatible — miracles simultaneously. The same action that saved the Children of Israel drowned the Egyptians.

In reality, the whole miracle was executed by means of the two

Rabbi Eliezer said: "How does one derive that every plague that the Holy One, Blessed is He, inflicted upon the Egyptians in Egypt was equal to four plagues? As it says, 'He sent upon them His fierce anger: wrath, fury, and trouble, a band of emissaries of evil.'[1] [Since each plague in Egypt consisted of] 1) wrath, 2) fury, 3) trouble, and 4) a band of emissaries of evil, therefore conclude that in Egypt they were struck by forty plagues and at the Sea by two hundred!"

Rabbi Akiva said: "How does one derive that each plague that the Holy One, Blessed is He, inflicted upon the Egyptians in Egypt was equal to five plagues? As it says, 'He sent upon them His fierce anger: wrath, fury, trouble, and a band of emissaries of evil.'[1] [Since each plague in Egypt consisted of] 1) fierce anger, 2) wrath, 3) fury, 4) trouble, and 5) a band of emissaries of evil, therefore conclude that in Egypt they were struck by fifty plagues and at the Sea by two hundred and fifty!"

---

(1) *Psalms* 78:49.

---

miraculous pillars — the pillar of fire and the pillar of dark cloud. During that night, the pillar of fire traveled *behind* the camp of Israel. Because it did not lead from the front as usual, this slowed the march of the Israelites and allowed the pursuing Egyptian army to advance close up behind them. Yet, they were unable to get too close, as their way was blocked by the two pillars — the pillar of darkness directly in front of them and beyond that, the pillar of fire. While the fiery pillar still bathed the Children of Israel in clear unrestricted light, the Egyptians' view was obscured by the pillar of darkness. Thus, they only caught vague glimpses of light and saw only random sectors of the Hebrew camp. Then the pillar of fire bore down on them with unbearable heat and "the flames consumed the wicked" (*Psalms* 106:18). Using these two pillars, God threw the Egyptian army into utter disarray.

(*Exodus* 14:4, 19, 21; 15:9; *Deuteronomy* 11:4.
For the Kabbalistic interpretation of the *"Yad HaGadolah"*
see *Exodus* 14:31, 15:2 and *Deuteronomy* 34:12)

כַּמָּה מַעֲלוֹת טוֹבוֹת לַמָּקוֹם עָלֵינוּ.

אִלּוּ הוֹצִיאָנוּ מִמִּצְרַיִם וְלֹא עָשָׂה בָהֶם שְׁפָטִים דַּיֵּנוּ.

אִלּוּ עָשָׂה בָהֶם שְׁפָטִים וְלֹא עָשָׂה בֵאלֹהֵיהֶם דַּיֵּנוּ.

אִלּוּ עָשָׂה בֵאלֹהֵיהֶם וְלֹא הָרַג אֶת בְּכוֹרֵיהֶם דַּיֵּנוּ.

אִלּוּ הָרַג אֶת בְּכוֹרֵיהֶם

וְלֹא נָתַן לָנוּ אֶת מָמוֹנָם דַּיֵּנוּ.

אִלּוּ נָתַן לָנוּ אֶת מָמוֹנָם

וְלֹא קָרַע לָנוּ אֶת הַיָּם דַּיֵּנוּ.

אִלּוּ קָרַע לָנוּ אֶת הַיָּם

וְלֹא הֶעֱבִירָנוּ בְתוֹכוֹ בֶּחָרָבָה דַּיֵּנוּ.

אִלּוּ הֶעֱבִירָנוּ בְתוֹכוֹ בֶּחָרָבָה

וְלֹא שִׁקַּע צָרֵינוּ בְּתוֹכוֹ דַּיֵּנוּ.

אִלּוּ שִׁקַּע צָרֵינוּ בְּתוֹכוֹ

וְלֹא סִפֵּק צָרְכֵּנוּ בַּמִּדְבָּר אַרְבָּעִים שָׁנָה דַּיֵּנוּ.

◆§ עָשָׂה בָהֶם שְׁפָטִים — *He executed judgments against them.* God Himself had decreed that the Children of Israel "should be enslaved and afflicted." So the Egyptians deserved no great punishment for doing precisely that. However, Egypt acted with evil intent, scheming "lest they multiply" to wipe them out completely. Also, Pharaoh commanded the midwives to murder the males at birth, and ordered his people to drown them in the Nile. It was because of these excesses that they were severely judged. God reognized their evil intentions and punished their wickedness as it is written ". . . for you knew how they sinned willfully against them. . ." (*Nehemiah* 9:10). God "searches the heart" (*I Samuel* 16:7) and brings justice to the oppressed. No one can withstand His wrath and vengeance. (*Exodus* 18:11)

◆§ עָשָׂה בֵאלֹהֵיהֶם — *He executed judgments against their gods.* Every nation has its own constellations and is controlled by Heavenly Angels (mentioned in *Daniel* 10:13 — which is why the nations served these as pagan gods). At the time of the Jewish People's exodus, the Egyptian constellations were so far in the ascendancy that the Children of Israel should have been unable to escape. However, God

The Omnipresent has bestowed so many favors upon us!
  Had He brought us out of Egypt,
    but not executed judgments against the Egyptians,
                    it would have sufficed us.
Had He executed judgments against them,
    but not upon their gods,
                    it would have sufficed us.
Had He executed judgments against their gods,
    but not slain their firstborn,
                    it would have sufficed us.
Had He slain their firstborn, but not given us their wealth,
                    it would have sufficed us.
Had He given us their wealth, but not split the Sea for us,
                    it would have sufficed us.
Had He split the Sea for us,
    but not let us through it on dry land,
                    it would have sufficed us.
Had He let us through it on dry land,
    but not drowned our oppresors in it,
                    it would have sufficed us.
Had He drowned our oppressors in it,
    but not provided for our needs in the desert for forty years,
                    it would have sufficed us.

---

judged those celestial forces and demoted their powers. In this way, the Jews were appropriated as His portion when He rescued them from the furnace of suffering. (*Deuteronomy* 4:15)

◄§ שְׁקַע צָרֵינוּ — *Drowned our oppressors.* By direct Divine intervention the Egyptians sank like lead and heavy stones. There must have been many in the Egyptian army capable of swimming; nor were they that distant from dry land. All those on horseback should have saved themselves, as horses are used to swimming. Also, anyone handling a shield could have used that as an aid in avoiding a watery grave. None, however, escaped. God shook up the Egyptian army, raised them with a heavy wind and then hurled them down, deep into the waters. (*Exodus* 15:10)

אִלּוּ סִפֵּק צָרְכֵּנוּ בַּמִּדְבָּר אַרְבָּעִים שָׁנָה
וְלֹא הֶאֱכִילָנוּ אֶת הַמָּן דַּיֵּנוּ.
אִלּוּ הֶאֱכִילָנוּ אֶת הַמָּן
וְלֹא נָתַן לָנוּ אֶת הַשַּׁבָּת דַּיֵּנוּ.
אִלּוּ נָתַן לָנוּ אֶת הַשַּׁבָּת
וְלֹא קֵרְבָנוּ לִפְנֵי הַר סִינַי דַּיֵּנוּ.

⧫§ הֶאֱכִילָנוּ אֶת הַמָּן — *Fed us the manna.* From the 16th of *Iyar,* God rained manna down on them. "He prepared a table for them in the wilderness. . . until they reached an inhabited land" (*Psalms* 78:19 and 35). This wondrous creation became their staple diet for many years. (Perhaps the quail, which was blown in from the sea, was generally available only for the pious or older people.)

Reliance on manna which they and "their forefathers knew not" (*Deuteronomy* 8:16) was a severe trial for them, particularly when they had no other source of food. They received only a day's supply at a time, yet they trusted God implicitly to follow Him even to arid destinations, devoid of sustenance. This was a deliberate test of their obedience, as God could equally have led them past inhabited cities with food supplies.

Manna was a great innovation, reminiscent of the Creation, and replete with almost every flavor they wished for. Moreover, as hinted by Rabbi Akiba in the Talmud (*Yoma* 75b), it is the "food of angels" who exist by Hashem's Glory. Equally, the Divine Glory sustained the Children of Israel in the desert. As stated in the *Mechilta* (16:25) this nourishment will be available in the World to Come.

(*Exodus* 16:2 ff., 12; *Deuteronomy* 8:3.
See also ibid. 29:5 and *Genesis* 2:17)

⧫§ נָתַן לָנוּ אֶת הַשַּׁבָּת — *Given us the Sabbath.* The Sabbath is inherently a celebration of Creation, the day God rested. So why is it also observed "in memoriam of the Exodus from Egypt"? *Rambam* (*Guide to the Perplexed* 2:31) explains that as slaves in Egypt, we were forced to work all day without any rest. Now we remember God's kindness in freeing us from slavery, by refraining from work and celebrating the Sabbath as a rest day.

This explanation is unclear to me. How does our merely relinquishing work on the Sabbath commemorate the Exodus or our liberation

Had He provided for our needs in the desert for forty years,
but not fed us the manna, it would have sufficed us.
Had He fed us the manna, but not given us the Sabbath,
it would have sufficed us.
Had He given us the Sabbath,
but not brought us before Mount Sinai,
it would have sufficed us.

---

from slavery? In which way are these principles revealed to the casual observer?

In reality, the miracles of the Exodus were ample evidence of the existence of God Who is the Eternal, the Creator, the Almighty. The miracles of the Exodus, proving God's will and power, enlightened all who doubted the act of Creation, which the Sabbath signifies. Thus the Exodus is also "a commemoration" of Creation. On Sabbath, by remembering these outstanding events of the Exodus, one bears witness that God must also be the Creator Who performs each miracle and can affect everything by His will. Observing the Sabbath commemorates the Exodus and therefore the Creation.

(*Deuteronomy* 5:15. See also *Exodus* 20:2 and *Ramban's* lecture *Toras Temimah*)

קֵרְבָנוּ לִפְנֵי הַר סִינַי — *Brought us before Mount Sinai.* We have a sacred duty to remember the thunder and lightning, Hashem's glory and greatness, and His words appearing amidst the fire. All these phenomena must be transmitted to every generation, so that our descendants will learn to fear God. This duty is reinforced with a number of commandments because its importance is fundamental to Judaism.

The Children of Israel were brought close to Mount Sinai and personally saw and heard the Revelation with their own eyes and ears. Consequently, the belief in Torah and commandments is stronger than if they had received these only through Moses.

Should any prophet arise to contradict Moses we will not accept him — even if he produces signs or wonders! Our ancestors have testified that they all personally witnessed the Giving of the Torah through their own senses and knew it to be true without question. Thus we shall "believe in [Moses] forever" (*Exodus* 19:9). Certainly, this is fundamental to our faith.

This is how the momentous events actually took place. In the

אִלּוּ קֵרְבָנוּ לִפְנֵי הַר סִינַי
וְלֹא נָתַן לָנוּ אֶת הַתּוֹרָה דַּיֵּנוּ.

morning, there were loud claps of thunder, flashes of lightning and the resounding call of the *shofar* — but the Holy *Shechinah* had not yet descended. The people still sheltering in their camp trembled in fear. Nonetheless, Moses coaxed them to approach the foot of the mountain.

While they were waiting and watching in anticipation, God descended onto the mountain, which was enveloped in fire, and the heavy clouds of thick, dark smoke rose to the center of Heaven. The mountain itself shook and quivered as if it were erupting in an earthquake — "The mountains skipped like rams. . .like young sheep" (*Psalms* 114:6), and that is not an empty figure of speech.

As the *shofar* blasts grew ever louder, the Children of Israel retreated to stand at a distance. For fear the shock would kill them, they requested that God should not speak to them at all. By the prophetic visions they had already witnessed, they were racked with pain and had lost all physical strength. Should they also hear Hashem's Words, they feared they would surely die.

Yet Moses encouraged them not to be afraid and they accepted his assurances. Still, they remained at a distance from their allotted places at the foot of Mount Sinai. When Moses approached the dark cloud — but did not enter it — God began to deliver the Ten Commandments.

After these Commandments were proclaimed, the elders and leaders of the tribes again approached Moses. They declared that if they continued to hear God's voice they would surely die! They felt unable to endure "hearing" His "voice" any longer, assuming that God intended to teach them all the commandments directly, and they begged Moses to act as their intermediary. God accepted their request as correct, for He had always intended to deliver directly only the Ten Commandments and He felt their fear was justified.

(*Exodus* 20:15, *Deuteronomy* 4:9.
See also 19:9, 20:17 and also appendices to *Sefer HaMitzvos*)

⧫§ **נָתַן לָנוּ אֶת הַתּוֹרָה** — *Given us the Torah.* God did not institute the commandments for His own advantage. Instead they are for the benefit of mankind: Some commandments prevent man from coming to harm, succumbing to false beliefs, or becoming accus-

Had He brought us before Mount Sinai,
   but not given us the Torah,   it would have sufficed us.

---

tomed to substandard behavior. Others encourage a person to recollect God's miracles or become more aware of God's presence and conduct.

As the Sages teach us (*Bereishis Rabbah* 44:1), commandments are designed to refine the human being and remove all impurities. They accustom us to the truth and eliminate false opinions. The *Midrash* (*Tanchuma, Shemini* 8) elaborates: What difference would it make to God whether we perform a correct ritual slaughter on an animal or stab it to death? Can either action bring positive harm or gain to God? What difference will it make to Him if we eat kosher or non-kosher animals? "Any wisdom gained is confined to yourself alone" (*Proverbs* 9:12). The commandments, concludes the *Midrash,* were given solely to refine human society, so the word of Hashem may protect us.

This *Midrash* establishes clearly that God receives no actual advantage from these commandments. Similarly, in the Sanctuary, He did not need the light from the golden *Menorah,* nor the smell of the incense, nor the food of the sacrifices.

Even commandments designed to commemorate the Creation or the Exodus are not for His benefit; they teach us to know and remember the truth, and thus earn God's protection. From God's perspective, all our declarations or commemorations of His miracles are of no benefit.

That we slaughter an animal correctly rather than from the back does not benefit the Creator. All the moral advantages are ours, to teach *us* compassion. Again, the eating of only kosher foods helps us develop a refined, sensitive soul more receptive to wisdom and truth. All the practical commandments (such as ritual slaughter) develop within us better character traits. The restrictions on non-kosher species purify our soul so that we should "not make our souls abominable" (*Leviticus* 20:25).

Ultimately these are all for our welfare. "If you sin how does that affect Him? If you are righteous, what do you give Him — what does He receive from your hands?" (*Job* 35:6 ff.).

According to the Sages, commandments such as *succah, lulav* and even *tefillin* (which commemorate "the mighty hand" of the Exodus) are not intended for Hashem's glory but to earn mercy for our souls

אֵלוּ נָתַן לָנוּ אֶת הַתּוֹרָה

וְלֹא הִכְנִיסָנוּ לְאֶרֶץ יִשְׂרָאֵל   דַּיֵּנוּ.

אֵלוּ הִכְנִיסָנוּ לְאֶרֶץ יִשְׂרָאֵל

וְלֹא בָּנָה לָנוּ אֶת בֵּית הַבְּחִירָה   דַּיֵּנוּ.

(*Yerushalmi Nedarim* 9:1). This is at the heart of the *Yom Kippur* prayer (at *Ne'ilah*) "You set Man apart, from the beginning, and considered him to be worthy to stand before You. For who can tell You what to do? And if he is righteous, what can he give You? . . ."

Similarly, the Torah clearly states, "And HASHEM commanded us to observe all the statutes, to fear HASHEM our God for our continual good" and ". . .commanded for your benefit" (*Deuteronomy* 6:24, 10:13). Note that they are for *our* good — not God's — to purify and refine, liberating us from unworthy character traits and evil thoughts.

The Sages also teach us (*Berachos* 33b), God's commandments are not merely instructing us to behave mercifully, but are Divine decrees. Were God solely concerned in showing mercy to animals, He would have forbidden slaughter or our exploitation of animals altogether. He forbade us to take the mother bird from the nest or to slaughter an animal and its mother on the same day, to teach *us* compassion so we refrain from brutality. For cruelty spreads easily within a man's soul. Those who regularly butcher large bulls and donkeys become callous, sadistic, and consumed with a blood lust. As the Sages say (*Kiddushin* 82a), "The most refined of these butchers remains a partner of Amalek!" The commandments are not primarily designed with mercy for birds and animals, but to train *us* in good character traits.   (*Deuteronomy* 22:6, see also 4:5 ff.)

◆§ הִכְנִיסָנוּ לְאֶרֶץ יִשְׂרָאֵל — *Brought us into the Land of Israel.* Unlike Egypt which possessed a reliable water supply from the Nile, the Land of Israel is an arid country, dependent on regular rainfall. Therefore, it is constantly under God's Providence. If His will is ignored, God will not shower it with "rains of blessings" (*Taanis* 19a), and the crops will wither. Although He could equally destroy Egypt through drought, the Land of Israel is more vulnerable. Similarly, a sick person requires more merit and prayers than someone who is perfectly healthy.

Also, the Land of Israel will not tolerate wickedness. It cannot bear immorality or idolatry and the land spews out evildoers. Other

Had He given us the Torah,
  but not brought us into the Land of Israel,
                    it would have sufficed us.
Had he brought us into the Land of Israel,
  but not built the Temple for us,
                    it would have sufficed us.

---

countries may be ruled by a celestial constellation, as it says, ". . .To nations their inheritance. . .He set the national borders. . ." (*Deuteronomy* 32:8 ff.). The Land of Israel, however, is directly controlled by God as His own estate, special to His Name. Consequently, the rules are far stricter there. Therefore, the Samaritans were molested by lions for serving idols in Samaria (Shomron). Yet they were not punished in Kuta, their birthplace, near Assyria (*II Kings* 17:26 ff.). Although the Canaanites apparently behaved no worse than the Egyptians did in their land, the Canaanites were driven from this land.

Jacob had to instruct his household to purify themselves and remove any idols when they entered the Holy Land (*Genesis* 35:2). Also, the Matriarch Rachel died as they reached the Land of Israel, since the land would not tolerate the Patriarch being married to two sisters.

God settled His chosen people in His chosen land where they would not be subject to control by foreign constellations. Abraham recognized its inherent superiority and felt drawn to this region even before God directed him there.

The Sages compared living abroad as almost tantamount to being outside God's domain (*Tosefta, Avodah Zarah* 5:5 — as if such a statement can possibly be understood at face value, since the whole world is Hashem's). Life outside the Land of Israel is guided by the impure influence of the celestial powers created for those lands, powers which the nations chose to worship.

Our Rabbis remarked (*Sifre Deuteronomy* 11:17) that when we are driven into exile, God tells us, "Observe the commandments in order that they should not feel strange to you when you finally return to *Eretz Yisrael.*" This refers even to duties like putting on *tefillin* or affixing *mezuzos,* which are not directly connected to the land (as are tithes, for instance). This is comparable to a king who was angered by his wife and sent her to her father's home, but instructed her, "Continue to wear your jewelry, so that when I take you back it will

עַל אַחַת כַּמָּה, וְכַמָּה טוֹבָה כְפוּלָה וּמְכֻפֶּלֶת לַמָּקוֹם עָלֵינוּ. שֶׁהוֹצִיאָנוּ מִמִּצְרַיִם, וְעָשָׂה בָהֶם שְׁפָטִים, וְעָשָׂה בֵאלֹהֵיהֶם, וְהָרַג אֶת בְּכוֹרֵיהֶם, וְנָתַן לָנוּ אֶת מָמוֹנָם, וְקָרַע לָנוּ אֶת הַיָּם, וְהֶעֱבִירָנוּ בְתוֹכוֹ בֶּחָרָבָה, וְשִׁקַּע צָרֵינוּ בְּתוֹכוֹ, וְסִפֵּק צָרְכֵּנוּ בַּמִּדְבָּר אַרְבָּעִים שָׁנָה, וְהֶאֱכִילָנוּ אֶת הַמָּן, וְנָתַן לָנוּ אֶת הַשַּׁבָּת, וְקֵרְבָנוּ לִפְנֵי הַר סִינַי, וְנָתַן לָנוּ אֶת הַתּוֹרָה, וְהִכְנִיסָנוּ לְאֶרֶץ יִשְׂרָאֵל, וּבָנָה לָנוּ אֶת בֵּית הַבְּחִירָה, לְכַפֵּר עַל כָּל עֲוֹנוֹתֵינוּ.

רַבָּן גַּמְלִיאֵל הָיָה אוֹמֵר. כָּל שֶׁלֹּא אָמַר שְׁלֹשָׁה דְּבָרִים אֵלּוּ בַּפֶּסַח, לֹא יָצָא יְדֵי חוֹבָתוֹ, וְאֵלּוּ הֵן,

פֶּסַח. מַצָּה. וּמָרוֹר.

פֶּסַח שֶׁהָיוּ אֲבוֹתֵינוּ אוֹכְלִים בִּזְמַן שֶׁבֵּית הַמִּקְדָּשׁ הָיָה קַיָּם, עַל שׁוּם מָה? עַל שׁוּם שֶׁפָּסַח הַקָּדוֹשׁ בָּרוּךְ

---

not seem strange to you." So too, God tells the Jews, "Continue to observe my commandments, so they not seem strange to you."

The Sages also declared that colonizing the Land is equal to all the commandments in the Torah (*Sifre Re'eh* 11:31).

In my opinion, it remains a bona fide *mitzvah* to conquer and settle the Land and we may not despise God's estate. Again, the Sages stress the importance of this commandment by restricting us from leaving the Land. They disparaged the wife who refused to accompany her husband to *Eretz Yisrael* as well as the husband who refused to accompany his wife (*Kesubos* 110b). The Torah frequently repeats this commandment. (*Leviticus* 18:25, *Numbers* 33:53, *Deuteronomy* 11:10 and *Ramban's* lecture on *Koheles*. See also *Ramban's* notes on *Sefer HaMitzvos: Lo Saaseh* 237 and appendices to *Mitzvos Aseh*)

◆§ בָּנָה לָנוּ אֶת בֵּית הַבְּחִירָה — *Built the Temple for us.* The Israelites' exile was not fully ended until they achieved the level of their forefathers. Thus, although they left Egypt, so long as they merely wandered through deserts and foreign lands, freedom from Egypt and slavery was incomplete until they arrived at Mount Sinai. When

Thus, how much more so should we be grateful to the Omnipresent for all the numerous favors He showered upon us: He brought us out of Egypt; executed judgments upon them and against their gods; slew their firstborn; gave us their wealth; split the Sea for us; led us through it on dry land; drowned our oppressors in it; provided for our needs in the desert for forty years; fed us the manna; gave us the Sabbath; brought us before Mount Sinai; gave us the Torah; brought us to the Land of Israel; and built for us the Temple to atone for all our sins.

Rabban Gamliel used to say: Whoever has not explained the following three things on Passover has not fulfilled his duty, namely:

Pesach — the Passover offeirng; **Matzah** — the Unleavened Bread; **Maror** — the Bitter Herbs.

Pesach — Why did our fathers eat a Passover offering during the period when the Temple still stood? Because the Holy One, Blessed is He, passed over the houses of our

---

they built the Sanctuary and God rested His Presence there, the Children of Israel finally achieved the status of the Patriarchs upon whose tents the Divine Presence had rested. Only then could their redemption be considered absolute.

After the Children of Israel received the Ten Commandments, they gave their pledge to accept God's every command. They entered into a Holy Covenant with God who assured them they shall remain His "Treasure. . .a kingdom of priests and a holy nation" (*Exodus* 19:5 ff.). As a measure of their new sanctity, they deserved a Sanctuary for the *Shechinah* to dwell amongst them; a House dedicated to His Name, from which His directives issued forth. Within the Holy House was concealed the Divine Glory, which had previously been revealed at Mount Sinai. (The esoteric secrets of both the Tabernacle and the Temple are hinted at in the description of the Giving of the Torah, *Exodus* 20:16, 24:10, and from the prayer of King Solomon, *I Kings* 8:23.)   (Preface to *Exodus* and 25:1. See also *Deuteronomy* 33:2)

◀§ פֶּסַח — *The Passover Offering.* The sign of the zodiac for the month of *Nissan* is Aries — the Ram. Yet, God ordered the Children of

הוּא עַל בָּתֵּי אֲבוֹתֵינוּ בְּמִצְרָיִם. שֶׁנֶּאֱמַר, וַאֲמַרְתֶּם, זֶבַח פֶּסַח הוּא לַיהוה, אֲשֶׁר פָּסַח עַל בָּתֵּי בְנֵי יִשְׂרָאֵל בְּמִצְרַיִם בְּנָגְפּוֹ אֶת מִצְרַיִם, וְאֶת בָּתֵּינוּ הִצִּיל, וַיִּקֹּד הָעָם וַיִּשְׁתַּחֲווּ.[1]

The broken *matzah* is lifted and displayed while the following paragraph is recited.

מַצָּה זוֹ שֶׁאָנוּ אוֹכְלִים, עַל שׁוּם מָה? עַל שׁוּם שֶׁלֹּא הִסְפִּיק בְּצֵקָם שֶׁל אֲבוֹתֵינוּ לְהַחֲמִיץ, עַד שֶׁנִּגְלָה עֲלֵיהֶם מֶלֶךְ מַלְכֵי הַמְּלָכִים הַקָּדוֹשׁ בָּרוּךְ הוּא וּגְאָלָם. שֶׁנֶּאֱמַר, וַיֹּאפוּ אֶת הַבָּצֵק אֲשֶׁר הוֹצִיאוּ מִמִּצְרַיִם עֻגֹת מַצּוֹת כִּי לֹא חָמֵץ, כִּי גֹרְשׁוּ מִמִּצְרַיִם, וְלֹא יָכְלוּ לְהִתְמַהְמֵהַּ, וְגַם צֵדָה לֹא עָשׂוּ לָהֶם.[2]

The *maror* is lifted and displayed while the following paragraph is recited.

מָרוֹר זֶה שֶׁאָנוּ אוֹכְלִים, עַל שׁוּם מָה? עַל שׁוּם שֶׁמֵּרְרוּ הַמִּצְרִים אֶת חַיֵּי אֲבוֹתֵינוּ בְּמִצְרָיִם. שֶׁנֶּאֱמַר, וַיְמָרְרוּ אֶת חַיֵּיהֶם, בַּעֲבֹדָה קָשָׁה, בְּחֹמֶר וּבִלְבֵנִים, וּבְכָל עֲבֹדָה בַּשָּׂדֶה, אֵת כָּל עֲבֹדָתָם אֲשֶׁר עָבְדוּ בָהֶם בְּפָרֶךְ.[3]

Israel to kill and eat their sheep, just when Aries was in its ascendancy. This revealed how we left Egypt without the assistance of the constellations, and only by God's Decree.

According to the Sages, the Egyptians worshiped the ram as a pagan idol and saw it as the source of their power (*Shemos Rabbah* 16:2 and *Targum Onkelos* 8:22). They did not eat its meat and regarded shepherds as an abomination. God destroyed all the Egyptian deities and images — and along with them with their baneful influence — just as they reached the peak of their ascendancy.

(*Exodus* 12:3 and *Ramban's* lecture *Toras Temimah*)

≈§ **וַיֹּאפוּ אֶת הַבָּצֵק** — *They baked the dough.* They baked their dough into *matzos,* as they had been forbidden to have any *chametz* among their possessions.

Because the Egyptians were so desperate to drive them out, the Children of Israel possessed no *matzos* nor had they the time to bake

fathers in Egypt, as it says, "You shall say: It is a Passover offering for Hashem, Who passed over the houses of the Children of Israel in Egypt when He struck the Egyptians, and spared our houses. And [upon hearing this] the people bowed down and prostrated themselves."[1]

The broken *matzah* is lifted and displayed while the following paragraph is recited.

Matzah — Why do we eat this unleavened bread? Because the dough of our fathers did not have time to become leavened before the King of kings, the Holy One, Blessed is He, revealed Himself to them and redeemed them, as it says, "They baked the dough which they had brought out of Egypt into unleavened bread, for it had not fermented, because they were driven out of Egypt and could not delay; nor had they prepared any provisions for themselves."[2]

The *maror* is lifted and displayed while the following paragraph is recited.

Maror — Why do we eat this bitter herb? Because the Egyptians embittered the lives of our fathers in Egypt, as it says, "They embittered their lives with hard labor, with mortar and bricks, and with all manner of labor in the field. All of the work which they made them do was with hard labor."[3]

---

(1) *Exodus* 12:27. (2) 12:39. (3) 1:14.

---

provisions inside the cities. Instead, they were forced to take with them their unbaked dough, together with their kneading bowls, wrapped in their clothes and slung over their shoulders. In their haste to prevent their dough from becoming leaven, they baked it either en route or when they stopped at Succos for a short break.   (*Exodus* 12:39)

⋙ מָרוֹר זֶה — *This bitter herb.* Unlike the separate commandments of *matzah* and the Passover sacrifice, the Biblical requirement to eat bitter herbs is not totally independent. The specific commandment to eat the bitter herbs depended on simultaneously eating the Passover meat. By contrast, the Passover sacrifice did not depend on the bitter herbs. Should one have eaten the paschal meat without also consuming bitter herbs, he would have still fulfilled his duty as far as the sacrifice was concerned. [The requirement to eat the bitter herbs in our times is of Rabbinic origin. — *Ed.*]   (*Exodus* 12:8)

בְּכָל דּוֹר וָדוֹר חַיָּב אָדָם לִרְאוֹת אֶת עַצְמוֹ כְּאִלּוּ הוּא יָצָא מִמִּצְרַיִם. שֶׁנֶּאֱמַר, וְהִגַּדְתָּ לְבִנְךָ בַּיּוֹם הַהוּא לֵאמֹר, בַּעֲבוּר זֶה עָשָׂה יהוה לִי, בְּצֵאתִי מִמִּצְרָיִם.[1] לֹא אֶת אֲבוֹתֵינוּ בִּלְבָד גָּאַל הַקָּדוֹשׁ בָּרוּךְ הוּא, אֶלָּא אַף אֹתָנוּ גָּאַל עִמָּהֶם. שֶׁנֶּאֱמַר, וְאוֹתָנוּ הוֹצִיא מִשָּׁם, לְמַעַן הָבִיא אֹתָנוּ לָתֶת לָנוּ אֶת הָאָרֶץ אֲשֶׁר נִשְׁבַּע לַאֲבוֹתֵינוּ.[2]

The *matzos* are covered and the cup is lifted and held until it is to be drunk. According to some customs, however, the cup is put down after the following paragraph, in which case the *matzos* should once more be uncovered.

לְפִיכָךְ אֲנַחְנוּ חַיָּבִים לְהוֹדוֹת, לְהַלֵּל, לְשַׁבֵּחַ, לְפָאֵר, לְרוֹמֵם, לְהַדֵּר, לְבָרֵךְ, לְעַלֵּה, וּלְקַלֵּס, לְמִי שֶׁעָשָׂה לַאֲבוֹתֵינוּ וְלָנוּ אֶת כָּל הַנִּסִּים הָאֵלּוּ,

────────────────────────────

⦿§ בְּכָל דּוֹר וָדוֹר — *In every generation.* Each of the amazing signs and wonders provided incontrovertible evidence to the existence of the Creator, Who rules over all life and matter. Nothing can withstand His Divine Will. Yet, it is not in every generation that God displays great miracles to confound every evildoer and skeptic as He did in Egypt. So it is of fundamental importance that we practice these commandments, instituted in memory of those momentous events, passing on the traditions intact to our descendants for all posterity.

(*Exodus* 13:16)

⦿§ כָּל הַנִּסִּים הָאֵלּוּ — *All these miracles.* Miracles usually take place for one of two reasons. Either they are displays of complete kindness when God graciously performs signs and wonders for the benefit of His Chosen People, or they are manifestations of Divine Justice when God angrily punishes those who transgress His will.

Generally, God does not interrupt the world's natural order. Exceptions to this rule occur when He wishes to reveal His Name, even to His enemies. This is what transpired regarding the miracles within Egypt, at the Splitting of the Sea and on other similar occasions.

Beyond those open miracles, which clearly contradict the natural order, the Torah is replete with countless hidden miracles. These work within natural events, as anybody perceptive will recognize.

In every generation one is obligated to view himself as though he has gone out of Egypt, as it is said, "And you shall tell your son on that day, saying, 'It is because of this that Hashem did so for me when I went out of Egypt.'"[1] Not only did the Holy One, Blessed is He, redeem our ancestors, but He redeemed us, too, with them, as it is said, "He took us out of there to bring us to and give us the land which He had sworn to our fathers."[2]

The *matzos* are covered and the cup is lifted and held until it is to be drunk. According to some customs, however, the cup is put down after the following paragraph, in which case the *matzos* should once more be uncovered.

Therefore it is our duty to thank, praise, laud, glorify, aggrandize, extol, bless, exalt and acclaim the One Who performed all these miracles for our ancestors and for us.

(1) *Exodus* 13:8. (2) *Deuteronomy* 6:23.

Certainly, all the Torah's assurances — whether for reward or for punishment — are not totally natural. If nature alone ruled the world, then our merit or misconduct would not affect the way we are treated.

When we obey God's Word and the rains arrive on time, when we earn peace from our enemies, or they become so fainthearted that a hundred of their soldiers flee from five of ours — these are all examples of hidden miracles. If disaster occurs when we work the land during the Sabbatical year, this obviously does not follow the dictates of nature. All are miracles, though in a different category to the Splitting of the Sea. Rather than publicly contradicting the natural order, these work within it.

When these unnatural phenomena happen constantly and continuously in the Holy Land — when an entire people enjoy timely rain and plenitude, peace and security, health and strength, and the amazing downfall of their enemies — these publicize God's power.

Unfortunately, with Divine punishment the opposite is true. When a healthy man dies before his time because he incurred the penalty of excision, that miracle is well hidden and the cause is unknown. However, when the land is cursed unnaturally, the heavens are as iron and awful sickness prevails, then God's hand is obvious. Even "a later generation . . .. the foreigner who will come from a distand land" (*Deuteronomy* 29:21 ff.) will recognize that the plagues and sickness are of Divine origin. As the Torah relates, they will ask, "Why has HASHEM acted so to this land?" Invariably, as these clandestine

הוֹצִיאָנוּ מֵעַבְדוּת לְחֵרוּת, מִיָּגוֹן לְשִׂמְחָה, וּמֵאֵבֶל לְיוֹם טוֹב, וּמֵאֲפֵלָה לְאוֹר גָּדוֹל, וּמִשִּׁעְבּוּד לִגְאֻלָּה, וְנֹאמַר לְפָנָיו שִׁירָה חֲדָשָׁה, הַלְלוּיָהּ.

הַלְלוּיָהּ הַלְלוּ עַבְדֵי יהוה, הַלְלוּ אֶת שֵׁם יהוה. יְהִי שֵׁם יהוה מְבֹרָךְ, מֵעַתָּה וְעַד עוֹלָם. מִמִּזְרַח שֶׁמֶשׁ עַד מְבוֹאוֹ, מְהֻלָּל שֵׁם יהוה. רָם עַל כָּל גּוֹיִם יהוה, עַל הַשָּׁמַיִם כְּבוֹדוֹ. מִי כַּיהוה אֱלֹהֵינוּ, הַמַּגְבִּיהִי לָשָׁבֶת. הַמַּשְׁפִּילִי לִרְאוֹת, בַּשָּׁמַיִם וּבָאָרֶץ.

---

miracles continue to an entire nation over an extended period, they become less hidden.
(*Deuteronomy* 20:9; *Numbers* 11:19 and *Ramban's* lecture *Toras Temimah*. See also *Genesis* 17:1, 46:15; *Exodus* 6:2, 23:25; *Leviticus* 18:29, 26:11; and *Deuteronomy* 11:13)

⊷§ הַלְלוּיָהּ — *Halleluyah!* I have been instructed by my teacher Rabbi Yehudah (Ben Yakar) who received this from his teacher, Rabbi Yitzchak Ben Avraham that the *Hallel* chanted at the *seder* ought to be preceded by the blessing: "Blessed are You . . . Who commanded us to complete the Hallel." However, the *Geonim* in the name of Rav Tzemach contended that no preceding blessing should be recited, since this *Hallel* is interrupted by the meal.

Yet, since *Hallel* ends with a prayer which is a blessing upon *completing* the *Hallel*, it follows that a blessing should likewise *precede Hallel*. These *Geonim* were forced to admit that this case was an exception to the general rule.

Later authorities claimed that the prayer which ends *Hallel* is a separate blessing recited at the *seder,* upon the fourth cup of wine, with no connection to *Hallel*. That too is incorrect — on the contrary, this prayer is a general hymn of praise and does not even mention the Exodus from Egypt.

Also, I have discovered the *Masechtas Sofrim* (20:10) confirming Rabbi Yitzchak's view, where it includes Passover night among those occasions when individuals complete the *Hallel*. It goes on to describe that the ideal custom is chanting the *Hallel* in unison at the synagogue. After a public blessing at the synagogue, there would no longer be any need at the *seder*. Obviously, without the blessing in

He has brought us from slavery to freedom, from anguish to joy, from mourning to festivity, from darkness to great light, and from servitude to redemption. And we will say before Him! Halleluyah!

Halleluyah! Praise, servants of Hashem. Praise the Name of Hashem! Blessed be the Name of Hashem from now and forever. From the dawning place of the sun to its setting place, praised is the name of Hashem. Exalted above all nations is Hashem. Above the heavens is His glory. Who is like Hashem our God, Who dwells on high, yet deigns to look upon heaven and earth?

---

the synagogue, one would have to recite one at the *seder*. The *Tosefta* (*Succah* 3:2) strikes a similar note. Although there is a Talmudic debate on this subject (*Yerushalmi Berachos* 1:5), all protagonists there agree on this basic issue: namely, that the *Hallel* should be preceded by a blessing.

Indeed, it would be strange if it did not require a blessing. Reciting this *Hallel* was a prerequisite to commemorating the Exodus, simultaneous to consuming the Passover sacrifice. As our Sages designed the *Hallel* to be interrupted by the meal, eating that meal does not constitute a break in *Hallel*. Similarly, the *Rosh Hashanah* prayers are not considered an interruption of the *shofar* blasts. Nor is the synagogue reading of the Torah an interference in the blessings on the Torah. All this is true and correct. (*Chiddushim, Pesachim* 117)

◆§ יְהִי שֵׁם ה׳ מְבֹרָךְ מֵעַתָּה וְעַד עוֹלָם — *Blessed be the Name of* HASHEM *from now and forever.* This refers to Hashem's Kingship and Rule, which were manifested when He saved His servants and destroyed those who rebelled against Him. May He continue this in future generations — neither forsaking the righteous nor ignoring the wicked, who perpetuate evil against innocents. There are many other similar verses with the identical interpretation. (*Exodus* 15:18)

◆§ הַמַּשְׁפִּילִי לִרְאוֹת בַּשָּׁמַיִם וּבָאָרֶץ — *Yet deigns to look upon heaven and earth?* Clearly and incontrovertibly, a belief in general and specific Divine Providence — God's knowledge of all important and lesser species and His control over both the general group and the individual — is fundamental to Torah tradition. The skeptic, who claims that the Creator has no knowledge of the activities and

מְקִימִי מֵעָפָר דָּל, מֵאַשְׁפֹּת יָרִים אֶבְיוֹן. לְהוֹשִׁיבִי עִם
נְדִיבִים, עִם נְדִיבֵי עַמּוֹ. מוֹשִׁיבִי עֲקֶרֶת הַבַּיִת, אֵם הַבָּנִים
שְׂמֵחָה, הַלְלוּיָהּ.[1]

בְּצֵאת   יִשְׂרָאֵל מִמִּצְרָיִם, בֵּית יַעֲקֹב מֵעַם לֹעֵז. הָיְתָה
יְהוּדָה לְקָדְשׁוֹ, יִשְׂרָאֵל מַמְשְׁלוֹתָיו. הַיָּם רָאָה
וַיָּנֹס, הַיַּרְדֵּן יִסֹּב לְאָחוֹר. הֶהָרִים רָקְדוּ כְאֵילִים, גְּבָעוֹת
כִּבְנֵי צֹאן. מַה לְּךָ הַיָּם כִּי תָנוּס, הַיַּרְדֵּן תִּסֹּב לְאָחוֹר.
הֶהָרִים תִּרְקְדוּ כְאֵילִים, גְּבָעוֹת כִּבְנֵי צֹאן. מִלִּפְנֵי אָדוֹן
חוּלִי אָרֶץ, מִלִּפְנֵי אֱלוֹהַ יַעֲקֹב. הַהֹפְכִי הַצּוּר אֲגַם מָיִם,
חַלָּמִישׁ לְמַעְיְנוֹ מָיִם.[2]

---

exertions of lowly humans, denies the whole Torah. So does the
nonbeliever who maintains that God exercises no Providence based
on whether people do good or evil. Nor can these skeptics accept the
principle of prophecy, as that too is integral to a Divine interest in
human affairs. He who insists we enjoy profit and deliverance (or
suffer pain and mishap) purely by chance and coincidence — and
not Divine Design — has no share in the World to Come, nor any
part in the Torah and commandments.

We are obligated to believe that the Lord Above knows all manner
of men, both humble and mighty, and treats them accordingly. He is
aware of all their thoughts and deeds — past, present and future —
since it was He Who created them all out of total nothingness.

However, non-humans who do not speak or recognize the Creator
are not subject to the same individual Providence. They are under a
more diffused Divine Providence that concerns only the general
breed of these creatures. Even within the human race, those whose
thoughts stray far from God shall be abandoned by Providence to
natural circumstance. By contrast, the truly pious who remain constantly close to God in every situation will merit greater individual
Providence in direct proportion to the devotion they exert.

(Preface to *Job*, ibid. 36:7. See also *Genesis* 18:19, 19:8;
Exodus 13:16, *Deuteronomy* 18:13)

⊷§ יִשְׂרָאֵל מַמְשְׁלוֹתָיו — *Israel, His dominion.* Mankind was created to
recognize their Creator and proclaim their gratitude to Him. When

He raises the impoverished from the dust. From the trash heaps He lifts the indigent. To seat them with nobles, with the nobles of His people. He transforms a barren woman into a happy mother of children. Halleluyah![1]

When Israel went out of Egypt, the house of Jacob from a slanderous nation, Judah became His holy one; Israel, His dominion. The Sea saw and fled. The Jordan stayed to the rear. The mountains skipped like rams; the hills — like lambs. What is it, Sea, that makes you flee? Jordan, what makes you stay back? Mountains, why do you prance like rams? Hills, why do you skip like lambs? Before the presence of the Master Who created the earth. Before the presence of the God of Jacob; Who turns the rock into a pond of water, the flint into a fountain of water.[2]

---

(1) *Psalms* 113.

---

the early generations willfully sinned and denied His Name, the Children of Israel — by being shown signs and wonders — were chosen as living witnesses to publicize the eternal truth to all nations. Should they disappear and their memory be lost, all His miracles and deeds will likewise be forgotten. Even if nations occasionally recall those events, they might falsely ascribe them to other causes. Thus, the purpose of Man's Creation will be thwarted.

The Children of Israel were chosen because God found them more worthy of His love than any other. They have earned this Divine devotion by stubbornly suffering everything imposed on them — willingly declaring "Either we remain loyal to Judaism or we will be nailed to the stake!"

The Jewish nation, God's Chosen People, are not subject to the stars and constellations. The occult, spells or sorcery cannot harm them. Hashem alone is their source of reward and punishment.
(*Numbers* 23:23; *Deuteronomy* 7:7, 32:26. See also *Leviticus* 18:25, *Numbers* 11:16, and *Deuteronomy* 18:13)

⇐ הַהֹפְכִי הַצּוּר אֲגַם מָיִם — *Who turns the rock into a pond of water.* The very substance of the rock itself is converted into a pond of water. The waters gushed forth from the center of the rock and not from the earth below, as occurs naturally with other springs.
(*Numbers* 20:8. See also ibid. 21:18 and *Exodus* 17:5)

The cup is lifted and the *matzos* covered during the recitation of the following blessing.
[On Saturday night substitute the bracketed phrase for the preceding phrase.]

בָּרוּךְ אַתָּה יהוה אֱלֹהֵינוּ מֶלֶךְ הָעוֹלָם, אֲשֶׁר גְּאָלֵנוּ וְגָאַל אֶת אֲבוֹתֵינוּ מִמִּצְרַיִם, וְהִגִּיעֵנוּ הַלַּיְלָה הַזֶּה לֶאֱכָל בּוֹ מַצָּה וּמָרוֹר. כֵּן יהוה אֱלֹהֵינוּ וֵאלֹהֵי אֲבוֹתֵינוּ, יַגִּיעֵנוּ לְמוֹעֲדִים וְלִרְגָלִים אֲחֵרִים הַבָּאִים לִקְרָאתֵנוּ לְשָׁלוֹם, שְׂמֵחִים בְּבִנְיַן עִירֶךְ וְשָׂשִׂים בַּעֲבוֹדָתֶךְ, וְנֹאכַל שָׁם מִן הַזְּבָחִים וּמִן הַפְּסָחִים [מִן הַפְּסָחִים וּמִן הַזְּבָחִים] אֲשֶׁר יַגִּיעַ דָּמָם עַל קִיר מִזְבַּחֲךָ לְרָצוֹן. וְנוֹדֶה לְךָ שִׁיר חָדָשׁ עַל גְּאֻלָּתֵנוּ וְעַל פְּדוּת נַפְשֵׁנוּ. בָּרוּךְ אַתָּה יהוה, גָּאַל יִשְׂרָאֵל.

בָּרוּךְ אַתָּה יהוה אֱלֹהֵינוּ מֶלֶךְ הָעוֹלָם, בּוֹרֵא פְּרִי הַגָּפֶן.

The second cup is drunk while leaning on the left side —
preferably the entire cup, but at least most of it.

רחצה

The hands are washed for *matzah* and the following blessing is recited. It is preferable to bring water and a basin to the head of the household at the *seder* table.

בָּרוּךְ אַתָּה יהוה אֱלֹהֵינוּ מֶלֶךְ הָעוֹלָם, אֲשֶׁר קִדְּשָׁנוּ בְּמִצְוֹתָיו, וְצִוָּנוּ עַל נְטִילַת יָדָיִם.

❧ **יַגִּיעֵנוּ לְמוֹעֲדִים אֲחֵרִים הַבָּאִים לִקְרָאתֵנוּ** — *Bring us to future festivals and holidays.* The Children of Israel were commanded to make three annual pilgrimages to the site of God's choice. Each person brought along offerings, according to the prosperity with which God had blessed him. The Jews rejoiced before Him in gratitude for all their good fortune, which had been granted by His mercy and great kindness.

The Third Temple — may it be speedily built within our days — will be established without arguments or feuding. Finally, God will enlarge our borders as He has promised. We shall become fruitful and all the nations will worship Hashem as one.

(*Deuteronomy* 16:4 and *Genesis* 26:20, 29:2. With regard to sacrifices generally, see *Leviticus* 1:9 and *Ramban's* lecture *Toras Temimah*)

The cup is lifted and the *matzos* covered during the recitation of the following blessing.
[On Saturday night substitute the bracketed phrase for the preceding phrase.]

Blessed are You, Hashem, our God, King of the Universe, Who has redeemed us and redeemed our ancestors from Egypt, and enabled us to live to this night, to eat on it *matzah* and *maror*. So, Hashem, our God and the God of our fathers, bring us to future festivals and holidays in peace, happy in the reconstruction of Your city and joyful in Your worship. May we eat there of the offerings and Passover sacrifices [the Passover sacrifices and the offerings] whose blood will reach the wall of Your altar for acceptance. And may we thank You with a new song for our redemption and the liberation of our soul. Blessed are You, Hashem, Who redeemed Israel.

Blessed are You, Hashem, our God, King of the Universe, Who creates the fruit of the vine.

The second cup is drunk while leaning on the left side — preferably the entire cup, but at least most of it.

RACHTZAH

The hands are washed for *matzah* and the following blessing is recited. It is preferable to bring water and a basin to the head of the household at the *seder* table.

Blessed are You, Hashem, our God, King of the Universe, Who has sanctified us with His commandments and commanded us with regard to washing the hands.

---

(1) *Psalms* 114.

◆§ רָחְצָה — *The hands are washed*. Washing is a way of displaying respect for the Lord Above. Similarly, anyone approaching the royal table, to serve the king food and drink, must first wash his hands. Furthermore, the *Kohanim* were commanded to also cleanse their feet, since they performed the Temple service barefoot.

According to the mystical teachings, this washing engenders greater holiness as the number of fingers on both the hands and feet reflect the סְפִירוֹת — the Ten Emanations of Hashem's Power. For the same reason, our Rabbis instructed us to wash our hand before prayers. (*Exodus* 30:19)

מוֹצִיא / מַצָה

The following two blessings are recited over *matzah;* the first is recited over *matzah* as food, and the second for the special *mitzvah* of eating *matzah* on the night of Pesach. [The latter blessing is to be made with the intention that it also apply to the *korach*, "sandwich," and the *afikoman*.] The head of the household raises all the *matzos* on the *seder* plate and recites the following blessings:

בָּרוּךְ אַתָּה יהוה אֱלֹהֵינוּ מֶלֶךְ הָעוֹלָם, הַמּוֹצִיא לֶחֶם מִן הָאָרֶץ.

Those who use three *matzos* put down the bottom *matzah* at this point.

בָּרוּךְ אַתָּה יהוה אֱלֹהֵינוּ מֶלֶךְ הָעוֹלָם, אֲשֶׁר קִדְּשָׁנוּ בְּמִצְוֹתָיו, וְצִוָּנוּ עַל אֲכִילַת מַצָּה.

Each participant is required to eat an amount of *matzah* equal in volume to an egg.

Since it is usually impossible to provide a sufficient amount of *matzah* from the two *matzos* for all members of the household, other *matzos* should be available at the head of the table from which to complete the required amounts. However, each participant should receive a piece from each of the top two *matzos*.

The *matzos* are to be eaten while reclining on the left side
and without delay; they need not be dipped in salt.

מָרוֹר

The head of the household takes a half-egg volume of the *maror,* dips it into *charoses,* and gives each participant a like amount. The following blessing is recited with the intention that it also apply to the *maror* of the "sandwich." The *maror* is eaten without reclining, and without delay.

בָּרוּךְ אַתָּה יהוה אֱלֹהֵינוּ מֶלֶךְ הָעוֹלָם, אֲשֶׁר קִדְּשָׁנוּ בְּמִצְוֹתָיו, וְצִוָּנוּ עַל אֲכִילַת מָרוֹר.

⊰§ אֲשֶׁר קִדְּשָׁנוּ §⊱ — *Who has sanctified us.* Despite these blessings beginning in the second person: "Blessed are **You**, HASHEM, our God, King of the Universe," they switch to the third person: "*Who has sanctified us with **His** commandments and commanded us . . .*" This happens whenever God's Kingship is mentioned (just as one would not address a king directly). These blessings were particularly formulated to show greater respect to the Divine Lord of all Creation by referring to Him in the third person. Likewise, the prayer "*Aleinu*"

MOTZI / MATZAH

The following two blessings are recited over *matzah;* the first is recited over *matzah* as food, and the second for the special *mitzvah* of eating *matzah* on the night of Pesach. [The latter blessing is to be made with the intention that it also apply to the *korach,* "sandwich," and the *afikoman.*] The head of the household raises all the *matzos* on the *seder* plate and recites the following blessings:

Blessed are You, Hashem, our God, King of the Universe, Who brings forth bread from the earth.

> Those who use three *matzos* put down the bottom *matzah* at this point.

Blessed are You, Hashem, our God, King of the Universe, Who has sanctified us with His commandments and commanded us with regard to eating *matzah.*

> Each participant is required to eat an amount of *matzah* equal in volume to an egg.

Since it is usually impossible to provide a sufficient amount of *matzah* from the two *matzos* for all members of the household, other *matzos* should be available at the head of the table from which to complete the required amounts. However, each participant should receive a piece from each of the top two *matzos.*

> The *matzos* are to be eaten while reclining on the left side
> and without delay; they need not be dipped in salt.

MAROR

The head of the household takes a half-egg volume of the *maror,* dips it into *charoses,* and gives each participant a like amount. The following blessing is recited with the intention that it also apply to the *maror* of the "sandwich." The *maror* is eaten without reclining, and without delay.

Blessed are You, Hashem, our God, King of the Universe, Who has sanctified us with His commandments and commanded us with regard to eating *maror.*

("It is our duty to praise the Master of All") is formulated in the third person since it also mentions that God is "The King Who reigns over all kings. . . .."

However, when a blessing makes no mention of His Kingship, the prayers are framed in the second person. To quote just two instances of many: The second and third blessing of the *Amidah* refer to God as respectively "You are Mighty. . . ," and "You are Holy. . ."

(Exodus 15:26)

כּוֹרֵךְ

The bottom *matzah* is now taken. From it, with the addition of other *matzos* if needed, each participant receives a half-egg's volume of matzah with an equal volume of *maror* (dipped into *charoses* which is shaken off). The following paragraph is recited and the "sandwich" is eaten while reclining.

זֵכֶר לְמִקְדָּשׁ כְּהִלֵּל. כֵּן עָשָׂה הִלֵּל בִּזְמַן שֶׁבֵּית הַמִּקְדָּשׁ הָיָה קַיָּם. הָיָה כּוֹרֵךְ (פֶּסַח) מַצָּה וּמָרוֹר וְאוֹכֵל בְּיַחַד. לְקַיֵּם מַה שֶׁנֶּאֱמַר, עַל מַצּוֹת וּמְרֹרִים יֹאכְלֻהוּ.[1]

שֻׁלְחָן עוֹרֵךְ

The meal should be eaten in a combination of joy and solemnity, for the meal, too, is a part of the *seder* service.

It is customary to eat an egg, in remembrance of the *chagigah* offering, and meat (but not roasted), in remembrance of the *pesach* offering.

While it is desirable that *zemiros* and discussion of the laws and events of Pesach be part of the meal, extraneous conversation should be avoided.

It should be remembered that the *afikoman* must be eaten while there is still some appetite for it. In fact, if one is so sated that he must literally force himself to eat it, he is not credited with the performance of the *mitzvah* of *afikoman*. Therefore, it is unwise to eat more than a moderate amount during the meal.

צָפוּן

From the *afikoman matzah* (and from additional *matzos* to make up the required amount), a half-egg's volume portion — according to some, a full egg's volume portion — is given to each participant. It should be eaten before midnight, while reclining, without delay, and uninterruptedly. Nothing may be eaten or drunk after the *afikoman* (with the exception of water and the like) except for the last two *seder* cups of wine.

⧫§ **כֵּן עָשָׂה הִלֵּל** — *As Hillel did*. This practice of Hillel — to combine the eating of *matzah* and *maror* — is a minority view, particularly nowadays. *Maror* is now of only Rabbinical ordinance (since we have no Passover sacrifice) whereas eating the *matzah* remains a Biblical commandment.

The verse "on (עַל) bitter herbs they shall eat it (the paschal

KORECH

The bottom matzah *is now taken. From it, with the addition of other* matzos *if needed, each participant receives a half-egg's volume of* matzah *with an equal volume of* maror *(dipped into* charoses *which is shaken off). The following paragraph is recited and the "sandwich" is eaten while reclining.*

In remembrance of the Temple we do as Hillel did in Temple times: He would combine Passover offering, *matzah* and *maror* in a sandwich and eat them together, to fulfill that which is written, "With *matzos* and *maror* they should eat it."[1]

SHULCHAN ORECH

*The meal should be eaten in a combination of joy and solemnity,
for the meal, too, is a part of the* seder *service.*
It is customary to eat an egg, in remembrance of the chagigah *offering,
and meat (but not roasted), in remembrance of the* pesach *offering.*
While it is desirable that zemiros *and discussion of the laws and events of Pesach
be part of the meal, extraneous conversation should be avoided.*
It should be remembered that the afikoman *must be eaten while there is still some
appetite for it. In fact, if one is so sated that he must literally force himself to eat it, he is
not credited with the performance of the* mitzvah *of* afikoman. *Therefore, it is unwise to
eat more than a moderate amount during the meal.*

TZAFUN

From the afikoman matzah *(and from additional* matzos *to make up the required amount),
a half-egg's volume portion — according to some, a full egg's volume portion — is given
to each participant. It should be eaten before midnight, while reclining, without delay, and
uninterruptedly. Nothing may be eaten or drunk after the* afikoman *(with the exception of
water and the like) except for the last two* seder *cups of wine.*

---

(1) *Bamidbar* 9:11.

---

sacrifice)" (*Exodus* 12:8) can be simply explained. The word used — עַל — which generally means "on," here means "with" (i.e. the *matzah* and *maror* should merely accompany the sacrifice). The Torah uses here the word עַל rather than the more common עִם ("together with") to teach us that we are *not* obliged to wrap them together in a sandwich.

(*Exodus* 12:8 and *Milchamos* to *Pesachim* 115)

בָּרֵךְ

The third cup is poured and *Bircas HaMazon* (Grace After Meals) is recited.
According to some customs, the Cup of Elijah is poured at this point.

שִׁיר הַמַּעֲלוֹת, בְּשׁוּב יהוה אֶת שִׁיבַת צִיּוֹן, הָיִינוּ
כְּחֹלְמִים. אָז יִמָּלֵא שְׂחוֹק פִּינוּ וּלְשׁוֹנֵנוּ רִנָּה, אָז
יֹאמְרוּ בַגּוֹיִם, הִגְדִּיל יהוה לַעֲשׂוֹת עִם אֵלֶּה. הִגְדִּיל יהוה
לַעֲשׂוֹת עִמָּנוּ, הָיִינוּ שְׂמֵחִים. שׁוּבָה יהוה אֶת שְׁבִיתֵנוּ,
כַּאֲפִיקִים בַּנֶּגֶב. הַזֹּרְעִים בְּדִמְעָה בְּרִנָּה יִקְצֹרוּ. הָלוֹךְ יֵלֵךְ
וּבָכֹה נֹשֵׂא מֶשֶׁךְ הַזָּרַע, בֹּא יָבֹא בְרִנָּה, נֹשֵׂא אֲלֻמֹּתָיו.

תְּהִלַּת יהוה יְדַבֶּר פִּי, וִיבָרֵךְ כָּל בָּשָׂר שֵׁם קָדְשׁוֹ
לְעוֹלָם וָעֶד.¹ וַאֲנַחְנוּ נְבָרֵךְ יָהּ, מֵעַתָּה וְעַד
עוֹלָם, הַלְלוּיָהּ.² הוֹדוּ לַיהוה כִּי טוֹב, כִּי לְעוֹלָם חַסְדּוֹ.³
מִי יְמַלֵּל גְּבוּרוֹת יהוה, יַשְׁמִיעַ כָּל תְּהִלָּתוֹ.⁴

If three or more males, aged thirteen or older, participate in the meal, the leader is
required to formally invite the others to join him in the recitation of *Bircas HaMazon.*
Following is the *zimun,* or formal invitation.
The leader begins:

רַבּוֹתַי נְבָרֵךְ.

The group responds:

יְהִי שֵׁם יהוה מְבֹרָךְ מֵעַתָּה וְעַד עוֹלָם.⁵

The leader continues [if ten men join the *zimun,* the words in parentheses are included]:

יְהִי שֵׁם יהוה מְבֹרָךְ מֵעַתָּה וְעַד עוֹלָם.⁵ בִּרְשׁוּת מָרָנָן
וְרַבָּנָן וְרַבּוֹתַי, נְבָרֵךְ (אֱלֹהֵינוּ) שֶׁאָכַלְנוּ מִשֶּׁלּוֹ.

The group responds:

בָּרוּךְ (אֱלֹהֵינוּ) שֶׁאָכַלְנוּ מִשֶּׁלּוֹ וּבְטוּבוֹ חָיִינוּ.

The leader continues:

בָּרוּךְ (אֱלֹהֵינוּ) שֶׁאָכַלְנוּ מִשֶּׁלּוֹ וּבְטוּבוֹ חָיִינוּ.

The following line is recited if ten men join the *zimun.*

בָּרוּךְ הוּא וּבָרוּךְ שְׁמוֹ.

BARECH

The third cup is poured and *Bircas HaMazon* (Grace After Meals) is recited.
According to some customs, the Cup of Elijah is poured at this point.

A song of the steps. When Hashem will bring the exiles back to Zion, it will be as if we were dreaming. Then our mouth will be filled with laughter and our tongue with joy. Then they will say among the nations, "Hashem is the One Who has done great things with these." Hashem has indeed done great things with us. We have been made happy. Hashem, return our captives like dry streams that run again in the south. Those who sow in tears will reap in song. He who goes crying, carrying his load of seed, will return singing, carrying his sheaves of grain.

May my mouth declare the praise of Hashem and may all flesh bless His Holy Name forever.[1] We will bless Hashem from this time and forever. Halleluyah![2] Give thanks to God for He is good, His kindness endures forever.[3] Who can express the mighty acts of Hashem? Who can declare all His praise?[4]

If three or more males, aged thirteen or older, participate in the meal, the leader is required to formally invite the others to join him in the recitation of *Bircas HaMazon*. Following is the *zimun*, or formal invitation.

The leader begins:

Gentlemen, let us make the blessing.

The group responds:

May the name of Hashem be blessed from this moment and forever![5]

The leader continues [if ten men join the *zimun*, the words in parentheses are included]:

May the name of Hashem be blessed from this moment and forever![5]

With the permission of the distinguished people present,
let us bless [our God], for we have eaten from what is His.

The group responds:

Blessed is [our God] He of Whose we have eaten
and through Whose goodness we live.

The leader continues:

Blessed is [our God] He of Whose we have eaten
and through Whose goodness we live.

The following line is recited if ten men join the *zimun*.

Blessed is He and Blessed is His Name.

---

(1) *Psalms* 145:21. (2) 115:18. (3) 118:1. (4) 106:2. (5) 113:2.

בָּרוּךְ אַתָּה יהוה אֱלֹהֵינוּ מֶלֶךְ הָעוֹלָם, הַזָּן אֶת הָעוֹלָם כֻּלּוֹ, בְּטוּבוֹ, בְּחֵן בְּחֶסֶד וּבְרַחֲמִים, הוּא נוֹתֵן לֶחֶם לְכָל בָּשָׂר, כִּי לְעוֹלָם חַסְדּוֹ.[1] וּבְטוּבוֹ הַגָּדוֹל, תָּמִיד לֹא חָסַר לָנוּ, וְאַל יֶחְסַר לָנוּ מָזוֹן לְעוֹלָם וָעֶד. בַּעֲבוּר שְׁמוֹ הַגָּדוֹל, כִּי הוּא אֵל זָן וּמְפַרְנֵס לַכֹּל, וּמֵטִיב לַכֹּל, וּמֵכִין מָזוֹן לְכָל בְּרִיּוֹתָיו אֲשֶׁר בָּרָא. בָּרוּךְ אַתָּה יהוה, הַזָּן אֶת הַכֹּל. (אָמֵן. —Others)

נוֹדֶה לְּךָ יהוה אֱלֹהֵינוּ, עַל שֶׁהִנְחַלְתָּ לַאֲבוֹתֵינוּ אֶרֶץ חֶמְדָּה טוֹבָה וּרְחָבָה. וְעַל שֶׁהוֹצֵאתָנוּ יהוה אֱלֹהֵינוּ מֵאֶרֶץ מִצְרַיִם, וּפְדִיתָנוּ מִבֵּית עֲבָדִים, וְעַל בְּרִיתְךָ שֶׁחָתַמְתָּ בִּבְשָׂרֵנוּ, וְעַל תּוֹרָתְךָ שֶׁלִּמַּדְתָּנוּ, וְעַל חֻקֶּיךָ שֶׁהוֹדַעְתָּנוּ, וְעַל חַיִּים חֵן וָחֶסֶד שֶׁחוֹנַנְתָּנוּ, וְעַל אֲכִילַת מָזוֹן שָׁאַתָּה זָן וּמְפַרְנֵס אוֹתָנוּ תָּמִיד, בְּכָל יוֹם וּבְכָל עֵת וּבְכָל שָׁעָה.

וְעַל הַכֹּל יהוה אֱלֹהֵינוּ אֲנַחְנוּ מוֹדִים לָךְ, וּמְבָרְכִים אוֹתָךְ, יִתְבָּרַךְ שִׁמְךָ בְּפִי כָּל חַי תָּמִיד לְעוֹלָם וָעֶד. כַּכָּתוּב, וְאָכַלְתָּ וְשָׂבָעְתָּ, וּבֵרַכְתָּ אֶת יהוה אֱלֹהֶיךָ, עַל

---

§ תָּמִיד לֹא חָסַר לָנוּ — *Nourishment has never been lacking for us.* The idol worshipers mistakenly thought their pagan practices would benefit their crops and water supply, bringing them general success. On the contrary, only through serving God will we earn success and protection. God will bless our "bread" — which includes every food — and "water," including all drinkable liquids, providing them for us in abundance.

By blessing our food and drink, God ensures our physical health, freeing us from sickness. When the air, food and water are clear and healthy, the body functions properly. Also, the scourge of barren-ness and miscarriages — symptoms of an unhealthy body — will then be eradicated. (*Exodus* 23:25. See also *Leviticus* 26:4 and 11)

Blessed are You, Hashem, our God, King of the Universe, Who nourishes the entire world with His goodness, with grace, kindness, and mercy. He gives nourishment to all flesh, for His kindness is eternal.[1] And in His great goodness, nourishment has never been lacking for us, nor may it ever be, for the sake of His great name. For He feeds and supports all and does good to all and readies food for all His creatures that He created. Blessed are You, Hashem, Who feeds all.

We thank You, Hashem, our God, for giving to our ancestors as a heritage a desirable, good, and spacious land, and for taking us out, Hashem, our God, from the land of Egypt, and redeeming us from the house of bondage, and for the covenant which You sealed into our flesh, and for Your Torah which You taught us, and for Your laws which You made known to us, and for life, grace, and kindness which You have bestowed upon us, and for the food with which You feed and sustain us every day, at every time, at every moment.

For it all, Hashem, our God, we thank You and bless You. May Your name be blessed by the mouths of all who live constantly, forever, as it is written, "You will eat and you will be satisfied, and bless Hashem, your God, for

---

(1) *Psalms* 136:25.

❧ בְּרִיתְךָ שֶׁחָתַמְתָּ בִּבְשָׂרֵנוּ — *Your covenant which You sealed into our flesh.* The *Radak* explains that circumcision is to serve as a constant warning to use the reproductive organs, associated with desire, only where it is a duty or permissible.

It is also a symbol of God's Covenant with the descendants of Abraham, who are circumcised to serve Hashem as one.

(*Genesis* 9:12, 17:9. See also *Emunah and Bitachon* Chap. 8)

❧ וְאָכַלְתָּ וְשָׂבָעְתָּ וּבֵרַכְתָּ — *You will eat and you will be satisfied and bless. . .* When recalling the slavery in Egypt or the suffering in the wilderness, we shall bless Hashem over the food we eat to satisfaction, in the good land. Traditionally, according to our Rabbis,

הָאָרֶץ הַטֹּבָה אֲשֶׁר נָתַן לָךְ.[1] בָּרוּךְ אַתָּה יהוה, עַל
הָאָרֶץ וְעַל הַמָּזוֹן. (אָמֵן. —Others)

רַחֵם יהוה אֱלֹהֵינוּ עַל יִשְׂרָאֵל עַמֶּךָ, וְעַל יְרוּשָׁלַיִם
עִירֶךָ, וְעַל צִיּוֹן מִשְׁכַּן כְּבוֹדֶךָ, וְעַל מַלְכוּת בֵּית
דָּוִד מְשִׁיחֶךָ, וְעַל הַבַּיִת הַגָּדוֹל וְהַקָּדוֹשׁ שֶׁנִּקְרָא שִׁמְךָ
עָלָיו. אֱלֹהֵינוּ אָבִינוּ רְעֵנוּ זוּנֵנוּ פַּרְנְסֵנוּ וְכַלְכְּלֵנוּ
וְהַרְוִיחֵנוּ, וְהַרְוַח לָנוּ יהוה אֱלֹהֵינוּ מְהֵרָה מִכָּל
צָרוֹתֵינוּ. וְנָא אַל תַּצְרִיכֵנוּ יהוה אֱלֹהֵינוּ, לֹא לִידֵי
מַתְּנַת בָּשָׂר וָדָם, וְלֹא לִידֵי הַלְוָאָתָם, כִּי אִם לְיָדְךָ
הַמְּלֵאָה הַפְּתוּחָה הַקְּדוֹשָׁה וְהָרְחָבָה, שֶׁלֹּא נֵבוֹשׁ וְלֹא
נִכָּלֵם לְעוֹלָם וָעֶד.

---

this is a specific *positive commandment*. Although the verse here
mentions the "good land," the commandment equally applies
outside *Eretz Yisrael* — wherever and whenever we eat our fill of
bread. This verse tells us to thank Hashem for both the food and the
Promised Land that remained ours for generations.

Bircas HaMazon and the blessing after eating any of the seven
products (for which *Eretz Yisrael* was distinguished) are Biblical
commandments. Consequently, if we are unsure whether we recited
the appropriate blessing, we have to repeat it again.

(*Deuteronomy* 8:10 and *Chiddushim* to *Berachos* 49)

◆§ מַלְכוּת בֵּית דָּוִד מְשִׁיחֶךָ — *The monarchy of the house of David*.

Jacob, our Patriarch, chose Judah to rule over his brethren
and awarded him royalty over Israel. Yet, a member of another
tribe — Saul, from the tribe of Benjamin — was crowned first.
However, once a king was chosen from Judah (i.e. David), the
prerogatives of royalty should never leave that tribe. Indeed, Saul
was only chosen as a temporary expedient, when God was dis-
pleased at the untimely request for a king. (Their legitimate ruler
then was still the prophet Samuel, who led them into battle under
God's Will.)

I believe that after David's reign, later kings who came from other

the good land which He has given you."[1] Blessed are You, Hashem, for the land and the food.

Have mercy, Hashem, our God, on Israel, Your people, and on Jerusalem, Your city, and on Zion, the abode of Your glory, and on the monarchy of the house of David, Your anointed, and on the great and holy House upon which Your name is called. Our God, our Father, tend us, nourish us, support us, sustain us, and rescue us. And rescue us, Hashem, our God, speedily from all of our troubles. Please, Hashem, our God, do not put us in need of gifts or loans from men. May we need only Your full, open, holy, and ample hand, so that we may never be ashamed or embarrassed.

---

(1) *Deuteronomy* 8:10.

---

tribes disobeyed Jacob's testament and were guilty of disinheriting the royal tribe of Judah. The Israelites based themselves on the precedent of the prophet Achijah, who crowned Jeroboam, the son of Nebat. However, God had intended that, too, as only a temporary expedient, and the Jews' continuing to anoint kings from other tribes was an error. Because they ignored the will of our Patriarch, the kingdom of Israel suffered accordingly, as the prophet Hosea proclaimed (*Hosea* 8:4).

This also explains why the Hasmonean family, who reigned during the Second Temple, were punished so severely. They were men of extreme piety. Without their heroic battles, the observance of Torah and commandments might have been blotted out. Yet despite their merits, despite their bravery and glorious victories, the four saintly sons of Mattisyahu died by their enemies' sword. Eventually the whole family was wiped out because of this sin. According to the Sages (*Bava Basra* 3b), anyone claiming Hasmonean descent today must be an impostor and is deemed a slave.

As priests, the Hasmoneans were not from the royal house of David nor even tribal descendants of Judah. Besides abandoning the priesthood, they had usurped the royal power. In measured retribution for their transgression, they fell under the sway of slaves (Herod and his clan) who destroyed the entire family.

(*Genesis* 49:10)

On the Sabbath add the following paragraph.

רְצֵה וְהַחֲלִיצֵנוּ יהוה אֱלֹהֵינוּ בְּמִצְוֹתֶיךָ, וּבְמִצְוַת יוֹם
הַשְּׁבִיעִי הַשַּׁבָּת הַגָּדוֹל וְהַקָּדוֹשׁ הַזֶּה, כִּי יוֹם זֶה
גָּדוֹל וְקָדוֹשׁ הוּא לְפָנֶיךָ, לִשְׁבָּת בּוֹ וְלָנוּחַ בּוֹ בְּאַהֲבָה
כְּמִצְוַת רְצוֹנֶךָ, וּבִרְצוֹנְךָ הָנִיחַ לָנוּ יהוה אֱלֹהֵינוּ, שֶׁלֹּא
תְהֵא צָרָה וְיָגוֹן וַאֲנָחָה בְּיוֹם מְנוּחָתֵנוּ, וְהַרְאֵנוּ יהוה
אֱלֹהֵינוּ בְּנֶחָמַת צִיּוֹן עִירֶךָ, וּבְבִנְיַן יְרוּשָׁלַיִם עִיר קָדְשֶׁךָ,
כִּי אַתָּה הוּא בַּעַל הַיְשׁוּעוֹת וּבַעַל הַנֶּחָמוֹת.

אֱלֹהֵינוּ וֵאלֹהֵי אֲבוֹתֵינוּ, יַעֲלֶה, וְיָבֹא, וְיַגִּיעַ, וְיֵרָאֶה,
וְיֵרָצֶה, וְיִשָּׁמַע, וְיִפָּקֵד, וְיִזָּכֵר זִכְרוֹנֵנוּ
וּפִקְדוֹנֵנוּ, וְזִכְרוֹן אֲבוֹתֵינוּ, וְזִכְרוֹן מָשִׁיחַ בֶּן דָּוִד עַבְדֶּךָ,
וְזִכְרוֹן יְרוּשָׁלַיִם עִיר קָדְשֶׁךָ, וְזִכְרוֹן כָּל עַמְּךָ בֵּית
יִשְׂרָאֵל לְפָנֶיךָ, לִפְלֵיטָה לְטוֹבָה לְחֵן וּלְחֶסֶד וּלְרַחֲמִים,
לְחַיִּים וּלְשָׁלוֹם בְּיוֹם חַג הַמַּצּוֹת הַזֶּה. זָכְרֵנוּ יהוה
אֱלֹהֵינוּ בּוֹ לְטוֹבָה, וּפָקְדֵנוּ בוֹ לִבְרָכָה, וְהוֹשִׁיעֵנוּ בוֹ
לְחַיִּים. וּבִדְבַר יְשׁוּעָה וְרַחֲמִים, חוּס וְחָנֵּנוּ וְרַחֵם
עָלֵינוּ וְהוֹשִׁיעֵנוּ, כִּי אֵלֶיךָ עֵינֵינוּ, כִּי אֵל חַנּוּן וְרַחוּם
אָתָּה.[1]

---

(1) Cf. *Nehemiah* 9:31

---

§ כִּי יוֹם זֶה גָּדוֹל וְקָדוֹשׁ — *For this day is great and holy.* The Sages
considered the Sabbath as equal to all other commandments
in the Torah combined. It bears witness to the pillars of our
religion: Creation, Providence, and prophecy. As the Sabbath is
crucial to our faith in God, we must also remember this important
day throughout the week — never ignoring it nor confusing it with
another day.

Other nations call each day by a separate name (usually denoting
the celestial spheres or pagan deities). By contrast, we should
describe them as the "First day of the Sabbath," the "Second day of

On the Sabbath add the following paragraph.

May it be Your will, Hashem, our God, that You fortify us through Your *mitzvos* and through the *mitzvah* of the seventh day, this great and holy *Shabbos*. For this day is great and holy before You, to desist from work on it, and to rest on it lovingly, in accordance with the command of Your will. May it be Your will, Hashem, our God, that You spare us any trouble, anguish, or sorrow on the day of our rest, and that You show us, Hashem, our God, the consolation of Zion, Your city, and the reconstruction of Jerusalem, Your sacred city, for You are the Master of salvations and the Master of consolations.

Our God and the God of our fathers, may there arise, come, arrive, be seen, be accepted, be heard, be taken note of, and be remembered a remembrance and recollection of us, and a remembrance of our ancestors, and a remembrance of Messiah, son of David, Your servant, and a remembrance of Jerusalem, Your holy city, and a remembrance of all of Your people, the House of Israel, before You, for deliverance, for goodness, for grace, for kindness and for mercy, for life, and for peace, on this day of the Festival of *Matzos*. Remember us on it, Hashem, our God, for good, take us into account for blessing, and save us so that we may live. And with a word of salvation and mercy, have pity and be gracious to us, and have mercy upon us and save us, for our eyes look to You, for You are a merciful and gracious God.[1]

---

the Sabbath," and so on.

We must also remember to keep the Sabbath holy, freeing our minds from daily trivialities and passing preoccupations. Even our cattle were commanded to rest on the Sabbath to prevent any unnecessary distractions. Instead, we can delight our soul in Hashem's Way and absorb God's Wisdom from our prophets and sages. Indeed, the ancient tradition (as mentioned in *II Kings* 4:23) was that the Sabbath and *Rosh Chodesh* were the opportune times to visit the prophet.   (*Exodus* 20:8)

וּבְנֵה יְרוּשָׁלַיִם עִיר הַקֹּדֶשׁ בִּמְהֵרָה בְיָמֵינוּ. בָּרוּךְ אַתָּה יהוה, בּוֹנֵה (בְּרַחֲמָיו) יְרוּשָׁלָיִם. אָמֵן. (אָמֵן. –Others)

בָּרוּךְ אַתָּה יהוה אֱלֹהֵינוּ מֶלֶךְ הָעוֹלָם, הָאֵל אָבִינוּ מַלְכֵּנוּ אַדִּירֵנוּ בּוֹרְאֵנוּ גּוֹאֲלֵנוּ יוֹצְרֵנוּ קְדוֹשֵׁנוּ קְדוֹשׁ יַעֲקֹב, רוֹעֵנוּ רוֹעֵה יִשְׂרָאֵל, הַמֶּלֶךְ הַטּוֹב וְהַמֵּטִיב לַכֹּל, שֶׁבְּכָל יוֹם וָיוֹם הוּא הֵטִיב, הוּא מֵטִיב, הוּא יֵיטִיב לָנוּ. הוּא גְמָלָנוּ הוּא גוֹמְלֵנוּ הוּא יִגְמְלֵנוּ לָעַד, לְחֵן וּלְחֶסֶד וּלְרַחֲמִים וּלְרֶוַח הַצָּלָה וְהַצְלָחָה, בְּרָכָה וִישׁוּעָה נֶחָמָה פַרְנָסָה וְכַלְכָּלָה וְרַחֲמִים וְחַיִּים וְשָׁלוֹם וְכָל טוֹב, וּמִכָּל טוּב לְעוֹלָם אַל יְחַסְּרֵנוּ. (אָמֵן. –Others)

הָרַחֲמָן הוּא יִמְלוֹךְ עָלֵינוּ לְעוֹלָם וָעֶד. הָרַחֲמָן הוּא יִתְבָּרַךְ בַּשָּׁמַיִם וּבָאָרֶץ. הָרַחֲמָן הוּא יִשְׁתַּבַּח לְדוֹר דּוֹרִים, וְיִתְפָּאַר בָּנוּ לָעַד וּלְנֵצַח נְצָחִים, וְיִתְהַדַּר בָּנוּ לָעַד וּלְעוֹלְמֵי עוֹלָמִים. הָרַחֲמָן הוּא יְפַרְנְסֵנוּ בְּכָבוֹד. הָרַחֲמָן הוּא יִשְׁבּוֹר עֻלֵּנוּ מֵעַל צַוָּארֵנוּ, וְהוּא יוֹלִיכֵנוּ קוֹמְמִיּוּת לְאַרְצֵנוּ. הָרַחֲמָן הוּא יִשְׁלַח לָנוּ בְּרָכָה מְרֻבָּה בַּבַּיִת הַזֶּה, וְעַל שֻׁלְחָן זֶה שֶׁאָכַלְנוּ עָלָיו.

◆§ הַטּוֹב וְהַמֵּטִיב לַכֹּל — *Who is good and beneficent to all.* In His Goodness, God remunerates men according to how they perform their good deeds. There are those who observe His commandments merely for their potential reward — to receive long life, wealth and honor in this world. Others, however, obey God's commandments out of fear, and hope for a repayment in the World to Come. They will merit being spared from the severe judgments reserved for evildoers, and their souls will shelter in the good life.

There are others — those who observe *mitzvos* in the ideal manner, serving God with love — who will earn many rewards in this world, yet this will not detract from their merits in the World to Come.

And build Jerusalem, the city of sanctity, quickly in our days. Blessed are You, Hashem, Who builds Jerusalem (in His mercy). Amen.

Blessed are You, Hashem, our God, King of the Universe, the Powerful One, our Father, our King, our Mighty One, our Creator, our Redeemer, our Shaper, our Holy One, the Holy One of Jacob our Shepherd, the Shepherd of Israel, the King Who is good and beneficent to all, Who in each and every day has done good, is doing good, and will do good to us. He has bestowed upon us, is bestowing upon us, and will forever bestow upon us grace, kindness, mercy, rescue, deliverance, success, blessing, salvation, consolation, livelihood, sustenance, mercy, life, peace, and all that is good. May He never let us lack for any good thing.

May the Merciful One rule over us forever. May the Merciful One be blessed in the heavens and the earth. May the Merciful One be praised for all generations, and may He take pride in us for eternity, and may we be a source of glory to Him forever and ever. May the Merciful One provide us an honorable livelihood. May the Merciful One break the yoke upon our shoulders and lead us upright to our land. May the Merciful One send us abundant blessing in this house, and upon this table at which we have eaten.

Furthermore, there are those who ignore all physical attractions of this world and direct all their plans and thoughts to their Sublime Creator. These idealists will — like the prophet Elijah and Enoch in our tradition — live forever in both body and soul. They are "Children of the World to Come" who will rise again at the Resurrection. Therefore, the Torah uses various expressions to describe our future rewards.   (*Leviticus* 18:4. See also *Deuteronomy* 11:22)

יִשְׁלַח לָנוּ בְּרָכָה מְרֻבָּה ⧽₪ — *Send us abundant blessing.* When the world was created, God saw that "all that He had made was exceedingly good" (*Genesis* 1:31). From then on, God's blessing will not produce something out of nothing. Yet, as soon as there exists the smallest

הָרַחֲמָן הוּא יִשְׁלַח לָנוּ אֶת אֵלִיָּהוּ הַנָּבִיא זָכוּר לַטּוֹב,
וִיבַשֶּׂר לָנוּ בְּשׂוֹרוֹת טוֹבוֹת יְשׁוּעוֹת וְנֶחָמוֹת.

The following text — for a guest to recite at his host's table —
appears in *Shulchan Aruch, Orach Chaim* 201.

יְהִי רָצוֹן שֶׁלֹּא יֵבוֹשׁ וְלֹא יִכָּלֵם בַּעַל הַבַּיִת הַזֶּה, לֹא
בָּעוֹלָם הַזֶּה וְלֹא בָּעוֹלָם הַבָּא, וְיַצְלֵיחַ בְּכָל
נְכָסָיו, וְיִהְיוּ נְכָסָיו מוּצְלָחִים וּקְרוֹבִים לָעִיר, וְאַל יִשְׁלוֹט
שָׂטָן בְּמַעֲשֵׂה יָדָיו, וְאַל יִזְדַּקֵּק לְפָנָיו שׁוּם דְּבַר חֵטְא וְהִרְהוּר
עָוֹן, מֵעַתָּה וְעַד עוֹלָם.

Those eating at their own table recite the following,
adding the appropriate parenthesized phrases:

הָרַחֲמָן הוּא יְבָרֵךְ
אוֹתִי (וְאֶת אִשְׁתִּי /בַּעְלִי וְאֶת זַרְעִי) וְאֶת כָּל אֲשֶׁר לִי.

Guests recite the following.
Children at their parents' table add the words in parentheses.

הָרַחֲמָן הוּא יְבָרֵךְ
אֶת (אָבִי מוֹרִי) בַּעַל הַבַּיִת הַזֶּה,
וְאֶת (אִמִּי מוֹרָתִי) בַּעֲלַת הַבַּיִת הַזֶּה,

All guests recite the following:

אוֹתָם וְאֶת בֵּיתָם וְאֶת זַרְעָם וְאֶת כָּל אֲשֶׁר לָהֶם.

---

amount of something, God's blessing can rest upon it and it can
increase.[1]

This is also the underlying concept of the display of Showbread in
the Temple, that spread contentment throughout Israel. As our Rabbis taught (*Yoma* 39a), although every priest received only a tiny
portion of this Showbread, eating that small amount sated them.

(*Exodus* 25:24)

אֶת אֵלִיָּהוּ הַנָּבִיא ◆§ — *The prophet Elijah.* Whatever Moses and
Joshua inflicted on Amalek at the beginning of our history,

---

1. We see this from the prophet Elisha and the jug of oil, or the prophet Elijah with both
the vessel of flour and the cruse of oil (*I Kings* 17:16, *II Kings* 4:2 ff.).

May the Merciful One send us the prophet Elijah, who is remembered for the good, and may he bring us good tidings, salvations, and consolations.

The following text — for a guest to recite at his host's table — appears in *Shulchan Aruch, Orach Chaim* 201.

May it be God's will that this host not be shamed nor humiliated in This World or in the World to Come. May he be successful in all his dealings. May his dealings be successful and conveniently close at hand. May no evil impediment reign over his handiwork, and may no semblance of sin or iniquitous thought attach itself to him from this time and forever.

Those eating at their own table recite the following, adding the appropriate parenthesized phrases:

May the Merciful One bless me,

(my wife/husband and children) and all that is mine.

Guests recite the following. Children at their parents' table add the words in parentheses.

May the Merciful One bless

([my father, my teacher] the master of this house, and [my mother, my teacher] the mistress of this house)

All guests recite the following:

them, their house, their family, and all that is theirs,

Elijah together with *Mashiach Ben Yosef* will repeat on Amalek's progeny in the Final Days. Because Amalek are descendants of Esau, who live by the sword, they are the "first among nations" (*Numbers* 24:20), and it was they who initiated the first war against us. Also, our present *Churban* and exile derives from Rome, another of Esau's progeny. The Final Redemption will arrive when they and their followers are defeated. As the prophet foretold (*Obadiah* 1:21), "And liberators will ascend Mount Zion to judge Esau's mountain; and the kingdom will be HASHEM's."

(*Exodus* 17:9. See also *Genesis* 36:43, 40:28, and *Sefer HaGeulah* Chap.3)

All continue here:

אוֹתָנוּ וְאֶת כָּל אֲשֶׁר לָנוּ, כְּמוֹ שֶׁנִּתְבָּרְכוּ אֲבוֹתֵינוּ
אַבְרָהָם יִצְחָק וְיַעֲקֹב בַּכֹּל מִכֹּל כֹּל,[1] כֵּן יְבָרֵךְ אוֹתָנוּ כֻּלָּנוּ
יַחַד בִּבְרָכָה שְׁלֵמָה, וְנֹאמַר, אָמֵן.

בַּמָּרוֹם יְלַמְּדוּ עֲלֵיהֶם וְעָלֵינוּ זְכוּת, שֶׁתְּהֵא לְמִשְׁמֶרֶת
שָׁלוֹם. וְנִשָּׂא בְרָכָה מֵאֵת יהוה, וּצְדָקָה מֵאֱלֹהֵי
יִשְׁעֵנוּ, וְנִמְצָא חֵן וְשֵׂכֶל טוֹב בְּעֵינֵי אֱלֹהִים וְאָדָם.[2]

On the Sabbath add the following sentence:

הָרַחֲמָן הוּא יַנְחִילֵנוּ יוֹם שֶׁכֻּלּוֹ שַׁבָּת וּמְנוּחָה לְחַיֵּי הָעוֹלָמִים.

The words in parentheses are added on the two *seder* nights in some communities.

הָרַחֲמָן הוּא יַנְחִילֵנוּ יוֹם שֶׁכֻּלּוֹ טוֹב (יוֹם שֶׁכֻּלּוֹ אָרוּךְ,
יוֹם שֶׁצַּדִּיקִים יוֹשְׁבִים וְעַטְרוֹתֵיהֶם בְּרָאשֵׁיהֶם
וְנֶהֱנִים מִזִּיו הַשְּׁכִינָה, וִיהִי חֶלְקֵנוּ עִמָּהֶם).

הָרַחֲמָן הוּא יְזַכֵּנוּ לִימוֹת הַמָּשִׁיחַ וּלְחַיֵּי הָעוֹלָם הַבָּא.
מִגְדּוֹל יְשׁוּעוֹת מַלְכּוֹ וְעֹשֶׂה חֶסֶד לִמְשִׁיחוֹ

---

§ בָּכֹּל . . . אֲבוֹתֵינוּ שֶׁנִּתְבָּרְכוּ כְּמוֹ — *Just as our forefathers ... were blessed in everything.* Our forefathers were eventually blessed with wealth, property, respect, longevity and children — everything that people could wish for. All their hearts' desires were fulfilled and they were content with their good fortune.

According to the Sages, the word בַּכֹּל alludes to deep mystical secrets. (*Genesis* 24:1, 25:8. See there at length and also 35:28)

§ הַבָּא הָעוֹלָם וּלְחַיֵּי — *And the life of the World to Come.* Clearly, this traditional prayer, repeated for many generations, echoes the belief that the World to Come is a future entity. It will become a reality only in the Messianic Era. There are countless corroborations from the Sages that the Garden of Eden, the Messianic Era, and the World to Come are all separate phenomena (*Sanhedrin* 89a ff., *Shabbos* 63a, *Kiddushin* 39b, *Arachin* 13b, *Bereishis Rabbah* 14:5, *Shemos Rabbah* 15:21, *Sifre Bamidbar* 6:24, *Sifre Devarim* 6:7, 6:24,

ours and all that is ours — just as our forefathers Abraham, Isaac, and Jacob were blessed in everything from everything, with blessing.[1] So may He bless us all together with perfect blessing, and let us say: Amen.

M ay there be a favorable report (of them and) of us in heaven that should preserve peace. May we receive blessing from Hashem, and charity from the God of our salvation, and may we find favor and good regard in the eyes of God and man.[2]

> On the Sabbath add the following sentence:
> May the Merciful One cause us to inherit the day which will be completely a Sabbath and rest day for eternal life.

The words in parentheses are added on the two *seder* nights in some communities.

M ay the Merciful One grant us a day which is entirely good (that everlasting day, the day when the righteous sit with crowns on their heads, enjoying the reflection of God's majesty — and may our portion be with them)!

M ay the Merciful One make us worthy to attain the days of Messiah and the life of the World to Come. He is a tower of salvation to His king, and does kindness to His anointed,

---

(1) Cf. *Genesis* 24:1; 27:33; 33:11. (2) Cf. *Proverbs* 3:4.

11:21, 33:12, 33:19).

The World to Come is not a reward available immediately after death as the Garden of Eden is. The World to Come will be a new Creation fashioned by God, for those who merit Resurrection. The sequence of events is as follows: At some date during this present thousand years — the sixth millennium of the world's existence — the crown of royalty will return to the House of David. After the final day of judgment — beginning at the seventh millennium, known as "The Sabbath" — the world, and those fortunate to experience it, will enter an infinite and totally different kind of life.

It will be a physical world where humans will enjoy a bodily existence. However, they will subsist from the Glory of the *Shechinah*

לְדָוִד וּלְזַרְעוֹ עַד עוֹלָם.[1] עֹשֶׂה שָׁלוֹם בִּמְרוֹמָיו, הוּא יַעֲשֶׂה שָׁלוֹם עָלֵינוּ וְעַל כָּל יִשְׂרָאֵל. וְאִמְרוּ, אָמֵן.

יְרְאוּ אֶת יהוה קְדֹשָׁיו, כִּי אֵין מַחְסוֹר לִירֵאָיו. כְּפִירִים רָשׁוּ וְרָעֵבוּ, וְדֹרְשֵׁי יהוה לֹא יַחְסְרוּ כָל טוֹב.[2] הוֹדוּ לַיהוה כִּי טוֹב, כִּי לְעוֹלָם חַסְדּוֹ.[3] פּוֹתֵחַ אֶת יָדֶךָ, וּמַשְׂבִּיעַ לְכָל חַי רָצוֹן.[4] בָּרוּךְ הַגֶּבֶר אֲשֶׁר יִבְטַח בַּיהוה, וְהָיָה יהוה מִבְטַחוֹ.[5] נַעַר הָיִיתִי גַּם זָקַנְתִּי, וְלֹא רָאִיתִי צַדִּיק נֶעֱזָב, וְזַרְעוֹ מְבַקֶּשׁ לָחֶם.[6] יהוה עֹז לְעַמּוֹ יִתֵּן, יהוה יְבָרֵךְ אֶת עַמּוֹ בַשָּׁלוֹם.[7]

Upon completion of *Bircas HaMazon* the blessing over wine is recited and the third cup is drunk while reclining on the left side. It is preferable to drink the entire cup, but at the very least, most of the cup should be drained.

בָּרוּךְ אַתָּה יהוה אֱלֹהֵינוּ מֶלֶךְ הָעוֹלָם, בּוֹרֵא פְּרִי הַגָּפֶן.

The fourth cup is poured. According to most customs, the Cup of Elijah is poured at this point, after which the door is opened in accordance with the verse, "It is a guarded night." Then the following paragraph is recited.

---

as Moses did for forty days and Elijah, according to tradition, does now. Similarly, the Children of Israel survived on a diet of manna for forty years. In the future world we will also merit a full understanding of the mystical secrets. (*Shaar HaGemul*, closing paragraphs)

◈§ יַעֲשֶׂה שָׁלוֹם עָלֵינוּ — *[May He] make peace over us.* There will be peace among us so that no one will quarrel with his fellow man. Foreign armies shall not pass through our territories. We shall pursue our enemies and they will flee in panic.

Nor will wild animals menace the land. When the commandments are observed, *Eretz Yisrael* will resemble the world when it was still pristine, unsullied by sin. Thus, the wild beasts will not prey upon mankind, as they only attack because of our sins. Otherwise, their natural instinct is to leave humans alone. Unfortunately, their blood lust intensifies with each attack.

At the time of Adam, the natural food for all beasts was pure

to David and his offspring forever.[1] May He Who makes peace in His heights make peace over us and over all of Israel. Now respond: Amen.

Fear Hashem, holy ones of His! For those who fear Him lack nothing.[2] Young lions may be poor and hungry, but those who seek Hashem will not be in need of any good thing. Praise Hashem for He is good, for His kindness is eternal.[3] You open Your hand and satisfy the wants of every living thing.[4] Blessed is the man who trusts Hashem; then Hashem will be his security.[5] I was a youth and also have aged, and I have not seen a righteous man forsaken with his children begging for bread.[6] Hashem will grant strength to His people. Hashem will bless His people with peace.[7]

Upon completion of *Bircas HaMazon* the blessing over wine is recited and the third cup is drunk while reclining on the left side. It is preferable to drink the entire cup, but at the very least, most of the cup should be drained.

Blessed are You, Hashem, our God, King of the Universe, Who creates the fruit of the vine.

The fourth cup is poured. According to most customs, the Cup of Elijah is poured at this point, after which the door is opened in accordance with the verse, "It is a guarded night." Then the following paragraph is recited.

---

(1) *Psalms* 18:51. (2) 34:10-11. (3) 136:1 et al. (4) 145:16.
(5) *Jeremiah* 17:7. (6) *Psalms* 37:25. (7) 29:11.

---

vegetation (*Genesis* 1:30). After the Flood, they were implicitly allowed to prey upon each other — though not on man (*Genesis* 9:5). When humans will finally achieve perfection (in the Messianic Age), the wild beasts of *Eretz Yisrael* will regress to their initial natural instincts and peace will return.

(*Leviticus* 26:26. See also *Genesis* 9:5)

וְלֹא רָאִיתִי צַדִּיק נֶעֱזָב ‎§— *And I have not seen a righteous man forsaken.* Keeping the commandments ensures that the righteous are not abandoned, nor need their children beg for bread. We have evidence for this from our sojourn in the wilderness. God miraculously supported us with manna when we observed His Torah.

(*Deuteronomy* 8:2)

שְׁפֹךְ חֲמָתְךָ אֶל הַגּוֹיִם אֲשֶׁר לֹא יְדָעוּךָ וְעַל מַמְלָכוֹת אֲשֶׁר בְּשִׁמְךָ לֹא קָרָאוּ. כִּי אָכַל אֶת יַעֲקֹב וְאֶת נָוֵהוּ הֵשַׁמּוּ.¹ שְׁפָךְ עֲלֵיהֶם זַעְמֶךָ וַחֲרוֹן אַפְּךָ יַשִּׂיגֵם.² תִּרְדֹּף בְּאַף וְתַשְׁמִידֵם מִתַּחַת שְׁמֵי יהוה.³

הלל

The door is closed and the recitation of the *Haggadah* is continued.

לֹא לָנוּ יהוה לֹא לָנוּ, כִּי לְשִׁמְךָ תֵּן כָּבוֹד, עַל חַסְדְּךָ עַל אֲמִתֶּךָ. לָמָּה יֹאמְרוּ הַגּוֹיִם, אַיֵּה נָא אֱלֹהֵיהֶם. וֵאלֹהֵינוּ בַשָּׁמָיִם, כֹּל אֲשֶׁר חָפֵץ עָשָׂה. עֲצַבֵּיהֶם כֶּסֶף וְזָהָב, מַעֲשֵׂה יְדֵי אָדָם. פֶּה לָהֶם וְלֹא יְדַבֵּרוּ, עֵינַיִם לָהֶם וְלֹא יִרְאוּ. אָזְנַיִם לָהֶם וְלֹא יִשְׁמָעוּ, אַף לָהֶם וְלֹא יְרִיחוּן. יְדֵיהֶם וְלֹא יְמִישׁוּן, רַגְלֵיהֶם וְלֹא יְהַלֵּכוּ, לֹא יֶהְגּוּ בִּגְרוֹנָם. כְּמוֹהֶם יִהְיוּ עֹשֵׂיהֶם, כֹּל אֲשֶׁר בֹּטֵחַ בָּהֶם.

◆§ שְׁפֹךְ חֲמָתְךָ — *Pour Your wrath.* Ultimately, God will avenge His enemies and repay those that are hateful. They were cruel to us due to their dislike of Hashem. Jews are resented because they keep themselves apart with His commandments — refusing to intermarry or eat at the the non-Jews' table. Furthermore, Jews despised heathen worship and destroyed their idols wherever they found them.

It is "For HASHEM's sake that we are killed every day" (*Psalms* 44:23). All their wickedness against us was ultimately directed at God. Obviously, this Divine Judgment has not yet taken place and will occur during the time of Messiah.

(*Deuteronomy* 32:40. See also *Numbers* 24:18 ff.)

◆§ עֲצַבֵּיהֶם — *Their idols.* Despite all the pomp and ceremony accorded by their worshipers, idols remain the lifeless stones they were before being fashioned into idols. They do not even achieve the paltry life and power of the average person. They have less value than the man who made them.

The idols see neither the suffering of those that worshiped them

Pour Your wrath upon the nations who do not know
You and upon the kingdoms who call not upon Your
name, for they have consumed Jacob and laid waste his
dwelling.[1] Pour Your fury on them and may Your rage
overtake them.[2] Pursue them with anger and obliterate
them from under Hashem's skies.[3]

HALLEL

The door is closed and the recitation of the *Haggadah* is continued.

Not for us, Hashem, not for us, but for Your name give
glory, for Your kindness and Your truth. Why should
the nations say: Where is their God? Our God in the
heavens does whatever He desires. Their idols are silver
and gold, the work of man's hands. They have a mouth,
but do not speak. They have eyes, but do not see.
They have ears, but do not hear. They have a nose, but
do not smell. Their hands do not feel. Their feet do not
walk. They do not utter sound with their throat. Their
makers will be like them, all those who trust in them.

---

(1) *Psalms* 79:6-7. (2) 69:25. (30) *Lamentations* 3:66.

---

nor do they hear their prayers. The idols are incapable of raising a
limb to save their followers from any predicament. The idols can
neither "eat" nor "smell": They cannot issue forth a fire to consume
sacrifices nor are they able savor the offerings. (*Deuteronomy* 4:28)

בֹּל אֲשֶׁר בֹּטֵחַ בָּהֶם — *All those who trust in them.* Essentially, there
were three types of idolatry. The first began when people
worshiped angels, as the ancients recognized that specific angels
had some sovereignty over the various nations (*Daniel* 10:13, 20).
Believing that these angels (which they described as "elohim") could
bestow good or inflict evil, each nation served its particular angel.
Yet they recognized that supreme power still rested with Hashem
and they described Him as the "God of gods" (*Menachos* 110a).

Another type of idol worship came into being when humans
served the celestial bodies: the sun, moon or stars. Again each
nation chose the particular body that had influence over them, and
sought by their worship to strengthen "its star." They erected

יִשְׂרָאֵל בְּטַח בַּיהוה, עֶזְרָם וּמָגִנָּם הוּא. בֵּית אַהֲרֹן בִּטְחוּ בַיהוה, עֶזְרָם וּמָגִנָּם הוּא. יִרְאֵי יהוה בִּטְחוּ בַיהוה, עֶזְרָם וּמָגִנָּם הוּא.

יהוה זְכָרָנוּ יְבָרֵךְ, יְבָרֵךְ אֶת בֵּית יִשְׂרָאֵל, יְבָרֵךְ אֶת בֵּית אַהֲרֹן. יְבָרֵךְ יִרְאֵי יהוה, הַקְּטַנִּים עִם הַגְּדֹלִים. יֹסֵף יהוה עֲלֵיכֶם, עֲלֵיכֶם וְעַל בְּנֵיכֶם. בְּרוּכִים אַתֶּם לַיהוה, עֹשֵׂה שָׁמַיִם וָאָרֶץ. הַשָּׁמַיִם שָׁמַיִם לַיהוה, וְהָאָרֶץ נָתַן לִבְנֵי אָדָם. לֹא הַמֵּתִים יְהַלְלוּ יָהּ, וְלֹא כָּל יֹרְדֵי דוּמָה. וַאֲנַחְנוּ נְבָרֵךְ יָהּ, מֵעַתָּה וְעַד עוֹלָם, הַלְלוּיָהּ.[1]

---

sculptured images of their chosen star and hoped to gain success and power whenever their astrological omens were in the ascendancy. Those pagans also had false prophets who used magic and the art of divination to foretell the future. Probably, this type of idolatry began at the Generation of the Dispersion (*Genesis* 11:8). As the nations dispersed across the earth, they came under the influence of the various constellations.

Similarly, people worshiped powerful men and kings. Whenever they noted the unusual success of a single individual, the masses thought that by worshiping him they might share in his ascendancy and their luck would rise together. This was the perspective of Pharaoh who declared himself a god (*Shemos Rabbah* 9:7) as did Sennacherib and Hiram (*Isaiah* 14:14, *Ezekiel* 28:2). These kings may have been wicked but they were not totally foolish.

Later, a third form of idol worship appeared, with people serving the spirits and demons. They believed that these paranormal beings could harm them unless they were appeased. The Torah scoffs at this type of idolatry, since these are "demons without power, gods whom they knew not, newcomers recently arrived, whom your ancestors did not dread." (*Deuteronomy* 32:17). Even Terach and Nimrod ignored them. The spirits had been deified only by the Egyptian magicians.

Of course, the Torah forbids all forms of pagan idolatry; we must serve Hashem alone. (*Exodus* 20:3, see also 13:16)

Israel, trust in Hashem — He is their help and shield. House of Aaron, trust in Hashem — He is their help and shield. Those who fear Hashem, trust in Hashem — He is their help and shield.

Hashem Who has remembered, He will bless. He will bless the house of Israel. He will bless the house of Aaron. He will bless those who fear Hashem, the small with the great. Hashem will add upon you, upon you and your children. You are blessed of Hashem, Maker of the heavens and the earth. The heavens are the heavens of Hashem, but the earth He has given to man. The dead will not praise Hashem, nor all those who descend into silence. But we will praise Hashem forever. Halleluyah![1]

---

(1) *Psalms* 115.

⋗ יִשְׂרָאֵל בְּטַח בַּה' — *Israel, trust in HASHEM!* We must direct our hearts to God alone, trusting that nothing takes place in this world unless He causes it to happen. We must approach only His prophets and righteous ones to find out what the future holds, as God alone truthfully knows the course of future events. We should ignore the predictions of the star-gazers and their ilk, knowing "Everything is in the hands of Heaven. . . for HASHEM distorts the constellations. . .and frustrates the signs of the impostors. . ." (*Isaiah* 44:25, *Berachos* 33b).

The Jewish People has no celestial ruler other than God, since we are "His portion and inheritance" (*Deuteronomy* 32:9). None of the heavenly powers, that have influence over other nations, have the right to rule over Israel. (*Deuteronomy* 18:13, 32:12. See also 13:5)

⋗ עֹשֵׂה שָׁמַיִם וָאָרֶץ — *Maker of the heavens and earth.* God created only these two out of total nothingness. All the other creations were made by the Creator from these two materials. The "earth" includes the basic elements and all living things: all the creatures on land and sea, the trees, vegetation and the Garden of Eden. The "heavens" also encompass the sun, moon, stars and the constellations. (*Genesis* 1:1)

אָהַבְתִּי כִּי יִשְׁמַע יהוה, אֶת קוֹלִי תַּחֲנוּנָי. כִּי הִטָּה אָזְנוֹ לִי, וּבְיָמַי אֶקְרָא. אֲפָפוּנִי חֶבְלֵי מָוֶת, וּמְצָרֵי שְׁאוֹל מְצָאוּנִי, צָרָה וְיָגוֹן אֶמְצָא. וּבְשֵׁם יהוה אֶקְרָא, אָנָּה יהוה מַלְּטָה נַפְשִׁי. חַנּוּן יהוה וְצַדִּיק, וֵאלֹהֵינוּ מְרַחֵם. שֹׁמֵר פְּתָאִים יהוה, דַּלּוֹתִי וְלִי יְהוֹשִׁיעַ. שׁוּבִי נַפְשִׁי לִמְנוּחָיְכִי, כִּי יהוה גָּמַל עָלָיְכִי. כִּי חִלַּצְתָּ נַפְשִׁי מִמָּוֶת, אֶת עֵינִי מִן דִּמְעָה, אֶת רַגְלִי מִדֶּחִי. אֶתְהַלֵּךְ לִפְנֵי יהוה, בְּאַרְצוֹת הַחַיִּים. הֶאֱמַנְתִּי כִּי אֲדַבֵּר, אֲנִי עָנִיתִי מְאֹד. אֲנִי אָמַרְתִּי בְחָפְזִי, כָּל הָאָדָם כֹּזֵב.

מָה אָשִׁיב לַיהוה, כָּל תַּגְמוּלוֹהִי עָלָי. כּוֹס יְשׁוּעוֹת אֶשָּׂא, וּבְשֵׁם יהוה אֶקְרָא. נְדָרַי לַיהוה אֲשַׁלֵּם, נֶגְדָה נָּא לְכָל עַמּוֹ. יָקָר בְּעֵינֵי יהוה, הַמָּוְתָה לַחֲסִידָיו. אָנָּה יהוה כִּי אֲנִי עַבְדֶּךָ, אֲנִי עַבְדְּךָ, בֶּן אֲמָתֶךָ, פִּתַּחְתָּ לְמוֹסֵרָי. לְךָ אֶזְבַּח זֶבַח תּוֹדָה, וּבְשֵׁם יהוה אֶקְרָא. נְדָרַי לַיהוה אֲשַׁלֵּם, נֶגְדָה נָּא לְכָל עַמּוֹ. בְּחַצְרוֹת בֵּית יהוה, בְּתוֹכֵכִי יְרוּשָׁלָיִם הַלְלוּיָהּ.[1]

ﬗﬢ נְדָרַי לַה׳ אֲשַׁלֵּם — *My vows to HASHEM I will pay.* There are two alternative methods in creating obligations to bring an animal sacrifice: through a vow or a freewill offering. According to the Sages (*Kinnim* 1:1), a vow occurs when a person freely promises to bring an offering. This is considered a *personal* obligation since he did not specify which animal or make it conditional on the availability of his livestock. Even if all his animals were to die, he remains obligated. This is not the case with a *freewill offering*. Here he designates a specific animal as a sacrifice. Should that animal die or get stolen, he is not liable. The obligation is limited to that animal and does not devolve on the owner.

However, I have noticed that the Torah in discussing the vow (*Leviticus* 22:21) uses an unusual term, לְפַלֵּא or יַפְלִא (ibid. 27:2) — which can mean to articulate, but also refers to something wondrous or "extraordinary." This implies that a vow concerns something

I love Him, because Hashem hears my voice, my supplications. For He has inclined His ear to me. In all my days I will call upon Him. Pangs of death have encompassed me, and the distress of the pit has found me. I meet with trouble and sorrow, and I call on the Name of Hashem: Please, Hashem, rescue my soul! Gracious is Hashem, and righteous. Our God has mercy. Hashem guards the simple. I was poor, and He saved me. Return, my soul, to your rest, for Hashem has been bountiful to you. You have delivered my soul from death, my eye from tears, my foot from stumbling. I will walk before Hashem in the lands of life. I believe that I will say: I was greatly afflicted. I said in my despondency: All men lie.

How can I repay Hashem for all His bounties to me? I will lift up a cup of salvations, and I will call out the Name of Hashem. My vows to Hashem I will pay in the presence of all His people. Precious in the eyes of Hashem is death for His pious ones. I beseech You, Hashem, for I am Your slave. I am Your slave, the son of Your slavewoman. You have loosened my fetters. I will sacrifice to You an offering of thanksgiving, and I will call out the Name of Hashem. I will pay my vows to Hashem in the presence of all His people. In the courtyards of the House of Hashem, in you, Jerusalem. Halleluyah.[1]

---

(1) *Psalms* 116.

---

beyond our capabilities. Usually, the vow is made when a person is in crisis and makes promises to Hashem. Similarly, Jacob "took a vow" (*Genesis* 28:20) on his precarious escape to Laban: "If God will be with me . . . I shall repeatedly tithe to You," (ibid. vs. 20-22). Also the Israelites, after defeat in battle, vowed to lay waste to the Canaanite cities (*Numbers* 21:2. See also *Jonah* 1:16). Consequently, these promises encumber a person with greater responsibility.

Therefore, a freewill offering is different. Generally, this is donated because a person's "spirit motivated him" (*Exodus* 35:21), and as a spontaneous donation he does not incur any personal obligations.
(*Leviticus* 22:18. See also *Deuteronomy* 23:23)

בְּחַצְרוֹת בֵּית ה' ‎‎&ᴥ — *In the courtyards of the House of* HASHEM. When a man and his family eat before Hashem at the Jerusalem Temple,

הַלְלוּ אֶת יהוה, כָּל גּוֹיִם, שַׁבְּחֽוּהוּ כָּל הָאֻמִּים. כִּי גָבַר
עָלֵינוּ חַסְדּוֹ, וֶאֱמֶת יהוה לְעוֹלָם, הַלְלוּיָהּ.¹

הוֹדוּ לַיהוה כִּי טוֹב,   כִּי לְעוֹלָם חַסְדּוֹ.

יֹאמַר נָא יִשְׂרָאֵל,   כִּי לְעוֹלָם חַסְדּוֹ.

יֹאמְרוּ נָא בֵית אַהֲרֹן,   כִּי לְעוֹלָם חַסְדּוֹ.

יֹאמְרוּ נָא יִרְאֵי יהוה,   כִּי לְעוֹלָם חַסְדּוֹ.

מִן הַמֵּצַר קָרָֽאתִי יָּהּ, עָנָֽנִי בַמֶּרְחָב יָהּ. יהוה לִי לֹא
אִירָא, מַה יַּעֲשֶׂה לִי אָדָם. יהוה לִי בְּעֹזְרָי,
וַאֲנִי אֶרְאֶה בְשֹׂנְאָי. טוֹב לַחֲסוֹת בַּיהוה, מִבְּטֹחַ בָּאָדָם.
טוֹב לַחֲסוֹת בַּיהוה, מִבְּטֹחַ בִּנְדִיבִים. כָּל גּוֹיִם סְבָבֽוּנִי,
בְּשֵׁם יהוה כִּי אֲמִילַם. סַבּֽוּנִי גַם סְבָבֽוּנִי, בְּשֵׁם יהוה כִּי
אֲמִילַם. סַבּֽוּנִי כִדְבֹרִים דֹּעֲכוּ כְּאֵשׁ קוֹצִים, בְּשֵׁם יהוה כִּי
אֲמִילַם. דָּחֹה דְחִיתַֽנִי לִנְפֹּל, וַיהוה עֲזָרָֽנִי. עָזִּי וְזִמְרָת יָהּ,
וַיְהִי לִי לִישׁוּעָה. קוֹל רִנָּה וִישׁוּעָה, בְּאָהֳלֵי צַדִּיקִים, יְמִין
יהוה עֹשָׂה חָֽיִל. יְמִין יהוה רוֹמֵמָה, יְמִין יהוה עֹשָׂה חָֽיִל.
לֹא אָמוּת כִּי אֶחְיֶה, וַאֲסַפֵּר מַעֲשֵׂי יָהּ. יַסֹּר יִסְּרַֽנִּי יָּהּ,
וְלַמָּֽוֶת לֹא נְתָנָֽנִי. פִּתְחוּ לִי שַׁעֲרֵי צֶֽדֶק, אָבֹא בָם אוֹדֶה יָּהּ.
זֶה הַשַּֽׁעַר לַיהוה, צַדִּיקִים יָבֹֽאוּ בוֹ. אוֹדְךָ כִּי עֲנִיתָֽנִי, וַתְּהִי
לִי לִישׁוּעָה. אוֹדְךָ כִּי עֲנִיתָֽנִי, וַתְּהִי לִי לִישׁוּעָה. אֶֽבֶן מָאֲסוּ
הַבּוֹנִים, הָֽיְתָה לְרֹאשׁ פִּנָּה. אֶֽבֶן מָאֲסוּ הַבּוֹנִים, הָֽיְתָה
לְרֹאשׁ פִּנָּה. מֵאֵת יהוה הָֽיְתָה זֹּאת, הִיא נִפְלָאת בְּעֵינֵֽינוּ.

---

they will "learn to fear God" (*Deuteronomy* 14:23). This is because the
Kohanim and judges "who officiate there, before God" (ibid. 18:7) are
the teachers of Torah. They will impart *fear of God* and instruct them
in the ways of Torah and commandments.   (*Deuteronomy* 14:22)

הִיא נִפְלָאת בְּעֵינֵֽינוּ ‏׈ — *It is wondrous in our eyes!* All the psalms of
King David are based upon miracles and wonders. Indeed, the

Praise Hashem! Praise Hashem, all nations! Laud Him, all states. For His love for us is strong, and the truth of Hashem is eternal. Halleluyah![1]

Give thanks to Hashem for He is good,
for His kindness is eternal.
Let Israel say: For His kindness is eternal.
Let the house of Aaron say: For His kindness is eternal.
Let those who fear Hashem say:
For His kindness is eternal.

Out of distress I called Hashem. He responded to me expansively. Hashem is for me. I shall not fear. What can man do to me? Hashem is for me through my helpers, and I shall see the downfall of my enemies. It is better to take shelter in Hashem than to trust in man. It is better to take shelter in Hashem than to trust in those who are generous. All nations have beset me. In the name of Hashem I cut them down. They have surrounded me and beset me. In the name of Hashem I cut them down. They have surrounded me like bees. They were extinguished like a fire of thorns — in the name of Hashem I cut them down. You have pushed at me and toppled me, but Hashem has assisted me. The strength and vengeance of Hashem has been my salvation. There is a voice of song and salvation in the tents of the righteous. The right hand of Hashem does valiantly. The right hand of Hashem is raised high. The right hand of Hashem does valiantly. I shall not die, for I shall live and tell of the deeds of Hashem. Hashem has chastised me, but He has not let me die. Open for me the gates of righteousness; I will enter them; I will thank Hashem. This is the gate of Hashem, the righteous will enter it. I thank You, for You have answered me and become my salvation. I thank You, for You have answered me and become my salvation. The stone the builders despised has become the cornerstone. The stone the builders despised has become the cornerstone. This emanated from Hashem; it is wondrous in our eyes.

---

(1) *Psalms* 117.

מֵאֵת יהוה הָיְתָה זֹּאת, הִיא נִפְלָאת בְּעֵינֵינוּ. זֶה הַיּוֹם
עָשָׂה יהוה, נָגִילָה וְנִשְׂמְחָה בוֹ. זֶה הַיּוֹם עָשָׂה יהוה,
נָגִילָה וְנִשְׂמְחָה בוֹ.

אָנָּא יהוה הוֹשִׁיעָה נָּא. אָנָּא יהוה הוֹשִׁיעָה נָּא.
אָנָּא יהוה הַצְלִיחָה נָא. אָנָּא יהוה הַצְלִיחָה נָא.

בָּרוּךְ הַבָּא בְּשֵׁם יהוה, בֵּרַכְנוּכֶם מִבֵּית יהוה.
בָּרוּךְ הַבָּא בְּשֵׁם יהוה, בֵּרַכְנוּכֶם מִבֵּית יהוה.
אֵל יהוה וַיָּאֶר לָנוּ, אִסְרוּ חַג בַּעֲבֹתִים, עַד קַרְנוֹת
הַמִּזְבֵּחַ. אֵל יהוה וַיָּאֶר לָנוּ, אִסְרוּ חַג בַּעֲבֹתִים, עַד
קַרְנוֹת הַמִּזְבֵּחַ. אֵלִי אַתָּה וְאוֹדֶךָּ, אֱלֹהַי אֲרוֹמְמֶךָּ. אֵלִי
אַתָּה וְאוֹדֶךָּ, אֱלֹהַי אֲרוֹמְמֶךָּ. הוֹדוּ לַיהוה כִּי טוֹב, כִּי
לְעוֹלָם חַסְדּוֹ. הוֹדוּ לַיהוה כִּי טוֹב, כִּי לְעוֹלָם חַסְדּוֹ.[1]

יְהַלְלוּךָ יהוה אֱלֹהֵינוּ כָּל מַעֲשֶׂיךָ, וַחֲסִידֶיךָ צַדִּיקִים
עוֹשֵׂי רְצוֹנֶךָ, וְכָל עַמְּךָ בֵּית יִשְׂרָאֵל בְּרִנָּה

---

(1) *Psalms* 118.

---

birth of David, our ruler, was a miracle in itself. He was a member of
the fifth generation of his family to be born from the time the Children
of Israel entered the Promised Land. He was preceded by only four
generations: Shalmon (the son of Nachshon, the son of Aminadav),
Boaz, Oved and Jesse (David's father). Yet, approximately three
hundred and seventy years had elapsed from the entry to Israel until
David's birth!

If this would have happened naturally, each of his ancestors would
have been, on the average, ninety-three years old when their son was
born. This would make them nearly as old as Abraham was when
Isaac was born. As the general life-span then was less than a hundred
years, each would have had his son in his very final years, which is
most unusual.

According to the Sages (*Bereishis Rabbah* 96:4 and *Bava Basra*
91b), Oved lived exceedingly long, as did his mother Ruth. All these

This emanated from Hashem; it is wondrous in our eyes. This is the day Hashem made; let us rejoice and be glad on it. This is the day Hashem made; let us rejoice and be glad on it.

We beseech You, Hashem, save us!
 We beseech You, Hashem, save us!
We beseech You, Hashem, grant us success!
 We beseech You, Hashem, grant us success!

Blessed is he who comes in the Name of Hashem; we bless you from the House of Hashem. Blessed is he who comes in the Name of Hashem; we bless you from the House of Hashem. Hashem is God and He will give us light. Bind the festival sacrifice with cords, leading it up to the corners of the altar. Hashem is God and He will give us light. Bind the festival sacrifice with cords, leading it up to the corners of the altar.You are my God and I will thank You. My God — I will exalt You. You are my God and I will thank You. My God — I will exalt You. Give thanks to Hashem for He is good, for His kindness is eternal. Give thanks to Hashem for He is good, for His kindness is eternal.[1]

All Your works, Hashem, our God, will praise You, and Your pious ones, the righteous who perform Your will. And all Your people, the House of Israel, with song,

---

were hidden miracles, not openly described in Scripture. Similarly, the birth of Moses must have been a miracle, as his mother Jochebed was Levi's own daughter. She must have been one hundred-thirty years old when Moses was born, since his birth took place eighty years before the Exodus from Egypt. His birth (and Aaron's) was delayed for many years because it was still too early for the Redemption.

Besides Jochebed's giving birth at so advanced an age, there are many other hidden miracles in the Torah. Indeed, though the whole Torah is based on miracles, it does not explicitly point out every one. It is only those miracles foretold or performed by a prophet or angel that are explicitly mentioned.

(*Genesis* 46:15. See also ibid. 11:28, 17:1, and *Leviticus* 26:11)

יוֹדוּ וִיבָרְכוּ וִישַׁבְּחוּ וִיפָאֲרוּ וִירוֹמְמוּ וְיַעֲרִיצוּ וְיַקְדִּישׁוּ
וְיַמְלִיכוּ אֶת שִׁמְךָ מַלְכֵּנוּ, כִּי לְךָ טוֹב לְהוֹדוֹת וּלְשִׁמְךָ
נָאֶה לְזַמֵּר, כִּי מֵעוֹלָם וְעַד עוֹלָם אַתָּה אֵל.

כִּי לְעוֹלָם חַסְדּוֹ.	**הוֹדוּ** לַיהוה כִּי טוֹב
כִּי לְעוֹלָם חַסְדּוֹ.	הוֹדוּ לֵאלֹהֵי הָאֱלֹהִים
כִּי לְעוֹלָם חַסְדּוֹ.	הוֹדוּ לַאֲדֹנֵי הָאֲדֹנִים
כִּי לְעוֹלָם חַסְדּוֹ.	לְעֹשֵׂה נִפְלָאוֹת גְּדֹלוֹת לְבַדּוֹ
כִּי לְעוֹלָם חַסְדּוֹ.	לְעֹשֵׂה הַשָּׁמַיִם בִּתְבוּנָה
כִּי לְעוֹלָם חַסְדּוֹ.	לְרֹקַע הָאָרֶץ עַל הַמָּיִם
כִּי לְעוֹלָם חַסְדּוֹ.	לְעֹשֵׂה אוֹרִים גְּדֹלִים
כִּי לְעוֹלָם חַסְדּוֹ.	אֶת הַשֶּׁמֶשׁ לְמֶמְשֶׁלֶת בַּיּוֹם
	אֶת הַיָּרֵחַ וְכוֹכָבִים לְמֶמְשָׁלוֹת בַּלָּיְלָה
כִּי לְעוֹלָם חַסְדּוֹ.	
כִּי לְעוֹלָם חַסְדּוֹ.	לְמַכֵּה מִצְרַיִם בִּבְכוֹרֵיהֶם
כִּי לְעוֹלָם חַסְדּוֹ.	וַיּוֹצֵא יִשְׂרָאֵל מִתּוֹכָם
כִּי לְעוֹלָם חַסְדּוֹ.	בְּיָד חֲזָקָה וּבִזְרוֹעַ נְטוּיָה
כִּי לְעוֹלָם חַסְדּוֹ.	לְגֹזֵר יַם סוּף לִגְזָרִים
כִּי לְעוֹלָם חַסְדּוֹ.	וְהֶעֱבִיר יִשְׂרָאֵל בְּתוֹכוֹ
כִּי לְעוֹלָם חַסְדּוֹ.	וְנִעֵר פַּרְעֹה וְחֵילוֹ בְיַם סוּף

---

§◈ **לְמֶמְשֶׁלֶת בַּיּוֹם** — *For the reign of day.* The sun and moon not only
provide light, they also "reign" over the seasons. By its power of
warmth and light, the sun causes the germination, growth and even-
tual deterioration of all living things. The moon exercises its sway
over the oceans and waters — everything liquid and cold.

According to the ancient astrologers, the constellations were in-
strumental in transferring the power that passes from the upper
worlds to our lower sphere. Perhaps this "reign" refers to that belief
too. Obviously, however, all powers originate and emanate from the
Almighty, according to His Will.   (*Genesis* 1:18. See also 1:3,14)

will thank, bless, laud, glorify, exalt, adulate, sanctify, and acknowledge the majesty of Your Name, our King, for to You it is good to give thanks, and to Your Name it is proper to sing, because You are God for eternity. Blessed are You, Hashem, the King Who is extolled in praises.

Give thanks to Hashem for He is good
— for His kindness is eternal.
Give thanks to the God of gods
— for His kindness is eternal.
Give thanks to the Master of masters
— for His kindness is eternal.
To Him Who does great wonders alone
— for His kindness is eternal.
To Him Who makes the heavens with understanding
— for His kindness is eternal.
To Him Who stretches the earth over the water
— for His kindness is eternal.
To Him Who makes the great lights
— for His kindness is eternal.
The sun for the reign of day   — for His kindness is eternal.
The moon and the stars for the reign of night
— for His kindness is eternal.
To Him Who smote the firstborn of the Egyptians
— for His kindness is eternal.
And brought Israel out from among them
— for His kindness is eternal.
With a strong hand and an outstretched arm
— for His kindness is eternal.
To Him Who divided the Reed Sea into parts
— for His kindness is eternal.
And had Israel pass through it
— for His kindness is eternal.
And tossed Pharaoh and his army into the Reed Sea
— for His kindness is eternal.

לְמוֹלִיךְ עַמּוֹ בַּמִּדְבָּר	כִּי לְעוֹלָם חַסְדּוֹ.
לְמַכֵּה מְלָכִים גְּדֹלִים	כִּי לְעוֹלָם חַסְדּוֹ.
וַיַּהֲרֹג מְלָכִים אַדִּירִים	כִּי לְעוֹלָם חַסְדּוֹ.
לְסִיחוֹן מֶלֶךְ הָאֱמֹרִי	כִּי לְעוֹלָם חַסְדּוֹ.
וּלְעוֹג מֶלֶךְ הַבָּשָׁן	כִּי לְעוֹלָם חַסְדּוֹ.
וְנָתַן אַרְצָם לְנַחֲלָה	כִּי לְעוֹלָם חַסְדּוֹ.
נַחֲלָה לְיִשְׂרָאֵל עַבְדּוֹ	כִּי לְעוֹלָם חַסְדּוֹ.
שֶׁבְּשִׁפְלֵנוּ זָכַר לָנוּ	כִּי לְעוֹלָם חַסְדּוֹ.

◆§ **לְמוֹלִיךְ עַמּוֹ בַּמִּדְבָּר** — *To Him Who led His people through the desert.*

The Torah (*Numbers* 33) details all the places where the Children of Israel encamped on their journeys through the desert. *Rambam* (*Guide to the Perplexed* 3:50) explains there was a good reason for this. The survival of an entire nation for forty years in an inhospitable wilderness, far from civilization, is a great and wondrous miracle. So too was the daily miracle of manna since a desert cannot provide fruit, bread or drink.

Hashem knew that later generations would be skeptical of these miracles, just as they distrust all ancient history. Probably, they would speculate that the Children of Israel must have encamped near natural habitats (as the Bedouins do today). Perhaps they had sojourned in cultivated settlements, areas with some food and water supply. So the Torah recorded every stage of their travels to publicize these great miracles.

Furthermore, their clothes never wore out. That was not merely because they lived on manna, which caused no perspiration (as the *Ibn Ezra* writes). Even new clothes would wear thin, just by being hung on a beam for forty years. It was nothing less than another of God's miracles.

He particularly wanted us to remember His great deeds: how the Children of Israel sheltered under His Clouds of Glory and were protected throughout their many years in the desert, far from cities and settlements.

(*Leviticus* 23:43, *Numbers* 33:1, *Deuteronomy* 8:4. See also 11:22)

◆§ **לְמַכֵּה מְלָכִים גְּדֹלִים** — *To Him Who smote great kings.* Generally, the Torah does not give the name of kings (such as the Edomites, or

To Him Who led His people through the desert
                    — for His kindness is eternal.
To Him Who smote great kings
                    — for His kindness is eternal.
And killed mighty kings   — for His kindness is eternal.
Sichon, king of the Emorites
                    — for His kindness is eternal.
And Og, king of Bashan
                    — for His kindness is eternal.
And gave their lands as an inheritance
                    — for His kindness is eternal.
An inheritance to Israel, His servant
                    — for His kindness is eternal.
Who remembered us in our lowliness
                    — for His kindness is eternal.

Canaanites mentioned in *Joshua* 12). However, the names of Sichon and Og are singled out as they were powerful enemies — a byword among the nations. Again, when we give thanks here to God *"For His kindness is eternal,"* we particularly mention the names of the Emorite kings: Sichon and Og.

(*Numbers* 20:14. See also ibid. 9:3)

§⊷ שֶׁבְּשִׁפְלֵנוּ זָכַר לָנוּ — *Who remembered us in our lowliness.* The Israelites might have fallen into the trap of unwarranted pride after fighting bravely in battle and defeating the Canaanites in open warfare. They may have fooled themselves into believing that their victories or wealth was solely due to "My strength and the might of my hand" (*Deuteronomy* 8:17). Alternatively, they might mistakenly have thought that God helped them succeed against their enemies because they were inherently more deserving.

However, that is manifestly not so. We must remember that God brought us out of Egypt when we possessed absolutely no prowess nor mighty hand at all. Moreover, all wealth and every success derive totally from God, Who grants us the strength and ability to accumulate wealth. Nor is it our spiritual merits that earn us success. Rather, it is the wickedness of our enemies that bring destruction down on their heads.   (*Deuteronomy* 8:18, 9:14)

וַיִּפְרְקֵנוּ מִצָּרֵינוּ   כִּי לְעוֹלָם חַסְדּוֹ.

נֹתֵן לֶחֶם לְכָל בָּשָׂר   כִּי לְעוֹלָם חַסְדּוֹ.

הוֹדוּ לְאֵל הַשָּׁמָיִם   כִּי לְעוֹלָם חַסְדּוֹ.[1]

נִשְׁמַת כָּל חַי תְּבָרֵךְ אֶת שִׁמְךָ יהוה אֱלֹהֵינוּ, וְרוּחַ כָּל בָּשָׂר תְּפָאֵר וּתְרוֹמֵם זִכְרְךָ מַלְכֵּנוּ תָּמִיד. מִן הָעוֹלָם וְעַד הָעוֹלָם אַתָּה אֵל, וּמִבַּלְעָדֶיךָ אֵין לָנוּ מֶלֶךְ גּוֹאֵל וּמוֹשִׁיעַ. פּוֹדֶה וּמַצִּיל וּמְפַרְנֵס וּמְרַחֵם בְּכָל עֵת צָרָה וְצוּקָה. אֵין לָנוּ מֶלֶךְ אֶלָּא אָתָּה. אֱלֹהֵי הָרִאשׁוֹנִים וְהָאַחֲרוֹנִים אֱלוֹהַּ כָּל בְּרִיּוֹת אֲדוֹן כָּל תּוֹלָדוֹת הַמְהֻלָּל בְּרֹב הַתִּשְׁבָּחוֹת הַמְנַהֵג עוֹלָמוֹ בְּחֶסֶד וּבְרִיּוֹתָיו בְּרַחֲמִים וַיהוה לֹא יָנוּם וְלֹא יִישָׁן. הַמְעוֹרֵר יְשֵׁנִים וְהַמֵּקִיץ נִרְדָּמִים וְהַמֵּשִׂיחַ אִלְּמִים וְהַמַּתִּיר אֲסוּרִים וְהַסּוֹמֵךְ נוֹפְלִים וְהַזּוֹקֵף כְּפוּפִים לְךָ לְבַדְּךָ אֲנַחְנוּ מוֹדִים. אִלּוּ פִינוּ מָלֵא שִׁירָה כַּיָּם וּלְשׁוֹנֵנוּ רִנָּה כַּהֲמוֹן גַּלָּיו וְשִׂפְתוֹתֵינוּ שֶׁבַח כְּמֶרְחֲבֵי רָקִיעַ וְעֵינֵינוּ מְאִירוֹת כַּשֶּׁמֶשׁ וְכַיָּרֵחַ וְיָדֵינוּ פְרוּשׂוֹת כְּנִשְׁרֵי שָׁמָיִם וְרַגְלֵינוּ קַלּוֹת כָּאַיָּלוֹת, אֵין אֲנַחְנוּ מַסְפִּיקִים לְהוֹדוֹת לְךָ יהוה אֱלֹהֵינוּ וֵאלֹהֵי אֲבוֹתֵינוּ

❧ וּמִבַּלְעָדֶיךָ אֵין לָנוּ מֶלֶךְ — *And besides for You we have no king.* God commanded Pharaoh to send out His people, "for this time I shall send all My plagues . . . so that you shall know that there is none like Me in all the world." (*Exodus* 9:14). The events of the Exodus flatly contradicted the theories of those who speculated that the world was not created. If that were so, nothing could have altered the fixed rules of nature.

By His limitless mastery of the elements — displayed with the miracles of the Exodus, and the accompanying plagues — it was finally proven that Hashem is the Eternal, existing through all time, preceding the Creation. Everything in the universe was brought into being by the All-Powerful. Therefore, we are duty bound to worship Him. The Exodus bears witness to all these eternal truths. (*Exodus* 20:2)

And redeemed us from our enemies
> — for His kindness is eternal.

He gives food to all living creatures
> — for His kindness is eternal.

Give thanks to God of the heavens
> — for His kindness is eternal.[1]

The soul of every living being will bless Your Name, Hashem, our God, and the spirit of all flesh will constantly glorify and exalt Your remembrance, our King. You are God forever, and besides You we have no king, redeemer, savior, liberator, deliverer, supporter, or source of mercy at any time of trouble or distress. We have no God but You, God of the first and the last, God of all creatures, Master of all generations, extolled with many praises, Who conducts His world with kindness and His creatures with mercy. Hashem does not doze or slumber. He wakes those who sleep and arouses those who slumber. He makes the mute speak. He releases the imprisoned, supports those who fall, and straightens those who are bent over. You alone we thank. Even if our mouths were as full of song as the sea, and our tongue full of joyous melody as its many waves, and our lips full of praise as the expanses of the firmament, and our eyes illuminating as the sun and the moon, and our arms spread wide as the eagles of the skies, and our feet as fleet as antelopes, we still could not sufficiently praise You or bless Your Name, Hashem, our God and the God of our fathers,

---

(1) *Psalms* 136.

◆§ לְךָ לְבַדְּךָ אֲנַחְנוּ מוֹדִים — *You alone we thank.* We shall always be mindful of God and His love. Our thoughts shall remain with Him when we are out on the road, lying down to sleep, or rising in the morning. Ideally, we should become so close to God that even while we hold conversations with others, our hearts remain united with the Divine Presence. It can be that those who truly achieve this level become "entwined with eternal life" (*I Samuel* 25:29), even during their lifetime. Their very being becomes a "residence" for the Divine Presence, as *Kuzari* (3:1) suggests. (*Deuteronomy* 11:22)

וּלְבָרֵךְ אֶת שִׁמְךָ עַל אַחַת מֵאָלֶף אֶלֶף אַלְפֵי אֲלָפִים וְרִבֵּי רְבָבוֹת פְּעָמִים הַטּוֹבוֹת שֶׁעָשִׂיתָ עִם אֲבוֹתֵינוּ וְעִמָּנוּ. מִמִּצְרַיִם גְּאַלְתָּנוּ יהוה אֱלֹהֵינוּ וּמִבֵּית עֲבָדִים פְּדִיתָנוּ בְּרָעָב זַנְתָּנוּ וּבְשָׂבָע כִּלְכַּלְתָּנוּ מֵחֶרֶב הִצַּלְתָּנוּ וּמִדֶּבֶר מִלַּטְתָּנוּ וּמֵחֳלָיִם רָעִים וְנֶאֱמָנִים דִּלִּיתָנוּ. עַד הֵנָּה עֲזָרוּנוּ רַחֲמֶיךָ וְלֹא עֲזָבוּנוּ חֲסָדֶיךָ וְאַל תִּטְּשֵׁנוּ יהוה אֱלֹהֵינוּ לָנֶצַח. עַל כֵּן אֵבָרִים שֶׁפִּלַּגְתָּ בָּנוּ וְרוּחַ וּנְשָׁמָה שֶׁנָּפַחְתָּ בְּאַפֵּינוּ וְלָשׁוֹן אֲשֶׁר שַׂמְתָּ בְּפִינוּ הֵן הֵם יוֹדוּ וִיבָרְכוּ וִישַׁבְּחוּ וִיפָאֲרוּ וִירוֹמְמוּ וְיַעֲרִיצוּ וְיַקְדִּישׁוּ וְיַמְלִיכוּ אֶת שִׁמְךָ מַלְכֵּנוּ. כִּי כָל פֶּה לְךָ יוֹדֶה וְכָל לָשׁוֹן לְךָ תִשָּׁבַע וְכָל בֶּרֶךְ לְךָ תִכְרַע וְכָל קוֹמָה לְפָנֶיךָ תִשְׁתַּחֲוֶה וְכָל לְבָבוֹת יִירָאוּךָ וְכָל קֶרֶב וּכְלָיוֹת יְזַמְּרוּ לִשְׁמֶךָ. כַּדָּבָר שֶׁכָּתוּב כָּל עַצְמֹתַי תֹּאמַרְנָה יהוה מִי כָמוֹךָ מַצִּיל עָנִי מֵחָזָק מִמֶּנּוּ וְעָנִי וְאֶבְיוֹן מִגֹּזְלוֹ.¹ מִי יִדְמֶה לָךְ וּמִי יִשְׁוֶה

---

§ וּמֵחֳלָיִם רָעִים — *From severe diseases.* By obeying God's wishes, we are spared from illness. As we saw from the terrible diseases of the Egyptians, sickness is a punishment for those that rebel against God's Will. (*Exodus* 15:26. See also *Deuteronomy* 7:15)

§ וְיַמְלִיכוּ אֶת שִׁמְךָ — *And do homage to Your Name.* When our leaders, elders and judges gather together, the Jews will proclaim that Hashem has become our King. All the tribes of Israel will join as one, to accept His Rule upon us throughout the generations, undertaking to observe His Torah and recognize His sovereignty for ever. This constitutes accepting the Heavenly Kingdom and God's Torah, while denying idolatry.

The Sages teach us (*Sifre, Devarim* 33:5): When the elders sit together in council in this world, Hashem's Great Name is glorified in the Heavens above. Thus, the Torah tells us "He became King over Jeshurun — when the leaders of the people gather, and all the tribes of Israel are united." Unfortunately, this is only true when there is a unified gathering. When we disintegrate into groups and factions, this is no longer the case. The *Midrash* (*Bamidbar Rabbah* 15:14)

for even a thousandth or a ten-thousandth of the good that You have done for our ancestors and for us. You redeemed us from Egypt, Hashem, our God, and delivered us from the house of bondage. You have fed us in famine and sustained us in plenty. You have saved us from the sword, rescued us from epidemic, and spared us from severe and enduring diseases. Your mercy has helped us until this time and Your kindness has not abandoned us. Hashem, our God, do not ever desert us. Therefore the limbs which You have carved in us, the spirit and soul that You have blown into our nostrils, the tongue that You have put into our mouths — they will thank, bless, laud, glorify, exalt, adulate, sanctify, and do homage to Your Name, our King. For every mouth gives thanks to You, every tongue vows allegiance to You, every knee bends to You, every stature bows before You, every heart fears You, and all internal organs sing out to Your Name. As it is written, "All my bones say, Hashem: Who is like You, Who saves the poor man from one stronger than he, and the poor and impoverished from the one who seeks to rob him?"[1] Who can resemble You? Who can compare

---

(1) *Psalms* 35:10.

---

confirms this: It is as if Hashem's Throne is secure only when the Jewish People are united into a single gathering. Such a statement — Hashem's Kingdom depends on our unity — can, obviously, not be understood on a simple level. (*Deuteronomy* 33:5)

⊰§ מַצִּיל עָנִי — *Who saves the poor man.* People make the mistake of thinking they can take advantage of the poor who have no one to protect them. In reality, the poor have greater protection than anyone else. While others may busy themselves seeking someone who could save them or help them take revenge, the poor man, in contrast, who has nowhere to turn, prays directly to God. All he has to do is to cry out to the Almighty. Immediately, Hashem hears his voice, and saves him from injustice and punishes those mistreating him — just as He saved us from oppression in Egypt.

(*Exodus* 22:22. See also ibid. 22:20 and *Deuteronomy* 15:11)

לָךְ וּמִי יַעֲרָךְ לָךְ הָאֵל הַגָּדוֹל הַגִּבּוֹר וְהַנּוֹרָא אֵל עֶלְיוֹן
קֹנֵה שָׁמַיִם וָאָרֶץ. נְהַלֶּלְךָ וּנְשַׁבֵּחֲךָ וּנְפָאֶרְךָ וּנְבָרֵךְ אֶת
שֵׁם קָדְשֶׁךָ כָּאָמוּר לְדָוִד בָּרְכִי נַפְשִׁי אֶת יהוה וְכָל קְרָבַי
אֶת שֵׁם קָדְשׁוֹ.¹

הָאֵל בְּתַעֲצֻמוֹת עֻזֶּךָ הַגָּדוֹל בִּכְבוֹד שְׁמֶךָ הַגִּבּוֹר לָנֶצַח
וְהַנּוֹרָא בְּנוֹרְאוֹתֶיךָ הַמֶּלֶךְ הַיּוֹשֵׁב עַל כִּסֵּא
רָם וְנִשָּׂא.

שׁוֹכֵן עַד מָרוֹם וְקָדוֹשׁ שְׁמוֹ. וְכָתוּב רַנְּנוּ צַדִּיקִים
בַּיהוה לַיְשָׁרִים נָאוָה תְהִלָּה.² בְּפִי יְשָׁרִים
תִּתְהַלָּל וּבְדִבְרֵי צַדִּיקִים תִּתְבָּרַךְ וּבִלְשׁוֹן חֲסִידִים
תִּתְרוֹמָם וּבְקֶרֶב קְדוֹשִׁים תִּתְקַדָּשׁ:

וּבְמַקְהֲלוֹת רִבְבוֹת עַמְּךָ בֵּית יִשְׂרָאֵל בְּרִנָּה יִתְפָּאַר
שִׁמְךָ מַלְכֵּנוּ בְּכָל דּוֹר וָדוֹר שֶׁכֵּן חוֹבַת כָּל
הַיְצוּרִים לְפָנֶיךָ יהוה אֱלֹהֵינוּ וֵאלֹהֵי אֲבוֹתֵינוּ לְהוֹדוֹת
לְהַלֵּל לְשַׁבֵּחַ לְפָאֵר לְרוֹמֵם לְהַדֵּר לְבָרֵךְ לְעַלֵּה וּלְקַלֵּס
עַל כָּל דִּבְרֵי שִׁירוֹת וְתִשְׁבְּחוֹת דָּוִד בֶּן יִשַׁי עַבְדְּךָ
מְשִׁיחֶךָ.

יִשְׁתַּבַּח שִׁמְךָ לָעַד מַלְכֵּנוּ הָאֵל הַמֶּלֶךְ הַגָּדוֹל וְהַקָּדוֹשׁ
בַּשָּׁמַיִם וּבָאָרֶץ כִּי לְךָ נָאֶה יהוה אֱלֹהֵינוּ

וּבְקֶרֶב קְדוֹשִׁים ❧ — *And amid the holy.* Holiness involves self-control in
   many areas. The Torah forbids immorality and certain foods. In
addition, one is not allowed to enjoy a life of sheer pleasure to excess,
even when confined to permissible activities. Otherwise a person will
freely indulge himself with many wives, glut himself with too much
meat and wine, and utter all sorts of profanities. Such a person will
become an outcast within the rules of the Torah!
   To attain holiness, we have to practice moderation and abstinence.

to You? Who can estimate You? The great, mighty, and awesome God, the supreme God, Creator of heavens and earth. We will praise You, laud You, glorify You, and bless Your holy Name, as it says: "Of David: my soul blesses Hashem, and all my insides bless His holy Name."[1]

O God, in the supremacies of Your might! You Who are great in the glory of Your name, Who are mighty forever and fearful through Your awe-inspiring deeds! The King Who sits upon a high and exalted throne!

He Who dwells in eternity, high and holy is His Name. As it is written, "Let the righteous rejoice in Hashem. It is fitting for the upright to extol."[2] By the mouth of the upright You shall be praised. And by the words of the righteous You shall be blessed. And by the tongue of the pious You shall be exalted. And amid the holy You shall be sanctified.

And in the assemblies of the myriads of Your people, the House of Israel, Your Name shall be extolled in song, our King, in each and every generation. For it is the duty of all that is created: in Your presence, Hashem, our God and the God of our fathers, to thank, praise, laud, glorify, exalt, adorn, bless, elevate, and celebrate beyond all the songs and praises of David the son of Yishai, Your servant, Your anointed.

May Your Name be praised forever, our King, the God and King, great and holy, in the heavens and the earth. For hymn and praise befit You, Hashem, our God

---

(1) *Psalms* 103:1. (2) 33:1.

We have to limit our intake of intoxicating drink, refrain from too frequent intercourse, and distance ourselves from impurity. Our mouths should not become debased with foul language or gluttony. We should sanctify our desires, needs and behavior until we reach the standard of abstinence and restraint. This involves separating ourselves from the crude people, who corrupt themselves with coarse pleasures and obscenities. By becoming holy, we can become closer to God — for He is the ultimate source of Holiness. (*Leviticus* 19:2)

וֵאלֹהֵי אֲבוֹתֵינוּ שִׁיר וּשְׁבָחָה הַלֵּל וְזִמְרָה עֹז וּמֶמְשָׁלָה נֶצַח גְּדֻלָּה וּגְבוּרָה תְּהִלָּה וְתִפְאֶרֶת קְדֻשָּׁה וּמַלְכוּת בְּרָכוֹת וְהוֹדָאוֹת מֵעַתָּה וְעַד עוֹלָם: בָּרוּךְ אַתָּה יהוה אֵל מֶלֶךְ גָּדוֹל בַּתִּשְׁבָּחוֹת אֵל הַהוֹדָאוֹת אֲדוֹן הַנִּפְלָאוֹת הַבּוֹחֵר בְּשִׁירֵי זִמְרָה מֶלֶךְ אֵל חֵי הָעוֹלָמִים.

The blessing over wine is recited and the fourth cup is drunk while reclining to the left side.
It is preferable that the entire cup be drunk, but at least one should drink most of it.

בָּרוּךְ אַתָּה יהוה אֱלֹהֵינוּ מֶלֶךְ הָעוֹלָם, בּוֹרֵא פְּרִי הַגָּפֶן.

After drinking the fourth cup, the concluding blessing is recited.
On the Sabbath include the passage in parentheses.

בָּרוּךְ אַתָּה יהוה אֱלֹהֵינוּ מֶלֶךְ הָעוֹלָם, עַל הַגֶּפֶן וְעַל פְּרִי הַגֶּפֶן וְעַל תְּנוּבַת הַשָּׂדֶה וְעַל אֶרֶץ חֶמְדָּה טוֹבָה וּרְחָבָה שֶׁרָצִיתָ וְהִנְחַלְתָּ לַאֲבוֹתֵינוּ לֶאֱכוֹל מִפִּרְיָהּ וְלִשְׂבּוֹעַ מִטּוּבָהּ. רַחֶם נָא יהוה אֱלֹהֵינוּ עַל יִשְׂרָאֵל עַמֶּךָ וְעַל יְרוּשָׁלַיִם עִירֶךָ וְעַל צִיּוֹן מִשְׁכַּן כְּבוֹדֶךָ וְעַל מִזְבְּחֶךָ וְעַל הֵיכָלֶךָ. וּבְנֵה יְרוּשָׁלַיִם עִיר הַקֹּדֶשׁ בִּמְהֵרָה בְיָמֵינוּ וְהַעֲלֵנוּ לְתוֹכָהּ וְשַׂמְּחֵנוּ בְּבִנְיָנָהּ וְנֹאכַל מִפִּרְיָהּ וְנִשְׂבַּע מִטּוּבָהּ וּנְבָרֶכְךָ עָלֶיהָ בִּקְדֻשָּׁה וּבְטָהֳרָה. [וּרְצֵה וְהַחֲלִיצֵנוּ בְּיוֹם הַשַּׁבָּת הַזֶּה] וְשַׂמְּחֵנוּ בְּיוֹם חַג הַמַּצּוֹת הַזֶּה. כִּי אַתָּה יהוה טוֹב וּמֵטִיב לַכֹּל וְנוֹדֶה לְךָ עַל הָאָרֶץ וְעַל פְּרִי הַגָּפֶן. בָּרוּךְ אַתָּה יהוה עַל הָאָרֶץ וְעַל פְּרִי הַגָּפֶן.

נרצה

חֲסַל סִדּוּר פֶּסַח כְּהִלְכָתוֹ. כְּכָל מִשְׁפָּטוֹ וְחֻקָּתוֹ. כַּאֲשֶׁר זָכִינוּ לְסַדֵּר אוֹתוֹ. כֵּן נִזְכֶּה לַעֲשׂוֹתוֹ.

and the God of our fathers — accolade and song, strength and sovereignty, eternity, greatness and might, fame and glory, sanctity and majesty, blessing and thanksgiving, for all eternity. Blessed are You, Hashem, God, King, great in praises, the God to whom we owe thanks, Master of wonders, Who is pleased with melodious song — King, God, Life of the worlds.

The blessing over wine is recited and the fourth cup is drunk while reclining to the left side. It is preferable that the entire cup be drunk, but at least one should drink most of it.

Blessed are You, Hashem, our God, King of the Universe, Who creates the fruit of the vine.

After drinking the fourth cup, the concluding blessing is recited. On the Sabbath include the passage in parentheses.

Blessed are You, Hashem, our God, King of the Universe, for the vine and the fruit of the vine, and the produce of the field, and for the precious, good, and spacious land that You willed to give as an inheritance to our ancestors, to eat of its fruit and to be sated by its goodness. Have mercy, please, Hashem, our God, on Israel, Your people, and on Jerusalem, Your city, and on Zion, the abode of Your glory, and on Your altar and on Your Temple. Rebuild Jerusalem, the city of sanctity, speedily in our lifetimes. Bring us up into it and let us rejoice in its reconstruction. Let us eat of its fruits and be sated by its goodness. May we bless You over it in holiness and purity (and may it be Your will to fortify us on this Sabbath day), and may You bring us joy on this day of the Festival of *Matzos*. For You, Hashem, are good and do good to all, and we thank You for the land and the fruit of the vine. Blessed are You, Hashem, for the land and the fruit of the vine.

NIRTZAH

The order of Pesach has come to its end in accordance with its Halachah, in accordance with all of its laws and statutes. Just as we have been worthy of making the *seder* this year, so may we be worthy of making it in the future.

זַךְ שׁוֹכֵן מְעוֹנָה. קוֹמֵם קְהַל עֲדַת מִי מָנָה. בְּקָרוֹב נַהֵל נִטְעֵי כַנָּה. פְּדוּיִם לְצִיּוֹן בְּרִנָּה.

לְשָׁנָה הַבָּאָה בִּירוּשָׁלָיִם.

---

§ **קְהַל עֲדַת מִי מָנָה** — *The countless congregation.* No man can count the dust of the earth or the sand of the sea. Similarly, the Jewish nation are beyond count. In the future, they will increase and shall not be diminished.

After King David ordered a census, the people were afflicted with a fierce plague (*II Samuel* 24:1 ff.). While the Torah forbids counting the Jewish nation without using coins (or other objects), I find it hard to accept that King David was not mindful of this. Even if it was an oversight on David's part, why did Joab — who personally conducted the census and was unhappy with the decision — not use shekels?

Therefore, I believe that the plague was brought because Heaven was angry with King David because he counted his people needlessly. He had no military or other reason to know their number. He was merely exhibiting pride in being king over so many people. Indeed, the *Midrash* (*Bamidbar Rabbah* 2:17) refers to David's counting as having been unnecessary and thus being the cause for loss of life.

Perhaps David also erred in having men under twenty years of age included in the count (as appears from *I Chronicles* 27:23 ff.), when one should not count those under twenty even with shekels — and maybe this was Joab's objection to the census.

Why, then, was the punishment of plague inflicted on the common people? The Sages (*Berachos* 62b) insist that David's error lay in conducting his census without using shekels. According to them, the people were probably punished for not offering shekels of their own accord. Yet, it appears (from *II Samuel* 24:1, as *Rashi* there notes) that God was already angry with the people, even before King David ordered the census.

Perhaps, they were found wanting for the delay in building a Temple, causing the Holy Ark to move from one temporary home to another, with the tribes not taking the initiative to build a permanent Sanctuary. When King David sought to build the Temple. God refused his offer because David's hands were stained with the blood

Pure One, Who dwells in His heavenly abode, raise up the countless congregation of Israel. In the near future, lead the shoots You have planted to Zion, redeemed, joyously.

Next year in Jerusalem!

of war (*II Samuel* 7:1 ff.) and thus it was postponed until the reign of Solomon. Had it been the people's undertaking, voiced by the tribal leaders, it could have been built earlier, either during the reign of the Judges, in the days of Saul or even under King David himself.

David's heavy personal involvement in bloody battles was only an impediment to his building the Temple *by himself*. Once David was no longer considered the prime mover, the fact that he had been a warrior should not have deterred the people from establishing a "House of Mercy." Had it originated as a national decision, building the Temple would not have been delayed until the days of King Solomon. God was therefore angry with the people, even before King David erred in counting them.

(*Numbers* 1:3, 16:21, 23:10. See also *Exodus* 3:12)

‎לְשָׁנָה הַבָּאָה בִּירוּשָׁלָיִם‏ — *Next year in Jerusalem*! The nations of old recognized that Jerusalem occupied the center of civilization. Perhaps, they knew from their ancient lore that Jerusalem occupies the site on earth directly opposite the Heavenly Sanctuary where the Divine Presence dwells. Furthermore, the *Midrash* (*Bereishis Rabbah* 43:6) teaches us that Jerusalem is described as "righteous," because it encourages its residents to righteousness.

Also, it is known as the "Gate of Heaven," for all prayers and sacrifices rise from there to heaven. Prayers held in Jerusalem are considered almost as if they are uttered at the Throne of Glory, since the Heavenly Gates are open to receive our prayers.

As this area is the closest link between heaven and earth, it is more likely that Heavenly visions might prevail here. The state of Divine prophecy is easier to attain in Jerusalem than anywhere else. It has been related that the souls of Jerusalem's inhabitants are cloaked in the Holy Spirit and they receive far greater Heavenly inspiration than is possible on an alien, impure soil.

(*Genesis* 14:18, 28:17. *Shaar HaGemul*. See also *Ramban's* lengthy "Lament at Jerusalem's Ruins," written in 1267)

On the first night recite the following. On the second night continue on page 126.

וּבְכֵן וַיְהִי בַּחֲצִי הַלָּיְלָה.

אָז רוֹב נִסִּים הִפְלֵאתָ   בַּלַּיְלָה.

בְּרֹאשׁ אַשְׁמוֹרֶת זֶה   הַלַּיְלָה.

גֵּר צֶדֶק נִצַּחְתּוֹ כְּנֶחֱלַק לוֹ   לַיְלָה.

וַיְהִי בַּחֲצִי הַלָּיְלָה.

דַּנְתָּ מֶלֶךְ גְּרָר בַּחֲלוֹם   הַלַּיְלָה.

הִפְחַדְתָּ אֲרַמִּי בְּאֶמֶשׁ   לַיְלָה.

וַיָּשַׂר יִשְׂרָאֵל לְמַלְאָךְ וַיּוּכַל לוֹ   לַיְלָה.

וַיְהִי בַּחֲצִי הַלָּיְלָה.

זֶרַע בְּכוֹרֵי פַתְרוֹס מָחַצְתָּ בַּחֲצִי   הַלַּיְלָה.

חֵילָם לֹא מָצְאוּ בְּקוּמָם   בַּלַּיְלָה.

טִיסַת נְגִיד חֲרוֹשֶׁת סִלִּיתָ בְּכוֹכְבֵי   לַיְלָה.

וַיְהִי בַּחֲצִי הַלָּיְלָה.

עֻ§ כְּנֶחֱלַק לוֹ לַיְלָה — *Dividing for him the night.* Abraham with his few troops chased the mighty enemy during daylight until the town of Dan. When it grew dark, he was unable to see their escape route. So he divided his entourage and servants into two or three units. He led one group down one road while the other groups chased the fleeing army down the remaining routes.

As is known, there is a substantial distance between Hebron (where Abraham set out from) and Chovah (the end of the chase) which is to the left of Damascus. So Abraham must have chased them for many days until he drove them from the country. Alternatively, this was a great miracle, for the Sages state (*Bereishis Rabbah* 43:7) that he covered great distances with each step he took. (*Genesis* 14:15)

עֻ§ וַיָּשַׂר יִשְׂרָאֵל לְמַלְאָךְ וַיּוּכַל לוֹ — *Israel [Jacob] fought with an angel and overcame him.* Although angels are "strong warriors who do His bidding" (*Psalms* 103:20), this angel could not overcome our patriarch Jacob, since he was restrained by Heaven. All he was permitted to do was to dislocate Jacob's thigh. This alluded to the effect the angel had on all Jacob's righteous descendants, according

הגדת של פסח / 124

On the first night recite the following. On the second night continue on page 126.

It happened at midnight.

Then You performed wondrous miracles at   night.
  At the first watch of this   night.
You brought victory to the righteous convert
[Abraham] by dividing for him the   night.
    It happened at midnight.
You judged the king of Gerar [Abimelech]
  in a dream of the   night.
You terrified the Aramean [Laban] in the dark of   night.
And Israel [Jacob] fought with an angel
  and overcame him at   night.
    It happened at midnight.
You bruised the firstborn seed
  of Pasros [Egypt] at   midnight.
They did not find their legions
  when they arose at   night.
The swift armies of the prince of Charoshes [Sisera]
  You crushed with the stars of   night.
    It happened at midnight.

---

to the *Midrash* (*Bereishis Rabbah* 77:4) referring to the generation of religious oppression.

The struggle between Jacob and the angel hinted at a future generation when Esau will be almost successful at eliminating Jacob's descendants entirely. This occurred during the time of the Sages, the *Tannaim* of the *Mishnah,* in the generation of Rabbi Yehudah Ben Bava and his colleagues.

Later, Rabbi Chiya bar Abba remarked (*Shir HaShirim Rabbah* 2:7), "Were I asked to surrender my life to sanctify His Name, I would willingly do it — but on the understanding I would be killed immediately. However, I would be unable to sustain this in the generation of religious oppression! What happened during that oppression? The Romans tortured them slowly with heated iron balls until they died in agony."

Similar and greater tortures occurred in other generations. Yet our nation has survived all encounters as the verse hints (*Genesis* 33:18): "And Jacob arrived intact." (*Genesis* 32:26)

בַּלַּיְלָה.	יָעַץ מְחָרֵף לְנוֹפֵף אִוּי הוֹבַשְׁתָּ פְגָרָיו
לַיְלָה.	כָּרַע בֵּל וּמַצָּבוֹ בְּאִישׁוֹן
לַיְלָה.	לְאִישׁ חֲמוּדוֹת נִגְלָה רָז חֲזוֹת
	וַיְהִי בַּחֲצִי הַלַּיְלָה.

בַּלַּיְלָה.	מִשְׁתַּכֵּר בִּכְלֵי קֹדֶשׁ נֶהֱרַג בּוֹ
לַיְלָה.	נוֹשַׁע מִבּוֹר אֲרָיוֹת פּוֹתֵר בִּעֲתוּתֵי
בַּלַּיְלָה.	שִׂנְאָה נָטַר אֲגָגִי וְכָתַב סְפָרִים
	וַיְהִי בַּחֲצִי הַלַּיְלָה.

לַיְלָה.	עוֹרַרְתָּ נִצְחֲךָ עָלָיו בְּנֶדֶד שְׁנַת
מִלַּיְלָה.	פּוּרָה תִדְרוֹךְ לְשׁוֹמֵר מַה
לַיְלָה.	צָרַח כַּשּׁוֹמֵר וְשָׂח אָתָא בֹקֶר וְגַם
	וַיְהִי בַּחֲצִי הַלַּיְלָה.

לַיְלָה.	קָרֵב יוֹם אֲשֶׁר הוּא לֹא יוֹם וְלֹא
הַלַּיְלָה.	רָם הוֹדַע כִּי לְךָ הַיּוֹם אַף לְךָ
הַלַּיְלָה.	שׁוֹמְרִים הַפְקֵד לְעִירְךָ כָּל הַיּוֹם וְכָל
לַיְלָה.	תָּאִיר כְּאוֹר יוֹם חֶשְׁכַּת
	וַיְהִי בַּחֲצִי הַלַּיְלָה.

On the first night continue on page 130.
On the second night recite the following.

וּבְכֵן וַאֲמַרְתֶּם זֶבַח פֶּסַח:

בַּפֶּסַח.	אֹמֶץ גְּבוּרוֹתֶיךָ הִפְלֵאתָ
פֶּסַח.	בְּרֹאשׁ כָּל מוֹעֲדוֹת נִשֵּׂאתָ
פֶּסַח.	גִּלִּיתָ לְאֶזְרָחִי חֲצוֹת לֵיל
	וַאֲמַרְתֶּם זֶבַח פֶּסַח.

The blasphemer [Sennacherib] schemed to raise
  his hand menacingly [over the precious city].
  You made his corpses rot at   night.
Bel [the Babylonian pagan deity] and his
  pedestal fell in the black of   night.
To the beloved man [Daniel] was revealed
  the secret of the visions of   night.
        It happened at midnight.
He who guzzled out of the sacred vessels
  [Belshazzar, king of Babylonia] was killed on that night.
The one who was saved from the lions' den
  interpreted the terrors of the   night.
The Aggagite [Haman] nurtured hatred
  and wrote decrees at   night.
        It happened at midnight.
You initiated Your triumph against him
  by disturbing the sleep [of Ahasuerus] at   night.
You will tread a winepress [in peace after victory]
  for him who cries out [Israel]: Our Guardian!
  What will be of this   night?
Like a guardian You will call out in response:
  The morning has come, as well as the   night.
        It happened at midnight.
The day is approaching which is neither day nor   night.
Most High! Make it known that Yours are
  both the day and the   night.
Appoint watchmen over Your city all day and all   night.
Illuminate like the light of day the darkness of   night.
        It will happen at midnight.

On the first night continue on page 130. On the second night recite the following.

And you will say: A feast of Passover.

The power of Your mighty deeds
  You showed wondrously on   Passover.
Foremost of all festivals You exalted   Passover.
You revealed to the oriental [Abraham]
  the events of the night of   Passover.
        And you will say: A feast of Passover.

127 / THE RAMBAN HAGGADAH

דְּלָתָיו דָּפַקְתָּ כְּחֹם הַיּוֹם   בְּפֶסַח.

הִסְעִיד נוֹצְצִים עֲגוֹת מַצּוֹת   בְּפֶסַח.

וְאֶל הַבָּקָר רָץ זֵכֶר לְשׁוֹר עֵרֶךְ   פֶּסַח.

וַאֲמַרְתֶּם זֶבַח פֶּסַח.

זוֹעֲמוּ סְדוֹמִים וְלוֹהֲטוּ בָּאֵשׁ   בְּפֶסַח.

חֻלַּץ לוֹט מֵהֶם וּמַצּוֹת אָפָה בְּקֵץ   פֶּסַח.

טִאטֵאתָ אַדְמַת מוֹף וְנוֹף בְּעָבְרְךָ   בְּפֶסַח.

וַאֲמַרְתֶּם זֶבַח פֶּסַח.

יָהּ רֹאשׁ כָּל אוֹן מָחַצְתָּ בְּלֵיל שִׁמּוּר   פֶּסַח.

כַּבִּיר עַל בֵּן בְּכוֹר פָּסַחְתָּ בְּדַם   פֶּסַח.

◆§ וְאֶל הַבָּקָר רָץ ◆§ — *And he ran to the cattle.* This reveals Abraham's
overwhelming zeal to practice kindness. Here was a prominent
personality, with three hundred and eighteen armed men about the
house, ready to do his bidding. Moreover, he was of old age and still
recovering from a painful operation. Yet, he went over to Sarah's tent
and encouraged her to prepare bread for the guests. Then he ran to
where his herd of cattle were stationed, to personally choose a young
and tasty calf for his guests. Although his servants awaited his orders,
he did not avail himself of their services, but saw to everything
himself.   (*Genesis* 18:7)

◆§ זוֹעֲמוּ סְדוֹמִים ◆§ — *The Sodomites provoked.* Sodom's inhabitants'
prime motive was to prevent strangers sharing their prosperity.
Because the land around them was very rich, "like the garden of
Hashem" (*Genesis* 13:10), they were apprehensive at being over-
whelmed by strangers and beggars. Typically, they disliked dispens-
ing charity. Lot was welcomed either because of his substantial
possessions or in Abraham's honor. Also, we see from the prophet
(*Ezekiel* 16:49) that Sodom sinned from pride, enjoying prosperity yet
failing to support the poor.

However, the Sages (*Sanhedrin* 109b) understand the Sodomites
were guilty of other crimes beyond oppressing the destitute.
Nonetheless, their fate was sealed because of their evil behavior

You knocked on his doors
   during the heat of the day on   Passover.
He gave bright angels a meal of cakes of
   matzah on   Passover.
He ran to fetch an ox in commemoration of
   the ox sacrificed [as the *korban chagigah* —
   the festival offering] on   Passover.
         And you will say: A feast of Passover.
The Sodomites provoked Hashem
   and were set ablaze on   Passover.
Lot escaped from them and baked *matzos*
   at the end of   Passover.
You swept clean the land of Mof and Nof
   [Egyptian cities] on   Passover.
         And you will say: A feast of Passover.
Hashem, the first issue of strength You bruised
   on the watchful night of   Passover.
Mighty One, You skipped over the firstborn son
   because of the blood of   Passover,

---

towards the poor and needy.

Sodom particularly was punished, because these crimes took place in *Eretz Yisrael*. The land of God's inheritance cannot tolerate men of evil. Just as it would later spew out whole nations because of their abominations, it destroyed the Sodomites for their unforgivable excesses. Because their pride derived from the blessed land around them, their land was totally destroyed for all time, never to be inhabited. Although other nations have also behaved appallingly, they were not similarly punished, for their sins were not committed within the Holy Land, the land which cannot tolerate evil.   (*Genesis* 19:5)

 musical_note§ בְּלֵיל שָׁמוּר פֶּסַח — *On the watchful night of Passover.* God watched and waited for this night, in which He would bring us out of Egypt. This was the night set aside by God, sanctified to His Name.

Also, it is a Night of Watchfulness for the Children of Israel throughout the generations. On this night, they observe His worship by consuming the Passover sacrifice, recalling His miracles and offering praise and gratitude to Hashem.   (*Exodus* 12:42)

	לְבִלְתִּי תֵּת מַשְׁחִית לָבֹא בִּפְתָחַי
בַּפֶּסַח.	
	וַאֲמַרְתֶּם זֶבַח פֶּסַח.
פֶּסַח.	מִסְגֶּרֶת סֻגְּרָה בְּעִתּוֹתֵי
פֶּסַח.	נִשְׁמְדָה מִדְיָן בִּצְלִיל שְׂעוֹרֵי עֹמֶר
פֶּסַח.	שׂוֹרְפוּ מִשְׁמַנֵּי פּוּל וְלוּד בִּיקַד יְקוֹד
	וַאֲמַרְתֶּם זֶבַח פֶּסַח.
פֶּסַח.	עוֹד הַיּוֹם בְּנֹב לַעֲמוֹד עַד גָּעָה עוֹנַת
בַּפֶּסַח.	פַּס יַד כָּתְבָה לְקַעֲקֵעַ צוּל
בַּפֶּסַח.	צָפֹה הַצָּפִית עָרוֹךְ הַשֻּׁלְחָן
	וַאֲמַרְתֶּם זֶבַח פֶּסַח.
בַּפֶּסַח.	קָהָל כִּנְּסָה הֲדַסָּה צוֹם לְשַׁלֵּשׁ
בַּפֶּסַח.	רֹאשׁ מִבֵּית רָשָׁע מָחַצְתָּ בְּעֵץ חֲמִשִּׁים
בַּפֶּסַח.	שְׁתֵּי אֵלֶּה רֶגַע תָּבִיא לְעוּצִית
פֶּסַח.	תָּעֹז יָדְךָ וְתָרוּם יְמִינֶךָ כְּלֵיל הִתְקַדֶּשׁ חַג
	וַאֲמַרְתֶּם זֶבַח פֶּסַח.

On both nights continue here:

כִּי לוֹ נָאֶה, כִּי לוֹ יָאֶה:

אַדִּיר בִּמְלוּכָה, בָּחוּר כַּהֲלָכָה, גְּדוּדָיו יֹאמְרוּ לוֹ, לְךָ וּלְךָ, לְךָ כִּי לְךָ, לְךָ אַף לְךָ, לְךָ יהוה הַמַּמְלָכָה, כִּי לוֹ נָאֶה, כִּי לוֹ יָאֶה.

⋙ **לְבִלְתִּי תֵּת מַשְׁחִית לָבֹא** — *Not to allow the destroyer to enter.* The "destroyer" here is the usual angel of destruction, who is abroad during all plagues. Yet it does not refer to an angel which actually participated in the destruction in Egypt. That was carried out by God alone. (*Exodus* 12:23. See also there 12:21)

⋙ **לְךָ ה׳ הַמַּמְלָכָה** — *Yours, HASHEM, is the sovereignty.* God has performed for us what He has never done for any other nation. He

Not to allow the destroyer to enter my doors on   Passover.
>> And you will say: A feast of Passover.
The closed city [Jericho] was handed over
>> [to the Jews] at the time of   Passover.
Midian was destroyed [by the Jews
>> under the leadership of Gidon]
>> through the merit of a cake of the *omer* on   Passover.
The mighty nobles of Pul and Lud [the Assyrians
>> in the days of King Hezekiah]
>> were burnt in a conflagration on   Passover.
>> And you will say: A feast of Passover.
He [Sennacherib] would have stood at Nob,
>> but the time of Passover arrived.
A hand wrote the decree of annihilation against Zul
>> [Babylonia] on   Passover.
Their scout went to look for the enemy while their table
>> was festively set on   Passover.
>> And you will say: A feast of Passover.
Hadassah [Esther] gathered an assembly for
>> a three-day fast on   Passover.
The head of the evil house [Haman] You killed
>> on a fifty-cubit pole on   Passover.
Bring bereavement and widowhood to Utzis
>> [Edom] in an instant on   Passover.
Strengthen Your hand, raise Your right hand
>> as on the night that the festival of Passover was sanctified.
>> And you will say: A feast of Passover.

On both nights continue here:

To Him it is fitting. To Him it is due.

Mighty in royalty, chosen by right, His legions say to Him:
Yours and only Yours; Yours, yes Yours, Yours, surely
Yours; Yours, Hashem, is the sovereignty of the world. To
Him it is fitting. To Him it is due.

---

allowed us, at the Giving of the Torah, to hear His Voice emerging
amid fire so that we should always fear Him, knowing that He is One.

דָּגוּל בִּמְלוּכָה, **הָדוּר** כַּהֲלָכָה, וָתִיקָיו יֹאמְרוּ לוֹ, לְךָ וּלְךָ, לְךָ כִּי לְךָ, לְךָ אַף לְךָ, לְךָ יהוה הַמַּמְלָכָה, כִּי לוֹ נָאֶה, כִּי לוֹ יָאֶה.

זַכַּאי בִּמְלוּכָה, **חָסִין** כַּהֲלָכָה, **טַפְסְרָיו** יֹאמְרוּ לוֹ, לְךָ וּלְךָ, לְךָ כִּי לְךָ, לְךָ אַף לְךָ, לְךָ יהוה הַמַּמְלָכָה, כִּי לוֹ נָאֶה, כִּי לוֹ יָאֶה.

יָחִיד בִּמְלוּכָה, **כַּבִּיר** כַּהֲלָכָה, **לִמּוּדָיו** יֹאמְרוּ לוֹ, לְךָ וּלְךָ, לְךָ כִּי לְךָ, לְךָ אַף לְךָ, לְךָ יהוה הַמַּמְלָכָה, כִּי לוֹ נָאֶה, כִּי לוֹ יָאֶה.

מוֹשֵׁל בִּמְלוּכָה, **נוֹרָא** כַּהֲלָכָה, **סְבִיבָיו** יֹאמְרוּ לוֹ, לְךָ וּלְךָ, לְךָ כִּי לְךָ, לְךָ אַף לְךָ, לְךָ יהוה הַמַּמְלָכָה, כִּי לוֹ נָאֶה, כִּי לוֹ יָאֶה.

עֲנָיו בִּמְלוּכָה, **פּוֹדֶה** כַּהֲלָכָה, **צַדִּיקָיו** יֹאמְרוּ לוֹ, לְךָ וּלְךָ, לְךָ כִּי לְךָ, לְךָ אַף לְךָ, לְךָ יהוה הַמַּמְלָכָה, כִּי לוֹ נָאֶה, כִּי לוֹ יָאֶה.

קָדוֹשׁ בִּמְלוּכָה, **ר**חוּם כַּהֲלָכָה, **שִׁנְאַנָּיו** יֹאמְרוּ לוֹ, לְךָ וּלְךָ, לְךָ כִּי לְךָ, לְךָ אַף לְךָ, לְךָ יהוה הַמַּמְלָכָה, כִּי לוֹ נָאֶה, כִּי לוֹ יָאֶה.

תַּקִּיף בִּמְלוּכָה, **תּוֹמֵךְ** כַּהֲלָכָה, **תְּמִימָיו** יֹאמְרוּ לוֹ, לְךָ וּלְךָ, לְךָ כִּי לְךָ, לְךָ אַף לְךָ, לְךָ יהוה הַמַּמְלָכָה, כִּי לוֹ נָאֶה, כִּי לוֹ יָאֶה.

Consequently, we will not descend into total corruption. From the heavens, we heard His Voice teaching us ethics and wisdom. On earth, we saw His great fire burning upwards to the very heavens when we heard His words emerging from the flames. Since Hashem is the One God in the heavens above and on the earth below, we must keep His commandments and statutes. By doing so we shall enjoy

Distinguished in royalty, glorious of right. His faithful say to Him: Yours and only Yours; Yours, yes Yours; Yours, surely Yours; Yours, Hashem, is the sovereignty of the world. To Him it is fitting. To Him it is due.

Pure in royalty, firm of right. His courtiers say to Him: Yours and only Yours; Yours, yes Yours; Yours, surely Yours; Yours, Hashem, is the sovereignty of the world. To Him it is fitting. To Him it is due.

Unique in royalty, mighty of right. His disciples say to Him: Yours and only Yours; Yours, yes Yours; Yours, surely Yours; Yours, Hashem, is the sovereignty of the world. To Him it is fitting. To Him it is due.

Ruling in royalty, feared of right. Those who surround Him say to Him: Yours and only Yours; Yours, yes Yours; Yours, surely Yours; Yours, Hashem, is the sovereignty of the world. To Him it is fitting. To Him it is due.

Humble in royalty, redeeming by right. His righteous ones say to Him: Yours and only Yours; Yours, yes Yours; Yours, surely Yours; Yours, Hashem, is the sovereignty of the world. To Him it is fitting. To Him it is due.

Holy in royalty, merciful of right. His angels say to Him: Yours and only Yours; Yours, yes Yours; Yours, surely Yours; Yours, Hashem, is the sovereignty of the world. To Him it is fitting. To Him it is due.

Powerful in royalty, sustaining of right. His perfect ones say to Him: Yours and only Yours; Yours, yes Yours; Yours, surely Yours; Yours, Hashem, is the sovereignty of the world. To Him it is fitting. To Him it is due.

---

goodness in heaven and our days will be extended in this world.

Furthermore, He chose us as His people, removing us from within another nation with signs and wonders, so we shall not serve any other deity. All this we saw with our own eyes, confirming to us that Hashem is the Eternal God, Who is One and His Name is One. Nothing else exists besides Him. (*Deuteronomy* 4:32)

אַדִּיר הוּא יִבְנֶה בֵיתוֹ בְּקָרוֹב, בִּמְהֵרָה, בִּמְהֵרָה, בְּיָמֵינוּ בְּקָרוֹב. אֵל בְּנֵה, אֵל בְּנֵה, בְּנֵה בֵיתְךָ בְּקָרוֹב.

בָּחוּר הוּא. **גָּ**דוֹל הוּא. **דָּ**גוּל הוּא. יִבְנֶה בֵיתוֹ בְּקָרוֹב, בִּמְהֵרָה, בִּמְהֵרָה, בְּיָמֵינוּ בְּקָרוֹב. אֵל בְּנֵה, אֵל בְּנֵה, בְּנֵה בֵיתְךָ בְּקָרוֹב.

הָדוּר הוּא. **וָ**תִיק הוּא. **זַ**כַּאי הוּא. **חָ**סִיד הוּא. יִבְנֶה בֵיתוֹ בְּקָרוֹב, בִּמְהֵרָה, בִּמְהֵרָה, בְּיָמֵינוּ בְּקָרוֹב. אֵל בְּנֵה, אֵל בְּנֵה, בְּנֵה בֵיתְךָ בְּקָרוֹב.

טָהוֹר הוּא. **יָ**חִיד הוּא. **כַּ**בִּיר הוּא. **לָ**מוּד הוּא. **מֶ**לֶךְ הוּא. **נוֹ**רָא הוּא. **סַ**גִּיב הוּא. **עִ**זּוּז הוּא. **פּוֹ**דֶה הוּא. **צַ**דִּיק הוּא. יִבְנֶה בֵיתוֹ בְּקָרוֹב, בִּמְהֵרָה, בִּמְהֵרָה, בְּיָמֵינוּ בְּקָרוֹב. אֵל בְּנֵה, אֵל בְּנֵה, בְּנֵה בֵיתְךָ בְּקָרוֹב.

קָדוֹשׁ הוּא. **רַ**חוּם הוּא. **שַׁ**דַּי הוּא. **תַּ**קִּיף הוּא. יִבְנֶה בֵיתוֹ בְּקָרוֹב, בִּמְהֵרָה, בִּמְהֵרָה, בְּיָמֵינוּ בְּקָרוֹב. אֵל בְּנֵה, אֵל בְּנֵה, בְּנֵה בֵיתְךָ בְּקָרוֹב.

אֶחָד מִי יוֹדֵעַ? אֶחָד אֲנִי יוֹדֵעַ. אֶחָד אֱלֹהֵינוּ שֶׁבַּשָּׁמַיִם וּבָאָרֶץ.

שְׁנַיִם מִי יוֹדֵעַ? שְׁנַיִם אֲנִי יוֹדֵעַ. שְׁנֵי לֻחוֹת הַבְּרִית, אֶחָד אֱלֹהֵינוּ שֶׁבַּשָּׁמַיִם וּבָאָרֶץ.

⦿§ יִבְנֶה בֵיתוֹ בְּקָרוֹב — *May He rebuild His House soon.* When Moses blessed the tribes at the end of his life (*Deuteronomy* 33:12), he referred to Benjamin as יְדִיד ה׳, "Hashem's beloved," because the Temple, where the Divine Presence rests, is on his territory. Likewise, King Solomon, the builder of the Temple, was known as "Hashem's beloved" (*II Samuel* 12:25).

Moses, in his blessing, refers to the dwelling of the Divine Presence in three separate ways, alluding to the three different Temples. About

Mighty is He. May He build His house soon; quickly, quickly, in our lifetimes, soon. God, build; God, build; build Your house soon.

Exalted is He, great is He, distinguished is He. May He build His house soon; quickly, quickly, in our lifetimes, soon. God, build; God, build; build Your house soon.

Glorious is He, faithful is He, guiltless is He, righteous is He. May He build His house soon; quickly, quickly, in our lifetimes, soon. God, build; God, build; build Your house soon.

Pure is He, unique is He, powerful is He, all-wise is He, the King is He, awesome is He, sublime is He, all-powerful is He, the Redeemer is He, all-righteous is He. May He build His house soon; quickly, quickly, in our lifetimes, soon. God, build; God, build; build Your house soon.

Holy is He, compassionate is He, Almighty is He, Omnipotent is He. May He build His house soon; quickly, quickly, in our lifetimes, soon. God, rebuild; God, build; build Your house soon.

Who knows one? I know one.

One is our God in the heavens and the earth.

Who knows two? I know two. Two are the Tablets of the Covenant. One is our God in the heavens and the earth.

---

the First Temple, he foretold, "He shall dwell securely." Similarly, it later says about the First Temple that "The Glory of the Divine Presence filled the House" (*II Chronicles* 7:1).

However, regarding the Second Temple, he predicted only that "He hovers over it all day," that God's Presence will not actually dwell there but will only "cover" the Temple — sheltering and protecting it. (According to the *Hachalos Rabbos,* His Presence literally only "hovered" over the Second Temple.)

As to the future Third Temple, Moses wrote Hashem "will dwell between his shoulders." This foresees the Messianic Age when Jerusalem will be known as "The Throne of HASHEM" (*Jeremiah* 3:17). (*Deuteronomy* 33:12. See also *Sefer HaGeulah* Chap. 1)

◆§ שְׁנֵי לֻחוֹת הַבְּרִית — *Two are the Tablets of the Covenant.* After God forgave the Children of Israel, He presented Moses with the second

שְׁלשָׁה מִי יוֹדֵעַ? שְׁלשָׁה אֲנִי יוֹדֵעַ. שְׁלשָׁה אָבוֹת,
שְׁנֵי לֻחוֹת הַבְּרִית, אֶחָד אֱלֹהֵינוּ שֶׁבַּשָּׁמַיִם וּבָאָרֶץ.

אַרְבַּע מִי יוֹדֵעַ? אַרְבַּע אֲנִי יוֹדֵעַ. אַרְבַּע אִמָּהוֹת,
שְׁלשָׁה אָבוֹת, שְׁנֵי לֻחוֹת הַבְּרִית, אֶחָד אֱלֹהֵינוּ
שֶׁבַּשָּׁמַיִם וּבָאָרֶץ.

חֲמִשָּׁה מִי יוֹדֵעַ? חֲמִשָּׁה אֲנִי יוֹדֵעַ. חֲמִשָּׁה חֻמְשֵׁי
תוֹרָה, אַרְבַּע אִמָּהוֹת, שְׁלשָׁה אָבוֹת, שְׁנֵי לֻחוֹת
הַבְּרִית, אֶחָד אֱלֹהֵינוּ שֶׁבַּשָּׁמַיִם וּבָאָרֶץ.

שִׁשָּׁה מִי יוֹדֵעַ? שִׁשָּׁה אֲנִי יוֹדֵעַ. שִׁשָּׁה סִדְרֵי מִשְׁנָה,
חֲמִשָּׁה חֻמְשֵׁי תוֹרָה, אַרְבַּע אִמָּהוֹת, שְׁלשָׁה אָבוֹת,
שְׁנֵי לֻחוֹת הַבְּרִית, אֶחָד אֱלֹהֵינוּ שֶׁבַּשָּׁמַיִם וּבָאָרֶץ.

שִׁבְעָה מִי יוֹדֵעַ? שִׁבְעָה אֲנִי יוֹדֵעַ. שִׁבְעָה יְמֵי שַׁבַּתָּא,
שִׁשָּׁה סִדְרֵי מִשְׁנָה, חֲמִשָּׁה חֻמְשֵׁי תוֹרָה, אַרְבַּע
אִמָּהוֹת, שְׁלשָׁה אָבוֹת, שְׁנֵי לֻחוֹת הַבְּרִית, אֶחָד
אֱלֹהֵינוּ שֶׁבַּשָּׁמַיִם וּבָאָרֶץ.

Tablets. Also, He made a new Covenant with them that His Presence
would continue to dwell among the Children of Israel. He returned to
His previous love for them as it was at the original "wedding."

The second Tablets were treated identical to the first pair (which
were previously broken). Likewise, the second Tablets were inscribed by Hashem with the "finger of Elokim" (*Exodus* 31:18).
Again, Moses stood for forty days in the presence of Hashem waiting
to receive the Torah. Earlier at the Giving of the first Tablets, he had
learned Torah for the same length of time, yet it was necessary to
repeat the process. (*Exodus* 34:28, 35:1)

⊷§ שְׁלשָׁה אָבוֹת — *Three are the Patriarchs.* It was God's wish to
proclaim an oath separately with each Patriarch. Each of our
forefathers was individually worthy of concluding a covenant with
God and the merit of each alone was an independent virtue for their
descendants. Every additional oath and covenant promoted more
value and honor for posterity.

Who knows three? I know three. Three are the Patriarchs. Two are the Tablets of the Covenant. One is our God in the heavens and the earth.

Who knows four? I know four. Four are the Matriarchs. Three are the Patriarchs. Two are the Tablets of the Covenant. One is our God in the heavens and the earth.

Who knows five? I know five. Five are the Books of the Torah. Four are the Matriarchs. Three are the Patriarchs. Two are the Tablets of the Covenant. One is our God in the heavens and the earth.

Who knows six? I know six. Six are the Orders of the *Mishnah.* Five are the Books of the Torah. Four are the Matriarchs. Three are the Patriarchs. Two are the Tablets of the Covenant. One is our God in the heavens and the earth.

Who knows seven? I know seven. Seven are the days of the week. Six are the Orders of the *Mishnah.* Five are the Books of the Torah. Four are the Matriarchs. Three are the Patriarchs. Two are the Tablets of the Covenant. One is our God in the heavens and the earth.

Later, the Torah promises, "I shall remember My Covenant with Jacob, and also My Covenant with Isaac, and also My Covenant with Abraham I shall remember. . ." (*Leviticus* 26:42), thus reiterating how each of the three Patriarchs had an individual covenant with the Lord. (*Genesis* 26:3)

שִׁבְעָה יְמֵי שַׁבַּתָּא ‌— *Seven days of the week.* As explained earlier, the six days of Creation reflect the six thousand years of the world's existence. The seventh day "is a Sabbath to HASHEM, Your God," representing the World to Come. Each Sabbath in the Temple, the Levites sang Psalm 92: "A psalm, a song for the Sabbath day. . ." According to the Sages (*Tamid* 7:4), "this is a song for the World to Come, for the time when there is everlasting rest and Sabbath."

Just as the weekly cycle reflects the Creation, so the seven-year cycle of *Shemittah,* the Sabbatical year, represents events throughout the years of the universe. Whoever denies the Sabbatical cycle does not believe in the Creation nor in the World to Come. Thus, the Torah is exceptionally strict regarding nonobservance of the Sabbat-

שְׁמוֹנָה מִי יוֹדֵעַ? שְׁמוֹנָה אֲנִי יוֹדֵעַ. שְׁמוֹנָה יְמֵי מִילָה, שִׁבְעָה יְמֵי שַׁבַּתָּא, שִׁשָּׁה סִדְרֵי מִשְׁנָה, חֲמִשָּׁה חֻמְשֵׁי תוֹרָה, אַרְבַּע אִמָּהוֹת, שְׁלֹשָׁה אָבוֹת, שְׁנֵי לֻחוֹת הַבְּרִית, אֶחָד אֱלֹהֵינוּ שֶׁבַּשָּׁמַיִם וּבָאָרֶץ.

תִּשְׁעָה מִי יוֹדֵעַ? תִּשְׁעָה אֲנִי יוֹדֵעַ. תִּשְׁעָה יַרְחֵי לֵדָה, שְׁמוֹנָה יְמֵי מִילָה, שִׁבְעָה יְמֵי שַׁבַּתָּא, שִׁשָּׁה סִדְרֵי מִשְׁנָה, חֲמִשָּׁה חֻמְשֵׁי תוֹרָה, אַרְבַּע אִמָּהוֹת, שְׁלֹשָׁה אָבוֹת, שְׁנֵי לֻחוֹת הַבְּרִית, אֶחָד אֱלֹהֵינוּ שֶׁבַּשָּׁמַיִם וּבָאָרֶץ.

---

ical year, punishing us with exile. The Biblical curses (*Leviticus* 26:14ff.) repeatedly warn this fate and it is confirmed in the *Mishnah* (*Avos* 5:9).

Also, the prophet Jeremiah (34:14ff.) decreed exile for those not freeing their slaves after six years. From the point of view of the slave, the seventh year of freedom is akin to the Jubilee year (when slaves are freed and most property which was sold reverts to its original owners). Similarly, the Jubilee hints at the world's progression, when everything will eventually return to its original state at Creation. This is the intrinsic meaning of the verse, "And the land shall maintain a Sabbath" (*Leviticus* 25:2). These are fundamental but esoteric truths. (*Leviticus* 25:2)

לֵידָה ⇛ — *Birth.* Mankind's physical elements derive from "the dust of the earth" (*Genesis* 2:7), similar to animals and beasts. However, their inner soul is on a higher plane since God "blew into his nostrils the breath of life" (ibid.). Human beings are born with these two distinct dimensions. Physically they resemble the earth from which they were formed, but spiritually they have similarities with loftier spheres. Therefore, souls do not die with the body. Thus, mankind is intrinsically different from the rest of creation — they are created in God's Image. According to *Psalms* (8:6), humans are crowned with honor and glory; this is because they strive towards wisdom and knowledge and are capable of talent and skill.

When describing our creation, the Torah uses the Divine Names of *Hashem Elokim*, thus revealing the sublime nature of the soul. It did not evolve from the heavens nor derive from the earthly elements. It emanated solely from the Great God — "From whose mouth issues

Who knows eight? I know eight. Eight are the days of circumcision. Seven are the days of the week. Six are the Orders of the *Mishnah.* Five are the Books of the Torah. Four are the Matriarchs. Three are the Patriarchs. Two are the Tablets of the Covenant. One is our God in the heavens and the earth.

Who knows nine? I know nine. Nine are the months of pregnancy. Eight are the days of circumcision. Seven are the days of the week. Six are the Orders of the *Mishnah.* Five are the Books of the Torah. Four are the Matriarchs. Three are the Patriarchs. Two are the Tablets of the Covenant. One is our God in the heavens and the earth.

---

knowledge and understanding" (*Proverbs* 2:6). Generally, when one breathes into another person, he imparts a bit of his own soul.

From the *Midrash* (*Bereishis Rabbah* 7:5) it appears that the living spirit that resided in Adam's blood was first formed from the earth in common with all other creatures. Later, he received the more sublime soul, uniquely breathed into him by God.

Some philosophers (*Rav Saadiah Gaon, Ibn Gabirol* and *Ibn Ezra*) speculated that humans have three separate types of soul. The first imparts life in common with all vegetation; another generates movement in common with fish, animals and all that move upon the earth; and the supreme soul that promotes rational thought. However, other philosophers (*Rambam* in *Shemoneh Perakim*) insist that, though the soul includes all three elements, it is but one entity since it emanates from the Almighty, Who is One Unity.

This latter view is confirmed by the literal meaning of the above verses in *Genesis.* After Adam was formed by God from earth, he lay dumb and lifeless until he received the breath of life. That soul was sufficient to generate life, movement and thought. Apparently, this is not the understanding of *Targum Onkelos* here. The *Targum* explains that God's breath specifically granted speech, implicitly suggesting that mankind possesses more than one level of soul and this assumption is confirmed in the Talmud (*Sanhedrin* 65b). Furthermore, the *Midrash* (*Vayikra Rabbah* 32:2) writes, mankind has at least a *neshamah,* both a soul and a moving spirit. If so, Adam was first formed into a being capable of movement, and only later did he receive the sublime soul that sustains understanding, speech and action. (*Genesis* 1:26, 2:7)

עֲשָׂרָה מִי יוֹדֵעַ? עֲשָׂרָה אֲנִי יוֹדֵעַ. עֲשָׂרָה דִבְּרַיָּא,
תִּשְׁעָה יַרְחֵי לֵדָה, שְׁמוֹנָה יְמֵי מִילָה, שִׁבְעָה יְמֵי שַׁבַּתָּא,
שִׁשָּׁה סִדְרֵי מִשְׁנָה, חֲמִשָּׁה חֻמְשֵׁי תוֹרָה, אַרְבַּע
אִמָּהוֹת, שְׁלֹשָׁה אָבוֹת, שְׁנֵי לֻחוֹת הַבְּרִית, אֶחָד
אֱלֹהֵינוּ שֶׁבַּשָּׁמַיִם וּבָאָרֶץ.

אַחַד עָשָׂר מִי יוֹדֵעַ? אַחַד עָשָׂר אֲנִי יוֹדֵעַ. אַחַד עָשָׂר
כּוֹכְבַיָּא, עֲשָׂרָה דִבְּרַיָּא, תִּשְׁעָה יַרְחֵי לֵדָה, שְׁמוֹנָה יְמֵי
מִילָה, שִׁבְעָה יְמֵי שַׁבַּתָּא, שִׁשָּׁה סִדְרֵי מִשְׁנָה, חֲמִשָּׁה
חֻמְשֵׁי תוֹרָה, אַרְבַּע אִמָּהוֹת, שְׁלֹשָׁה אָבוֹת, שְׁנֵי לֻחוֹת
הַבְּרִית, אֶחָד אֱלֹהֵינוּ שֶׁבַּשָּׁמַיִם וּבָאָרֶץ.

שְׁנֵים עָשָׂר מִי יוֹדֵעַ? שְׁנֵים עָשָׂר אֲנִי יוֹדֵעַ. שְׁנֵים
עָשָׂר שִׁבְטַיָּא, אַחַד עָשָׂר כּוֹכְבַיָּא, עֲשָׂרָה דִבְּרַיָּא,

---

§ עֲשָׂרָה דִבְּרַיָּא — *Ten are the Commandments.* Five of these
commandments deal with the Glory of the Creator and the other
five benefit human society. However, the commandment to "Honor
your father" is included in the first category. God's Glory demands
honoring parents, who are partners in creating the next generation.

Apparently, the first five commandments, which refer to God's
Glory, were inscribed on one stone tablet and the last five
commandments, which include the interpersonal commandments,
appeared on the second stone tablet. In this way, there were five
commandments opposite five.[1]

Also, the first set of commandments, through "Honor your father,"
reflects the Written Torah and the other set mirrors the Oral Law.

Apparently, this is what the Sages meant (*Shemos Rabbah* 41:7)
when they stated that the two Tablets reflect heaven and earth; a
groom and a bride (or their escorts acting on their behalf) and the
two worlds — this world and the World to Come. All these examples
refer to one central theme and those learned in Kabbalah will readily
understand the mystic secret. (*Exodus* 20:13)

---

1. The *Sefer Yetzirah* (1:3) compares this Kabbalistically to the Ten Divine Emanations, and
to the ten fingers which are similarly situated: "Five opposite five on each hand, and the
single covenant is exactly in the middle. . . ."

Who knows ten? I know ten. Ten are the Commandments. Nine are the months of pregnancy. Eight are the days of circumcision. Seven are the days of the week. Six are the Orders of the *Mishnah*. Five are the Books of the Torah. Four are the Matriarchs. Three are the Patriarchs. Two are the Tablets of the Covenant. One is our God in the heavens and the earth.

Who knows eleven? I know eleven. Eleven are the stars [of Yosef's dream]. Ten are the Commandments. Nine are the months of pregnancy. Eight are the days of circumcision. Seven are the days of the week. Six are the Orders of the *Mishnah*. Five are the Books of the Torah. Four are the Matriarchs. Three are the Patriarchs. Two are the Tablets of the Covenant. One is our God in the heavens and the earth.

Who knows twelve? I know twelve. Twelve are the tribes. Eleven are the stars. Ten are the Commandments.

⊷§ שְׁנֵים עָשָׂר שִׁבְטַיָּא — *Twelve are the tribes.* The Torah constantly counts the tribes as twelve in number. When Jacob blessed his sons (*Genesis* 49:28), he roundly declared, "All these are the tribes of Israel — twelve." In that context, he designated Joseph as only one tribe.

Later — when dedicating the Altar, delineating encampments in the desert, or allocating the tribal inheritance (*Numbers* 2:18ff., 7:48ff., 34:23ff.) — the Torah enumerated Joseph's sons, Manasseh and Ephraim, as two separate tribes and omitted the Levites.

When Moses blessed the tribes at the end of his life, he likewise reckoned Ephraim and Manasseh separately (*Deuteronomy* 33:17). Moses wanted to single out Joshua, a descendant of Ephraim, who had been chosen to capture and partition the Promised Land. However, he wished to also bless the Levites in particular. By virtue of their Temple service with the sacrifices, their blessing would indirectly benefit all of Israel. So Moses found it imperative to pass over another tribe (Simon) to keep the number down to twelve.

At the blessings and curses on Mount Gerizim and Mount Ebal (*Deuteronomy* 27:12) where Levi (and Simon) are included, the tribes of Joseph are only considered as one tribe. When the prophet Ezekiel (48:4 ff.) parcels out the land, he reckons Joseph as two separate tribes and omits the Levites. Yet when the prophet

תִּשְׁעָה יַרְחֵי לֵדָה, שְׁמוֹנָה יְמֵי מִילָה, שִׁבְעָה יְמֵי שַׁבַּתָּא, שִׁשָּׁה סִדְרֵי מִשְׁנָה, חֲמִשָּׁה חֻמְשֵׁי תוֹרָה, אַרְבַּע אִמָּהוֹת, שְׁלֹשָׁה אָבוֹת, שְׁנֵי לֻחוֹת הַבְּרִית, אֶחָד אֱלֹהֵינוּ שֶׁבַּשָּׁמַיִם וּבָאָרֶץ.

שְׁלֹשָׁה עָשָׂר מִי יוֹדֵעַ? שְׁלֹשָׁה עָשָׂר אֲנִי יוֹדֵעַ. שְׁלֹשָׁה עָשָׂר מִדַּיָּא, שְׁנֵים עָשָׂר שִׁבְטַיָּא, אַחַד עָשָׂר כּוֹכְבַיָּא, עֲשָׂרָה דִבְּרַיָּא, תִּשְׁעָה יַרְחֵי לֵדָה, שְׁמוֹנָה יְמֵי מִילָה, שִׁבְעָה יְמֵי שַׁבַּתָּא, שִׁשָּׁה סִדְרֵי מִשְׁנָה, חֲמִשָּׁה חֻמְשֵׁי תוֹרָה, אַרְבַּע אִמָּהוֹת, שְׁלֹשָׁה אָבוֹת, שְׁנֵי לֻחוֹת הַבְּרִית, אֶחָד אֱלֹהֵינוּ שֶׁבַּשָּׁמַיִם וּבָאָרֶץ.

חַד גַּדְיָא, חַד גַּדְיָא, דְּזַבִּין אַבָּא בִּתְרֵי זוּזֵי, חַד גַּדְיָא חַד גַּדְיָא.

וְאָתָא **שׁוּנְרָא** וְאָכְלָה לְגַדְיָא, דְּזַבִּין אַבָּא בִּתְרֵי זוּזֵי, חַד גַּדְיָא חַד גַּדְיָא.

וְאָתָא **כַלְבָּא** וְנָשַׁךְ לְשׁוּנְרָא, דְּאָכְלָה לְגַדְיָא, דְּזַבִּין אַבָּא בִּתְרֵי זוּזֵי, חַד גַּדְיָא חַד גַּדְיָא.

וְאָתָא **חוּטְרָא** וְהִכָּה לְכַלְבָּא, דְּנָשַׁךְ לְשׁוּנְרָא, דְּאָכְלָה לְגַדְיָא, דְּזַבִּין אַבָּא בִּתְרֵי זוּזֵי, חַד גַּדְיָא חַד גַּדְיָא.

וְאָתָא **נוּרָא** וְשָׂרַף לְחוּטְרָא, דְּהִכָּה לְכַלְבָּא, דְּנָשַׁךְ לְשׁוּנְרָא, דְּאָכְלָה לְגַדְיָא, דְּזַבִּין אַבָּא בִּתְרֵי זוּזֵי, חַד גַּדְיָא חַד גַּדְיָא.

---

describes the future City Gates of Jerusalem (further in the same chapter), he allocates one gate to Levi and only one for both tribes of Joseph. Thus, the tribes are never numbered more than twelve.

Consistent with that number, they reflect the twelve constellations

Nine are the months of pregnancy. Eight are the days of circumcision. Seven are the days of the week. Six are the Orders of the *Mishnah*. Five are the Books of the Torah. Four are the Matriarchs. Three are the Patriarchs. Two are the Tablets of the Covenant. One is our God in the heavens and the earth.

Who knows thirteen? I know thirteen. Thirteen are the Attributes of Hashem. Twelve are the tribes. Eleven are the stars. Ten are the Commandments. Nine are the months of pregnancy. Eight are the days of circumcision. Seven are the days of the week. Six are the Orders of the *Mishnah*. Five are the Books of the Torah. Four are the Matriarchs. Three are the Patriarchs. Two are the Tablets of the Covenant. One is our God in the heavens and the earth.

One kid, one kid that father bought for two *zuzim*. One kid, one kid.

And the cat came and ate the kid that father bought for two *zuzim*. One kid, one kid.

And the dog came and bit the cat that ate the kid that father bought for two *zuzim*. One kid, one kid.

And the stick came and beat the dog that bit the cat that ate the kid that father bought for two *zuzim*. One kid, one kid.

And the fire came and burned the stick that beat the dog that bit the cat that ate the kid that father bought for two *zuzim*. One kid, one kid.

---

of the Zodiac (*Bamidbar Rabbah* 14:29), the twelve months of the year, and the twelve edges of a cube.[1]

The Sages reiterate this in the Talmud (*Berachos* 32b). "The Holy One, Blessed is He, told the prophet to inform the community of Israel that the twelve constellations were created in the heavens to mirror the twelve tribes." (*Deuteronomy* 33:6. See also *Numbers* 17:17)

---

1. Kabbalistically, this refers to the Emanations deriving from combinations of Hashem's Name — *Sefer HaBahir* 95.

וְאָתָא **מַיָּא** וְכָבָה לְנוּרָא, דְּשָׂרַף לְחוּטְרָא, דְּהִכָּה לְכַלְבָּא, דְּנָשַׁךְ לְשׁוּנְרָא, דְּאָכְלָה לְגַדְיָא, דְּזַבִּין אַבָּא בִּתְרֵי זוּזֵי, חַד גַּדְיָא חַד גַּדְיָא.

וְאָתָא **תוֹרָא** וְשָׁתָה לְמַיָּא, דְּכָבָה לְנוּרָא, דְּשָׂרַף לְחוּטְרָא, דְּהִכָּה לְכַלְבָּא, דְּנָשַׁךְ לְשׁוּנְרָא, דְּאָכְלָה לְגַדְיָא, דְּזַבִּין אַבָּא בִּתְרֵי זוּזֵי, חַד גַּדְיָא חַד גַּדְיָא.

וְאָתָא **הַשּׁוֹחֵט** וְשָׁחַט לְתוֹרָא, דְּשָׁתָא לְמַיָּא, דְּכָבָה לְנוּרָא, דְּשָׂרַף לְחוּטְרָא, דְּהִכָּה לְכַלְבָּא, דְּנָשַׁךְ לְשׁוּנְרָא, דְּאָכְלָה לְגַדְיָא, דְּזַבִּין אַבָּא בִּתְרֵי זוּזֵי, חַד גַּדְיָא חַד גַּדְיָא.

וְאָתָא **מַלְאַךְ הַמָּוֶת** וְשָׁחַט לְשׁוֹחֵט, דְּשָׁחַט לְתוֹרָא, דְּשָׁתָה לְמַיָּא, דְּכָבָה לְנוּרָא, דְּשָׂרַף לְחוּטְרָא, דְּהִכָּה לְכַלְבָּא, דְּנָשַׁךְ לְשׁוּנְרָא, דְּאָכְלָה לְגַדְיָא, דְּזַבִּין אַבָּא בִּתְרֵי זוּזֵי, חַד גַּדְיָא חַד גַּדְיָא.

⇛ וְאָתָה הַשּׁוֹחֵט — *And the slaughterer came.* The term slaughtering refers to the cutting of the windpipe and gullet in the neck. In the desert, the Children of Israel were at first permitted to eat meat only from the peace-offerings. Later they were allowed the meat of ordinary, non-consecrated animals, once these were slaughtered correctly.

Originally, Adam and his progeny ate only fruit and vegetables. They were forbidden to slaughter meat for consumption because living creatures also have souls. (Apparently, the Greek philosopher Aristotle concurs that animals have souls.) This soul is sufficient to generate movement, allows animals to exercise some degree of choice concerning food or other benefits, and enables them to avoid death or pain. Animals can also recognize and show love towards those they are familiar with. (Dogs, for instance, may adore their masters and often reveal an uncanny recognition of their masters'

And the water came and doused the fire that burned the stick that beat the dog that bit the cat that ate the kid that father bought for two *zuzim*. One kid, one kid.

And the ox came and drank the water that doused the fire that burned the stick that beat the dog that bit the cat that ate the kid that father bought for two *zuzim*. One kid, one kid.

And the slaughterer came and slaughtered the ox that drank the water that doused the fire that burned the stick that beat the dog that bit the cat that ate the kid that father bought for two *zuzim*. One kid, one kid.

And the angel of death came and slaughtered the slaughterer who slaughtered the ox that drank the water that doused the fire that burned the stick that beat the dog that bit the cat that ate the kid that father bought for two *zuzim*. One kid, one kid.

---

households. Pigeons also display unusual recognition and knowledge.)

However, when all creatures sinned before the Flood, they should have been obliterated, just as the humans were. Therefore, after Noah saved some creatures to preserve the various species, God allowed their slaughter and consumption. They had only survived in Noah's merit. God also allowed men to harness animals for their own needs.

Yet, though their meat can now be eaten, their blood remains forbidden, as this is where their soul resides. The Sages also teach us (*Shabbos* 128b) that we have a Biblical duty to prevent animal suffering. This is the Divine design behind the kosher method of slaughter and is reflected in the blessing recited by the ritual slaughterer.

(*Genesis* 1:29, *Leviticus* 17:11 and *Deuteronomy* 12:21.
See also *Genesis* 9:5, *Leviticus* 26:6
and *Deuteronomy* 22:6)

וְאָתָא הַקָּדוֹשׁ בָּרוּךְ הוּא וְשָׁחַט לְמַלְאַךְ הַמָּוֶת, דְּשָׁחַט לְשׁוֹחֵט, דְּשָׁחַט לְתוֹרָא, דְּשָׁתָה לְמַיָּא, דְּכָבָה לְנוּרָא, דְּשָׂרַף לְחוּטְרָא, דְּהִכָּה לְכַלְבָּא, דְּנָשַׁךְ לְשׁוּנְרָא, דְּאָכְלָה לְגַדְיָא, דְּזַבִּין אַבָּא בִּתְרֵי זוּזֵי, חַד גַּדְיָא חַד גַּדְיָא.

Although the Haggadah formally ends at this point, one should continue to occupy himself with the story of the Exodus, and the laws of Passover, until sleep overtakes him.

◆§ וְאָתָא הַקָּדוֹשׁ בָּרוּךְ הוּא וְשָׁחַט לְמַלְאַךְ הַמָּוֶת — *The Holy One, Blessed is He, then came and slaughtered the angel of death.* The Sages teach us (*Bava Basra* 16a) that Satan is synonymous with the angel of death, and also the evil inclination. They believe this is not a natural force but an angel created to cause discord and inflict harm.

This angel provokes destruction and strife, inflicts injuries and plague, incites quarrels and schisms, and is behind the baneful influence of the constellations. Also, our Rabbis believed, he is the Heavenly Master over Esau, the nation that lives by the sword of war. Furthermore, he rules over the demons — which the Sages describe as "those who inflict damage" and the Torah (*Leviticus* 17:7, *Isaiah* 13:21) describes these as שְׂעִירִים, "goats." This term probably arose because they appear to crazed persons in the form of goats. Similarly, Esau (who will be judged at the end of days) is known by the name שֵׂעִיר.

According to the Sages, this angel descends into this world and leads men astray (as the evil inclination). Subsequently, he returns with the evidence to enrage Heaven (as Satan). Eventually he

הגדה של פסח / 146

The Holy One, Blessed is He, then came and slaughtered the angel of death who slaughtered the slaughterer who slaughtered the ox that drank the water that doused the fire that burned the stick that beat the dog that bit the cat that ate the kid that father bought for two *zuzim*. One kid, one kid.

Although the *Haggadah* formally ends at this point, one should continue to occupy himself with the story of the Exodus, and the laws of Passover, until sleep overtakes him.

---

receives permission to remove men's souls (in his guise as the angel of death). Apparently, the death of human beings capable of speech is not merely a cessation of life, according to the Sages, but also a positive act by this angel, who can remove the intangible life-force that is the soul.

Those learned in the natural sciences believe that all human beings must eventually die since we are formed from a combination of elements. According to them, had Adam not sinned, he would inevitably have perished at a later date.

The Sages (*Shabbos* 58b, *Avodah Zarah* 8a, *Bereishis Rabbah* 17:8), however, tell us that Adam should never have died. His sublime soul could sustain immortality and he would have lived by God's Will. Only those who lack faith in God insist that anything created from a combination of elements must eventually disintegrate. However, this universe was created with God's Will and will continue to exist for as long as Hashem wishes it. This is true and self-evident.

(*Genesis* 2:17 and preface to *Job*.
See also *Genesis* 5:4, *Leviticus* 17:7 and 18:29 regarding *kares*)